FROM EDISON TO ENRON

Also by Richard Munson

The Power Makers

Cousteau: The Captain and His World

The Cardinals of Capitol Hill

FROM EDISON TO ENRON

The Business of Power and What It Means for the Future of Electricity

RICHARD MUNSON

Westport, Connecticut
London

Library of Congress Cataloging-in-Publication Data

Munson, Richard.
    From Edison to Enron : the business of power and what it means for the future of
electricity / Richard Munson.
        p.   cm.
    Includes bibliographical references and index.
    ISBN 0–275–98740–X (alk. paper)
    1. Electric utilities—United States—History.   I. Title.
HD9685.U5M858   2005
333.793'2'0973—dc22   2005017480

British Library Cataloguing in Publication Data is available.

Library of Congress Catalog Card Number: 2005017480
ISBN: 0-275-98740-X

First published in 2005

Praeger Publishers, 88 Post Road West, Westport, CT 06881
An imprint of Greenwood Publishing Group, Inc.
www.praeger.com

Printed in the United States of America

The paper used in this book complies with the
Permanent Paper Standard issued by the National
Information Standards Organization (Z39.48-1984).

10 9 8 7 6 5 4 3 2 1

Dedicated to Diane, Daniel, and Dana

Contents

1

An Industry in Transition

Name the last century's greatest technical feat. You might suggest the automobile or the internal combustion engine. Maybe the airplane or the computer chip. No, say the professional engineers. The twentieth century's most significant accomplishment was to generate and harness an invisible stream of electrons.

The blackout of 2003 highlighted our dependence on electricity as some 50 million people in eight states and two provinces could no longer watch television, microwave dinners, obtain cash from ATM machines, or check email messages. Such a massive power interruption forced us to reflect on the usual wonder of flipping a switch and brightening a room. It caused us to consider the scientific marvel of submicroscopic particles moving like waves inside a wire and causing bulbs to glow. It highlighted the enormous expense, as well as vulnerability, of the generators, transformers, transmission lines, and switch boxes needed to tap and deliver electric power.

Electricity may be wondrous, but the politics of power spark controversies and conflicts. Blackouts, polluted air, and corporate bankruptcies are only a few of the electricity issues that fill today's headlines and mobilize the army of lobbyists trying to control this giant industry's future.

Despite its mystery and controversy, electricity is simply the movement of electrons. Each tiny particle of the atom flows only a short distance as it displaces another around a circuit, but the speed of this transfer is a staggering 186,000 miles per second. The electromagnetic wonder occurs virtually everywhere in nature, transmitting signals from our brains to contract our muscles, bonding molecules and atoms together, and even causing our compasses to point north. What's relatively new is our ability to put electricity to work.

The first observations of this power's bizarre properties occurred in ancient Greece, but we've been able to generate and transmit electric currents for only a little more than 100 years. The resulting innovations and lifestyle changes have been remarkable and rapid. Electric lights lengthened our days, imposed a regimentation divorced from natural rhythms, and caused the cornucopia of stars to fade from the night sky. Electric-powered elevators and streetcars heightened and enlarged the cityscape. Motors transformed industrial societies.

Electricity's profound impacts can be traced over only a few generations. My grandparents were born in houses that relied on candles and kerosene lamps for light and on wood-burning stoves for heat and hot water. Their first refrigerator was a leaky chest on the back porch into which my grandfather regularly placed fifty-pound blocks of ice. By the time my father entered high school, his family enjoyed running water warmed by an electric heater. Still, my parents initially had to put their wash through a hand-powered wringer and place those clothes on an outside line because their washing machine lacked a spin cycle and they had no dryer. Only when I became a teenager did wall-mounted air conditioners make hot summers more tolerable, and my own children now cannot imagine that I suffered through school without a computer or electronic games.

As my grandparents attested, the now-simple task of boiling water required wood to be chopped, stacked, and carried to the house. Starting and regulating the stove proved to be an art form, and the burning wood produced unbearable temperatures in the summer. Even lighting a kerosene lamp proved difficult. If the wick was too high, the lamp would smoke, and after every few minutes, it had to be readjusted.

Electric-powered lights and appliances curtailed these challenges and lessened life's burdens. The electrical phenomenon also became the foundation for the telephone, radio, television, electronics, long-range communication, computing, and radar systems. Electricity even plays a critical role in many industrial processes, such as precision machinery, the electroplating of metals, and electrostatic precipitators that remove waste particles from manufacturing furnaces.

Despite the impressive expansion of electric systems in developed countries, two-thirds of rural residents in Africa, Latin America, and Asia—some two billion people—lack access to power. Worse still, population growth in many areas is outstripping expansion of electrical wires; the percentage of connected people, sadly, is decreasing rather than increasing. The chasm between the haves and the have-nots of electricity is stark, glaring, and deepening steadily.[1]

International electrification, while critical, could be enormously costly. Assuming current trends and technologies, the International Energy Agency estimates world electrical demand will require over the next thirty years the addition of six times the current U.S. electric-generating capacity. Direct expenses for power plants and lines will surpass $10.8 trillion, and associated global carbon dioxide emissions will soar at least 70 percent.[2]

Electricity is a superior energy form—clean at the point of use, capable of performing many tasks, and easily controlled. Such attributes have increased its share of total energy use over the past three decades from 25 percent to nearly 40 percent. Yet unlike water and natural gas, electricity is not a substance, but a physical effect occurring throughout the wires that conduct it. This power does not exist naturally in quantities that can be manipulated for our benefit. It also cannot be easily stored. Its delivery, in fact, requires the ultimate just-in-time enterprise that balances supply and demand at every instant.

Controlling this drudgery-saving, hard-working wonder has been an ongoing struggle for engineers, politicians, and entrepreneurs alike. Competition flourished, sometimes chaotically, in the late nineteenth and early twentieth centuries before a few tycoons formed government-approved monopolies. Those electric trusts expanded rapidly for several decades, yet their momentum began to shatter in the 1960s and their efficiency waned. Long dominated by regulated monopolies, the electricity industry has been slow to innovate, yet entrepreneurs are advancing scores of modern technologies that challenge the status quo and offer increased efficiency and reduced pollution.

Electricity is a huge business. The traditional generators and deliverers of power—electric utilities—hold assets exceeding $600 billion and have annual sales above $260 billion. They are this nation's largest industry—roughly twice the size of telecommunications and almost 30 percent larger than the U.S.-based manufacturers of automobiles and trucks. Generating and delivering electricity is extremely capital intensive, requiring far more investment than the average manufacturing industry and even ten to 100 times more per unit of delivered energy than gas and oil systems.

Giant utilities employ some of the most effective lobbyists, working on many fronts to maintain their monopolistic benefits. Their federal campaign contributions in 2002 exceeded $21 million, approximately two-thirds of which went to Republicans. The largest donors were the Southern Company, which has opposed competition successfully in the South, and the National Rural Electric Cooperative Association, which has preserved the many tax subsidies for rural co-ops. Utilities also have counted on political support from Wall Street (which profits from marketing utility bonds) and the U.S. Chamber of Commerce and other business associations (which depend heavily upon power companies for dues and contributions).

North America's integrated wires from Manitoba and Nebraska to the Atlantic Ocean and the Gulf of Mexico constitute the world's largest machine. While that system impressively and instantaneously balances supply and demand for a product that's traveling at the speed of light, the status quo suffers numerous shortcomings. The utility industry's efficiency, for instance, has not increased since the late 1950s. Two-thirds of the fuel burned to generate electricity is lost, and Americans pay roughly $100 billion too much each year for heat and power; put another way, the typical utility consumes three lumps of coal to deliver one lump of electricity.[3] Unreliable power—the result of blackouts or temporary surges and sags—annually costs Americans another $119 billion,[4] and those costs will only increase as technology-dependent businesses and even individual consumers demand steadier supplies of electricity; to provide some perspective, today's unreliable power adds a 44-percent surcharge to the cost of U.S. electricity. Generators also are the nation's largest polluters, spewing tons of mercury, sulfur dioxide, and other contaminants into America's air and waters.

The U.S. power system, moreover, is a rickety antique. The average generating plant was built in 1964 using 1959 technology, and more than one-fifth of U.S. power plants are more than fifty years old. Today's high-voltage transmission lines were designed before planners ever imagined that enormous amounts of electricity would be sold across state lines, and, consequently, the wires often are overloaded and subject to blackouts. One outcome of this overloading has been an increase in line losses from 5 percent in the early 1980s to 10 percent today, placing a $12-billion annual "tax" on consumers that did not exist twenty years ago.

On the other hand, the United States is on the verge of a tremendous explosion in energy innovation. Entrepreneurs advancing modern technologies could double the electric system's efficiency, cut the generation of pollutants and greenhouse gases, expand consumer choices, enhance productivity and economic development, spawn a multi-billion-dollar export industry, and bring power to millions of the world's poor. Following the computer industry's recent shift from centralized mainframes to networked microcomputers, most of today's electric innovations reflect a move toward decentralized generators as well as the cogeneration of power and heat.

Marketing these efficient technologies requires the elimination of numerous policy barriers. Congress in 1978 opened monopoly markets slightly, and the Federal Energy Regulatory Commission and several state regulators have sought to further electricity competition. Yet scores of laws and regulations still protect old-line monopolies and may lock out the most promising innovations. The struggle to control electricity's future promises to accelerate.

2

Early Competition

Electricity's story begins long before Thomas Edison or George Westinghouse, although their business competition in the late nineteenth century launched our electric age and created the first power businesses. Observant individuals began writing about unique energy properties some 2,600 years ago. The first known recordings came from Thales, a brilliant Greek philosopher who devised mathematical formulas, identified the phenomenon of magnetism, and developed astronomical tables capable of predicting solar eclipses.

We can only guess how Thales actually achieved his electrical insight. Perhaps he was using a piece of fur or wool to polish amber, a yellowish-brown and translucent resin (which in Greek is "electron"). He might have laid the rubbed stone near straw, and to Thales's surprise, the straw jumped and clung to the amber. He probably repeated the experiment several times, noticing that nothing happened when he placed non-rubbed amber near the straw.

Centuries passed before other scientists began to measure and capture this mysterious energy source, but static electricity long remained something of a sideshow wonder. Even monks got into the act. To bedazzle King Louis XV, for example, Abbe Jean-Antoine Nollet assembled 700 friars at a monastery in Paris. Somehow he convinced the monks to join hands, with the man at one end holding onto one electrical contact. When the man at the other end of this circuitous line touched the other contact point, completing a circuit and allowing the electrons to flow, all 700 monks simultaneously leaped into the air. The king and his court gasped with delight at the entertaining demonstration of electrified friars.

Electricity also attracted confusion and superstition. Quacks (and even some "legitimate" doctors) advanced electricity as a cure for constipation, paralysis, cancer, nervous disorders, and even infertility. Before Benjamin Franklin's famous kite experiment, most people believed evil spirits rode with the storms and created lightning. That notion, in fact, led to the curious custom of church bell ringers warning villages of approaching storms and wickedness. Innocently, those ringers climbed to the highest spires, where lightning often struck, traveled through the metal bell, and descended the wet rope. Scores of ringers died before officials finally outlawed the practice.

It was September 1752 when Franklin attached a stiff wire to his kite and a metal key to the end of an attached string, predicting that lightning's electrical charge would flow from the kite to the key. Perhaps remembering the fate of the bell ringers, Franklin did take some precautions, such as standing inside the doorway of a building and holding onto a dry silk ribbon rather than the wet string. A Swedish scientist of the same period tried a similar experiment but died when lightning struck the rod he was holding high in the air during a thunderstorm. Fortunately for Franklin, only a gentle rain fell that September day, but it was enough for an electric charge to build up in the kite and for small sparks to travel down the string to the key. Those sparks proved that lightning was electricity.

Franklin, of course, was just one of the scientific giants who painstakingly built the foundation for our understanding of electricity and magnetism. William Gilbert, one of Queen Elizabeth's physicians, devised the first instrument to measure electricity. Otto Von Guericke in the mid-seventeenth century constructed the first machine to generate static electricity, and he demonstrated that power could be transmitted. Stephen Gray in the late seventeenth century identified "electric conduction" when he demonstrated that objects touching an electrified body will themselves become electrified.

Although the public from the late seventeenth until the early nineteenth centuries sought evermore dramatic sparks and crackles, almost no one thought electricity could do anything useful. Even Franklin felt "chagrined that we have been hitherto able to produce nothing in this way of use to mankind."[1] In fact, static electricity and lightning were quite impractical since their discharges came in bursts that were hard to control. A ready and steady stream of electrons was needed, yet it took a series of scientists several decades to envision that stream and to pave the way for now-famous inventions by Thomas Edison, George Westinghouse, and Nikola Tesla. Pieter Van Musschenbroek and Ewald von Kleist, around 1746, separately created a "capacitor," the first device to store static electricity. Alessandro Volta, professor of physics at Italy's University of Padua, invented a voltaic pile, the forerunner of an electric cell or battery. Hans Christian Oersted, a physics professor at the University of Copenhagen, showed for the first time that electricity and magnetism were similar. It was Michael Faraday, however, who took the dramatic step of demonstrating how magnets could generate electricity. And James Clark Maxwell, a physics professor at Cambridge University, put many of the theories into mathematical form, allowing later scientists and inventors to understand and calculate electromagnetic forces.

A progression of other scientists subsequently clarified the principles of electricity and magnetism, and by the 1840s the telegraph marked electricity's first practical application. Within only a few short decades, Alexander Graham Bell transferred his voice from vibrations on a steel disk, to the current passing through an electromagnet, and to audible vibrations at the other end of a wire. In 1901, Guglielmo Marconi, building on the theories of Nikola Tesla and Heinrich Hertz, transmitted wireless electromagnetic waves across the Atlantic, from Cornwall to Newfoundland, and launched the era of radio and television.

Thomas Edison explored several of these paths made possible by electricity—including the telegraph, telephone, and motion pictures. Although simple batteries could power a telegraph or telephone, Edison understood that a generator and distribution system were needed in order to take advantage of electricity's enormous power. His inventions associated with light and power would revolutionize America and much of the world.

WIZARD OF MENLO PARK

Thomas Edison is an American icon, proclaimed in textbooks as the "Napoleon of Science" or the "Purveyor of Light." More than two million tourists each year reverently view his laboratory that was moved by an admiring Henry Ford from Menlo Park, New Jersey, to Greenfield Village, Michigan, outside Detroit.

Thomas Edison. Courtesy of the Department of the Interior, National Parks Service, Edison National Historic Site.

History's most prolific inventor, Edison claimed 1,093 patents. A list of his discoveries reads like a litany of modern technologies: the stock ticker, automatic telegraph, phonograph, telephone transmitter, motion picture camera, multiplex telegraph, electric storage battery, mimeograph machine, and the industrial research lab. His most famous practical invention, of course, is the incandescent lamp, or electric light bulb. But more importantly, Edison created an entire electric system—inventing, developing, financing, and managing the generators, parallel distribution lines, and switches needed to bring power to consumers.

Young Edison appeared destined to be neither prolific nor famous. Called Al by his friends, he descended from a line of rebels. His grandfather, a prosperous Tory, fought against George Washington and the American Revolution in 1776. Convicted of treason and sentenced to hang, he fled to Canada. Al's father also narrowly escaped, this time from Canada to

Michigan after participating in an unsuccessful coup against the Royal Canadian government.

Born in 1847 in Milan, Ohio, the family's seventh and final child spent his early years dreaming, drifting, and getting into trouble. Although possessing an encyclopedic memory and visual imagination, Thomas Alva Edison performed poorly at his one-room school, with one teacher describing the student as "a little addled." His mother eventually home schooled him and nurtured his love of reading and science. "My mother was the making of me," Edison declared later. "She understood me. She let me follow my bent."[2]

One of Edison's first experiments burned his father's barn to the ground, but Al's whipping in the public square failed to deter his curiosity. A practiced practical joker, he also knocked down any friend or relative gullible enough to touch his electric generator. Edison gained a few knocks himself. While selling newspapers at various railroad stations, he tried to board a moving train with a heavy load. A friendly conductor tried to help, took Edison by the ears, and lifted him aboard. According to the inventor, "I felt something snap inside my head, and my deafness started from that time."[3]

Teenage Edison and his family moved to Port Huron, Michigan, where he proved to be a decent telegraph transmitter and adept tinkerer. According to one biographer, "A young boy learning telegraphy in Edison's day is roughly equivalent to a teenager learning how to build and program his own computers today."[4] Edison was clearly clever, and he demonstrated an intense curiosity by spending two-days' pay to join Detroit's public library and by devouring the three volumes of Michael Faraday's dense *Experimental Researches in Electricity and Magnatism*.

Moving to Stratford, a crossing point for the Grand Trunk Railroad, a restless and distracted Edison was hired to operate the track switch during the night shift. One evening, with his mind on other matters, he failed to warn an approaching train of a flipped switch, causing the engine, the tender, and one boxcar to jump the tracks. Edison quickly left for Cincinnati, where he took advantage of a workers' strike to grab another telegraph assignment; but his union-busting opportunism did not endear him to other telegraph operators and he again decided to move on.

By the age of twenty-four, when he drifted through Boston and settled in Newark, New Jersey, Edison exhibited recklessness, a lack of discipline, and stubbornness, yet an extreme confidence in his own abilities.

Although obviously adroit, this young man with a jutting jaw and large head seemed little different from the many other experimenters working in telegraph offices. Horatio Alger would not have been impressed.

But Edison's persistent dabbling eventually produced useful products that brought him to the attention of industrialists and Wall Street financiers. His stock ticker overcame many of the telegraph industry's bottlenecks by operating at 200 to 300 words per minute, and his automatic duplex allowed two messages to be sent simultaneously on a single wire. To use Edison's inventions, Western Union provided him with what he most wanted—money—although not enough to cover Edison's extravagant plans. To escape Newark's high rent, he and his new wife, Mary, moved twelve miles south to a large lot in Menlo Park. Here Edison spent far more time at work than with his family, two children of which he nicknamed "Dot" and "Dash" after the telegraph code. Here the researcher also built his now-famous laboratory, the first corporate research center, where he promised to develop "a minor invention every ten days and a big thing every six months or so."[5]

Menlo Park is also where Edison entertained and bedazzled financiers and newspaper reporters. Western Union president Hamilton McK. Twombly and banker J. Pierpont Morgan visited the Edison laboratory early on and witnessed only bursting bulbs, but they shared Edison's dream of making a fortune from a successful electric system. Viewing their competition as gas and whale-oil lamps, they relished Edison's prediction: "There will be neither blaze nor flame, no singeing or flickering; it will be whiter and steadier than any known lamp. It will give no obnoxious fumes nor smoke, will prove one of the healthiest lights possible, and will not blacken ceilings or furniture."[6] Edison, in essence, promised to break the age-old tie between light and fire, to create illumination without flame or smoke.

Twombly and Morgan assembled a group of financial backers to incorporate the Edison Electric Light Company, gaining control of Edison's future lamp inventions for a mere $50,000 investment. Edison received the cash and $250,000 of the new firm's stock. The initial twelve-member board also included Edison, his lawyer Grosvenor Lowrey, representatives of the Vanderbilts (family members did not want to be publicly associated with Edison because of their gas company holdings), and directors of Morgan's banking firm.

Edison, as he would on many occasions, glowed with optimism and expressed grand predictions beyond just electric lighting. "The same wire that brings the light," predicted the innovator, "will also bring power and heat—with the power you can run an elevator, a sewing machine, or any other mechanical contrivance, and by means of the heat you may cook your food."[7] This vision of a technological revolution generated no small amount of controversy. Professor Silvanus Thompson in London, for example, labeled Edison's predictions "sheer nonsense." Edison, according to Thompson, demonstrated "the most airy ignorance of the fundamental principles of both electricity and dynamics."[8]

In a sense, Thompson was right. Edison had almost no formal schooling and did not appreciate scientific theories. "At the time I experimented on the incandescent lamp I did not understand Ohm's law," admitted the experimenter. "Moreover, I do not want to understand Ohm's law. It would prevent me from experimenting."[9] Edison's was a dogged approach to problem solving. According to Nikola Tesla, "If Edison had a needle to find in a haystack, he would proceed at once with the diligence of the bee to examine straw after straw until he found the object of his search. . . . A little theory and calculation would have saved him 90 percent of his labor."[10]

Success did not come in a flash of genius, in isolation, or quickly. As Edison himself put it, "Invention is 1 percent inspiration and 99 percent perspiration." To power a long-lasting incandescent bulb, Edison and his associates certainly needed a high-resistant lamp filament, or thin thread, which the electric current would heat to a glow; but they also had to make a vastly improved vacuum globe within which the filament would burn without burning up; they needed to create a parallel circuit where lights could be operated independently of each other; and they demanded a better dynamo to generate electricity. Noting the complexities and costs, Edison laid aside his initial lighting efforts, arguing that "the results of the carbon [filament] experiments, and also of the boron and silicon experiments, were not considered sufficiently satisfactory, when looked at in the commercial sense."[11]

Edison worked best when he worked with a team. Throughout the hectic and productive years of 1878–80, he collaborated with Charles Batchelor, Francis Upton, John Kruesi, and Francis Jehl. Like Edison, Batchelor was a wanderer and tinkerer; a cotton-mill mechanic from England, the dark-bearded technician first worked with Edison at the American Telegraph works where they designed stock tickers. Upton, five years younger than Edison, provided some order and discipline to the lab; trained in mathematics and abstract science at Princeton and Berlin universities, Upton became Edison's calculator and data-retrieval system. Kruesi, a master Swiss mechanist, translated Edison's rough drawings into working models. Once attorney Grosvenor Lowrey's office boy, young Francis Jehl was initially responsible for developing the lab's vacuum pump; his tedious efforts to extract air required ten hours for each bulb. After Batchelor fell ill from breathing mercury fumes, Jehl became the lab's chief technician. He later declared, "Edison is in reality a collective noun and means the work of many men."[12] Edison, however, remained the lab's driving force, whose will and vision prompted continual experimentation and invention.

Renewed efforts to perfect an incandescent lamp produced only failure. Edison, for instance, ordered $3,000 worth of copper to build a series of thin pipes that were to be heated by steam, and polished-copper reflectors were to focus the heat onto a small point to bring "vivid incandescence." The frustrated experimenter eventually smashed the device with a hammer.

Attempts with a platinum filament were no more satisfying. At $5 an ounce, platinum would have raised the bulb's cost three to four times above that of a gas lamp. The first experiment with platinum filaments also produced only a series of Roman candles as the bulbs exploded and flared brilliantly throughout the lab.

Edison persevered with unorthodox, if dogged, work habits. According to his secretary, Edison "was just as likely to be at work in his laboratory at midnight as midday. He cared not for the hours of the day or the days of the week."[13]

Edison tried almost every imaginable chemical (e.g., chromium, molybdenum, boron, silicon, and zirconium oxide) to coat almost every imaginable substance (e.g., fish lines, cotton, cardboard, wood shavings, visiting cards, and beards). He initially dismissed carbon as a possible "burner" because of its presumed weakness when exposed to the 3,000-degree-Fahrenheit heat of an electric current, until he read about Joseph Swan's experiments in England where a thin carbon rod had been brightly lit for several minutes in a vacuum globe.

Building on Swan's work, Edison began in early October 1879 to bake carbonized sewing thread and to wire the charred ribbon to a stem assembly within a globe. After his new pump exhausted the bulb of its air, he switched on the electric current. The first eight attempts produced only broken threads. Francis Upton, reflecting the lab's profit motivation, grumbled that the electric light was "a continual trouble. For a year we cannot make what we want and see the untold millions roll in."[14]

Yet on October 21, 1879, the mood changed, when, according to Batchelor's lab notes, "we made some interesting experiments on straight carbons made from carbon thread."[15] The threads, however, proved to be delicate. "Just as we reached the glass blower's house, the wretched carbon broke," Edison remembered. "We turned back to the main laboratory and set to work again. It was late in the afternoon before we produced another carbon, which was broken by a jeweler's screwdriver falling against it. But we turned back again and before nightfall the carbon was completed and inserted in the lamp. The bulb was exhausted of air and sealed, the current turned on, and the sight we had so long desired to see met our eyes."[16]

The horseshoe-shaped carbonized cotton-thread filament lasted forty straight hours. It might have burned longer, but Edison, ever the investigator, increased the voltage until the filament expired. Uncharacteristically, he waited almost two months before publicly announcing his accomplishment, during which time he experimented with other substances, particularly strips of tough cardboard and bamboo. Over the same period, the Menlo Park lab designed an improved generator since existing models worked only for arc lights wired in series.

When the success was reported—the *New York Herald*'s front page declared "The Great Inventor's Triumph in Electric Illumination"[17]—the stock market reacted quickly. Gas company securities plummeted, with Manhattan Gas Light Company's value falling 21 percent in only six weeks. Stock in the Edison Electric Light Company, on the other hand, skyrocketed to $3,500 per share.

Yet not everyone was convinced of Edison's achievement. Professor Henry Morton of the Stevens Institute labeled the lamp "a conspicuous failure, . . . a fraud upon the public." The *London Times' Sunday Review*, suggesting Edison's results were based on trickery, declared: "There is a strong flavor of humbug about the whole matter."[18] Even Edison acknowledged that his production of bulbs, held to only three units a day because most of the delicate globes broke, would not achieve substantial profits.

The public, however, was intrigued, and curiosity seekers began to flood into Menlo Park. Brought by special trains on New Year's Eve from

Philadelphia and New York, more than 3,000 visitors descended on the one-store village for a demonstration of sixty lamps mounted on poles throughout the laboratory grounds. According to an impressed reporter for the *New York Herald*, "Many had come in the expectation of seeing a dignified, elegantly dressed person, and were much surprised to find a simple young man attired in the homeliest manner, using not high-sounding technical terms, but the plainest and simplest language."[19] Even Edison admitted to his rough appearance: "Holding a heavy cigar constantly in my mouth has deformed my upper lip, it has a sort of Havana curl."[20]

Edison, however, proved to be a preeminent promoter, as well as a clever and dogged inventor. To silence skeptics, for instance, he outfitted a 3,200-ton steamship, the *Columbia*, with 115 electric lamps, and after the two-and-one-half-month voyage around the tip of South America, the ship arrived in San Francisco to great fanfare with half its bulbs still working. Even in the midst of busy experiments, Edison would grant interviews, always claiming to be on the verge of a revolutionary breakthrough. Noting his past accomplishments, the media increasingly considered the crusty and opinionated innovator to be good copy.

More importantly, Edison was an entrepreneur, an avid experimenter with a clear purpose—to make money. The long-lasting incandescent bulb was a substantial achievement, but it remained only part of Edison's vision for a complete industry that would profitably generate and deliver electricity to homes, commercial buildings, and industries. That monumental task required designing and constructing a vast array of new electrical equipment, including dynamos, power lines, cables, sockets, switches, insulators, meters, voltage regulators, fuses, and junction boxes.

Edison, of course, didn't invent everything electric. The emerging industry ultimately depended upon Nikola Tesla's induction motor, William Stanley's transformer, Charles Steinmetz's mathematical formulas for alternating-current machinery, Oliver Shallenberg's induction meter, and Benjamin Lamme's dynamo-electric machine.

It was Edison, however, who in December 1880 created a new firm, the Edison Electric Illuminating Company of New York, to build the first electric generating plant and distribution system. As usual, the promoter announced unrealistic projections, which the media enthusiastically reprinted. He claimed a $160,000 investment would build a plant to supply electricity to a square mile of downtown Manhattan, and that within two and one-half years he would power all of New York City. The facts were that $160,000 purchased only two buildings on Pearl Street, that the generator supplied power to a sixth of a square mile, and that the first station alone took over two years to build. Yet Edison cleverly selected a service area that included the stock exchange, the major banking and financing houses, and the city's leading newspapers, ensuring that a successful project would prompt brokers, bankers, and editors to ensure his financial success and fame.

Edison's vision called for capturing the power plant's heat as well as its electricity. Rather than waste the thermal energy produced by burning coal, the innovator planned to pipe steam to warm the offices of Drexel Morgan and other potential investors. Edison, as a result, is credited with launching the first cogeneration or combined-heat-and-power unit, a technology, as will be discussed later, that has been modernized in the twenty-first century.

Obstacles abounded. Consider just the challenge of insulation. Rather than add to the array of telegraph wires that littered the New York skyline, Edison decided to bury his cables. Each night, crews of Irishmen dug up the horse-manure-laden streets of New York's slum district and installed into wooden boxes copper wires that were coated with tar for protection against the weather. Yet Francis Upton tested the lines after three months of labor and discovered that "some of the circuits are very badly insulated and all more or less defective."[21] Two other insulation experiments failed, until Edison devised a compound of parafine, tar, linseed oil, and asphaltum to coat several layers of muslin.

To reduce costs, Edison also needed to devise a new distribution network, one that did not rely on thick copper trunk lines carrying electricity into each building. His solution was a network of thin "feeder" wires that powered clusters of lights.

Such developments took time, leaving reporters and investors increasingly concerned with Edison's slow progress. On December 2, 1981, the *New York Times* complained that the Edison company had "laid a considerable quantity of wire, but so far as lighting up the downtown district is concerned, they are as far away from that as ever."

In addition to new technologies, Edison needed to produce political miracles. The Tammany Hall political machine dominated New York and corrupt aldermen demanded payoffs in exchange for the franchise needed to dig up city streets and lay electrical cables. The city's six gas companies also went out of their way to hinder Edison's efforts. The inventor's influential backers, therefore, needed to flex their political muscle in order to compete in the energy marketplace. Grosvenor Lowrey, attorney for Edison, Wells Fargo & Company, and Western Union, arranged a lobbying extravaganza for city commissioners at the Menlo Park laboratory, spent money to "work up an agitation in the daily press having in view the injury of the gas interests," and made payments to legislators in support of a bill allowing electric companies to do business in the state. Lowrey and Edison knew the franchise was as necessary for commercial success as a well-functioning dynamo or a durable lamp.

Edison scheduled the Pearl Street station's debut for September 4, 1882, and assembled his company's directors at J. P. Morgan's office on Wall Street to witness the event. Moments before the demonstration, one director bet "a hundred dollars the lights don't go on." "Taken," snapped Edison.

Precisely at 3:00 P.M., an electrician threw the switch that fed current from a Jumbo generator (named after the great elephant brought to America by P. T. Barnum) to 106 lamps throughout Morgan's office. Fifty-two additional bulbs glowed in the *New York Times'* editorial office. The simultaneous lighting must have astonished the financiers and reporters who were used to setting a flame to each gas lamp individually. The next day's paper described the artificial electric light as "soft, mellow, and grateful to the eye . . . without a particle of flicker to make the head ache. . . . The decision was unanimous in favor of the Edison electric lamp as against gas."

Edison, obviously pleased with his performance, declared, "I've accomplished all I promised."[22]

COMPETITION

Thomas Edison believed in competition. His experiments were spurred by rivals and motivated by money. "I can only invent under powerful incentive," said Edison. "No competition means no invention."[23]

Fortunately for Edison, competition flourished in the emerging electricity industry of the late nineteenth century. Scores of experimenters struggled to devise and market better lamps and dynamos. Lawyers battled over patents, while bankers viewed the new technologies as means to enormous riches. Gas companies, meanwhile, retrenched to protect their monopolies.

Among the competitors was William Sawyer, who convinced patent commissioners in October 1883 that his incandescent bulb with a carbon-baked filament preceded Edison's. Several of Edison's patent applications, it seems, were so slipshod and chaotically drawn that the regulators rejected them.

Hiram Maxim strengthened Edison's fragile filament by filling a bulb with hydrocarbon vapors and igniting them. *Illustrated Science News*, commenting on this "flashing process," predicted, "In connection with electric illumination (Maxim's) name will be remembered long after that of his boastful rival (Edison) is forgotten." A Maxim incandescent lighting system, in fact, was illuminating New York's Mercantile Safe Deposit Company two months before Edison's Pearl Street Station began distributing power.

Two professors from Philadelphia—Elihu Thomson and Edwin Houston—also were designing dynamos for commercial installations and obtaining contracts in several U.S. cities. The pair proved to be particularly skillful at improving and commercializing the inventions of others.

Moses Farmer, meanwhile, displayed his glaring arc lights at Philadelphia's Centennial Exposition of 1876, and Charles Brush installed scores of such lamps to brighten urban centers from Boston to San Francisco. On the very night Edison was entertaining New York commissioners in Menlo Park, the young Cleveland-based chemist launched seventeen powerful arc lamps, illuminating Union Square and three-quarters of a mile of Broadway, in what became known as "the Great White Way." The *New York Evening Post* described the effect as a "clear, sharp, bluish light resembling intense moonlight, with the same deep shadows that moonlight casts."[24]

Competition was fierce by 1890 when more than thirty firms manufactured incandescent lamps. After a rival won the contract to illuminate eight Hudson River ferries, Edison complained bitterly about the "lies of these infamous shysters." Although he obviously felt strongly about making money, Edison described his inventing impetus by stating, "I don't care so much for a fortune, as I do for getting ahead of the other fellow."[25]

Success was not certain since early electric equipment demonstrated both complexities and dangers. In 1883, for example, Edison's associates staged an elaborate unveiling of 1,200 bulbs at the new railroad station in Strasbourg, Germany. Emperor William I arrived to witness the grand event, but rather than see illumination he heard a loud explosion that tore down a wall. An embarrassed Edison sent several engineers to repair the system.

Employing the new electric systems proved difficult even for someone as wealthy and daring as J. Pierpont Morgan. The financier, who enjoyed testing the new technologies in which he invested, decided that his refurbished mansion on Madison Avenue would be the first residence to use Edison's lights and generator. However, his neighbor, the aristocratic Mrs. James Brown, complained about her house shaking as a result of the dynamo in Morgan's basement. The banker responded by ordering Edison to raise the machinery onto thick rubber pads and to pile sandbags around the walls of his cellar. Mrs. Brown subsequently charged that the generator's fumes were tarnishing her silver. Morgan responded by purchasing a different kind of coal, yet he had to survive a string of setbacks within his own house. Despite an on-site engineer, the electric lights flickered off regularly, leaving the financier and his guests groping about the huge and darkened house for candles and lanterns. Morgan also returned one evening to a fire—caused by a spark from a short-circuited electric wire—that destroyed the desk and expensive rug in his library.

Still, early predictions of electricity's might were intoxicating, even if sometimes a little tipsy. "Electricity occupies the twilight zone between the world of the spirit and the world of matter," wrote an early electrical engineer. "Electricians are all proud of their business. They should be. God is the Great Electrician."[26]

Marketing was key, and promoters of electricity had to overcome a range of consumer suspicions and change an array of habits. Success, said one analyst, "required many people to wire their houses, overcome fear of electrocution, discard those whale oil lanterns, and stay up after sundown."[27]

Edison sometimes placed signs near early electric lights stating: "This room is equipped with Edison Electric light. Do not attempt to light with match. Simply turn key on wall by the door. The use of electricity for lighting is in no way harmful to health, nor does it affect the soundness of sleep." The public remained fascinated but skeptical. Security officials even made sure President Benjamin Harrison did not touch the White House's first light switch.

Since gas consumers didn't need to purchase lamps and because electric lights remained brittle, Edison-the-marketer decided to supply and replace his bulbs free of charge. Noting the need for catchy advertising, he promoted his lamps as "the sun's only rival."

Edison's advantage among his electric competitors proved to be his relations with wealthy investors. Already well known for his successful telegraph inventions, the entrepreneur obtained more than $500,000 on the basis solely of his vision for an electric power system. Most other inventors had to show a positive financial return before they could attract underwriters.

Edison viewed gas companies as his "bitter enemies," and he complained that they were "keenly watching our every move and ready to pounce upon us at the slightest failure. Success meant world-wide adoption of our central-station plan. Failure meant loss of money and prestige and setting back our enterprise."[28] Gas lighting systems had evolved throughout the eighteenth and nineteenth centuries as wicks, enclosed containers, and polished reflectors continued to improve. The 1859 discovery of oil sparked a boom in kerosene lighting, displacing whale oil and volatile compounds drawn from heated coal, and investments in the gas industry had soared from $6.5 million in 1850 to $72 million in 1870. Yet Edison understood the system's shortcomings—each gas lamp, for instance, had to be lighted and snuffed out individually; the flame flickered and emitted small quantities of ammonia and sulfur; fumes would blacken the glass globe, as well as the interior of rooms; and people often felt sick after a gas light sucked the oxygen from a room. The innovator felt electricity offered a clearly better alternative.

Contemporary gas companies tended to enjoy exclusive service territories. As monopolists, they had become complacent with their slow but steady growth, and they thought little about marketing gas for anything other than lighting. When faced with competition from electric entrepreneurs, the gas utilities initially tried to consolidate and block the challengers. In 1880, six gas firms merged to form the Consolidated Gas Company of New York, and they began to lower their prices. Ironically, it was Edison who saw a brighter future for the gas companies: "Gas will be manufactured less for lighting as a result of electrical competition and more for heating, etc., thus enlarging its market and increasing its income."[29]

Arc light companies continued for more than a decade to dominate the lighting of public spaces within large cities. Charles Brush had installed twelve arc lamps in Cleveland several months before Edison developed his high-resistance filament, and his firm and the Thomson-Houston Electric Company over the next few years obtained contracts in most major urban areas, from New York to San Francisco.

Competition raged in courts and boardrooms, as well as in the marketplace. Edison eventually won most of his legal battles over contested patents, but at a severe cost. According to the inventor in his later years, again reflecting his habit of exaggeration, "My electric light inventions have brought me no profits, only 40 years of litigation."[30]

Early competition in the electricity industry, undoubtedly, was messy. It involved bribing aldermen for the permits needed to string wires across or under city streets. It resulted in incompatible standards—different-sized plugs or varying voltages—so that people moving across town from one power supplier to another often would not be able to use their fans, irons, and other early appliances. It also involved questionable business deals, as evidenced by Charles Coffin, the former shoe salesman who had purchased the Thomson-Houston firm, and Henry Villard, the railroad organizer interested in selling arc lighting equipment, agreeing to fix prices and split the business of supplying power to city streetcars. Their maneuvers prompted Congress to pass the Sherman Antitrust Act and stifle such arrangements.

Competition also was not pretty. Some twenty electric light, telegraph, and telephone companies strung separate wires on poles and buildings throughout Manhattan. According to the *New York Times*, the downtown streets were "darkened by wires, carried upon towering structures erected on the roofs of fatuously good-natured owners."[31] Even when electric companies went out of business, their lines usually remained, often fraying and creating short circuits. Faulty insulation and exposed wires threatened linemen, as well as tram-pulling horses with metal shoes. Cynics referred to the wire approved by underwriting insurance companies as the "undertaker's wire." Brooklyn's professional baseball team was said to have later taken its name from the citizens dodging trolley tracks for fear of electric shock.

Despite competition from all sides, the Edison Electric Illuminating Company initially achieved steady, but not spectacular, growth. Two months after the Pearl Street Station began service, the number of its customers increased from 59 to 203. A year later, there were 513, yet the venture was losing money. "We were not very commercial," Edison explained about the electric company's early days. "We put many customers on, but did not make out many bills." During these times, Edison faced constant cash shortages.

Outside the Pearl Street service area, however, Edison's fortunes looked brighter. By 1889, at the age of thirty-nine, he was a millionaire and his companies' combined assets totaled almost $10 million. His construction firm had built 500 isolated power plants for buildings and 58 larger units for communities, including Detroit, New Orleans, St. Paul, Chicago, Philadelphia, and Brooklyn. New electric companies were paying royalties to Edison's Electric Light Company for use of his lighting and electrical patents.

Edison's fortune might have been much greater if he had been a better manager. In fact, credit for the business order that did exist goes to Samuel Insull, Edison's personal secretary who for twelve years arranged the innovator's financial records and purchased his clothes. Stubborn and egotistical, Edison also alienated many of his clever colleagues by limiting their responsibilities and rejecting their ideas.

One of these was Frank Sprague. Academically trained at the U.S. Naval Academy, the brilliant mathematician came to New York in 1883 and provided Edison with time-saving formulas to reduce the amount of copper (and thus expense) required for electrical wiring. Sprague's calculations allowed Edison to acquire a lucrative patent but did not earn Sprague the freedom to experiment. After only a year, the mathematician told Edison that unless he was given more independence, he would resign. Edison bluntly responded, "I think it would be the better plan for you to resign."[32] Yet within a month of leaving Sprague patented a unique electric motor that maintained a constant speed regardless of load. Since Edison had failed to design such a practical motor, the Edison Electric Light Company's directors were forced to pay Sprague for the right to manufacture his invention. A few years later, Sprague built the first electric railway, providing a large, daytime demand for electricity. By the turn of the century, the Sprague Electric Railway and Motor Company and other firms had constructed more than 22,000 miles of track and replaced 99 percent of the nation's horse-drawn streetcars.

Edison also lost Nikola Tesla, a moody electrical wizard who began his career at the Edison telephone company in Yugoslavia. The European director of Edison's firms had sent a note to the inventor saying, "I know two great men and you are one of them; the other is this young man."[33] Despite the glowing recommendation, as noted in more detail below, Edison assigned Tesla to routine electrical work. The young engineer solved many difficult problems at the Edison lab, but he continued to earn only $18 a week, and Edison rejected his many requests for a raise. More importantly, Edison rejected Tesla's proposal to utilize alternating rather than direct current. "His ideas are splendid," complained Edison, "but they are utterly impractical."[34] Two years after leaving Edison's lab, Tesla formed the

Tesla Electric Company and filed for a patent on a more efficient motor and an electric distribution system that could carry power hundreds of miles with relatively little loss of voltage. Short of cash, Tesla accepted $1 million from George Westinghouse for his patents, which would revolutionize the electricity business, transforming it from a supplier of nighttime lighting to a twenty-four-hour service for residential and industrial customers, and enabling large generators and long-distance transmission.

WAR OF THE CURRENTS

Westinghouse emerged as Edison's chief competitor in the electricity market. In fact, the Edison-Westinghouse conflict—labeled by the popular press as the "war of the currents"—lasted several years and took odd and gruesome turns. Although partly a simple but aggressive struggle between two corporations, the entrepreneurs' battle proved to be critical to the electricity industry's future.

Edison advanced the use of direct current (DC), which maintained the same low voltage or thrust from the power station to the ultimate consumer. Focusing on safety, Edison argued that DC was not strong enough to cause dangerous electric shocks. "We're set up for direct current in America," he declared. "People like it, and it's all I'll ever fool with. . . . Spare me that nonsense. [Alternating current is] dangerous."[35] Yet direct current wasn't forceful enough to be transmitted over long distances. Contemporary Manhattan would have required at least three dozen DC generators to meet the demand for electricity, stirring complaints about the power plants' noxious fumes and the noise and congestion associated with coal-laden wagons.

Westinghouse, although a latecomer to electrical development, was an inventor in his own right, having perfected the railroad air brake, but he proved to be particularly innovative in his purchase of other peoples' patents. He clearly recognized the benefits of an alternating current (AC) that could convert electricity to higher voltages and send it long distances without significant power losses. Westinghouse acquired the patent for an efficient AC motor from Nikola Tesla and an effective transformer—which "steps up" or increases the electric current outside a large power plant and "steps down" the voltage before its reaches homes and offices—from William Stanley. (Both Tesla and Stanley offered the innovations originally to Edison, who dismissed them as not his own.)

Edison was not alone in his criticism of AC. Leading scientists—including Lord Kelvin, Werner von Siemans, Franklin Pope, and Elihu Thomson—also initially argued that a short-circuited AC transformer or an accidentally grounded high-tension power line could electrocute innocent bystanders. (Several of those researchers, particularly Lord Kelvin, eventually changed their minds and accepted AC's advantages.)

Edison's fears were justified since several electrical workers for arc lighting companies, which employed AC to power their blazing lights, had been shocked and even killed by contact with the high-voltage current. Yet the inventor's flaw was his unwillingness to see the potential for technologies not of his development, and he had become, according to a biographer, "the stubborn, reactionary old man of the electrical industry."[36] Edison lashed out aggressively at Westinghouse's advances, declaring, "The first man who touches a wire in a wet place is a dead man. Just as certain as death, Westinghouse will kill a customer within six months after he puts in a system of any size."[37]

Much of the controversy resulted from simple commercial competition. Edison may have been the celebrated pioneer, but he was losing the electricity market. In 1887, after eight years in business, Edison had sold 121 DC central stations, while Westinghouse, in his first year, constructed or contracted for sixty-eight AC units. In 1888, Edison reported central station orders that could power 44,000 lights, while Westinghouse announced contracts equaling 48,000 lights for the single month of October. Wanting to fight back, Edison issued an eighty-four-page diatribe that assailed Westinghouse and pleaded for electrical engineers to rise up against the infidels of AC: "All electricians who believe in the future of electricity ought to unite in a war of extermination against cheapness in applied electricity, whenever they see that it involves inefficiency and danger."[38]

Westinghouse, recognizing that he possessed the commercial upper hand, sought to limit the controversy with a personal note to Edison: "I believe there has been a systematic attempt on the part of some people to do a great deal of mischief and create as great a difference as possible between the Edison Company and The Westinghouse Electric Co. when there ought to be an entirely different condition of affairs." Westinghouse invited Edison to Pittsburgh, saying: "I have a lively recollection of the pains that you [Edison] took to show me through your works at Menlo Park when I was in pursuit of a plant for my house."[39] Edison rebuffed the gesture, responding curtly, "My laboratory work consumes the whole of my time."[40]

When the New York State legislature asked Edison's opinion of electrocution as a more humane method of capital punishment than hanging, he decided execution by electricity could damage Westinghouse's efforts and reputation. In December 1887, he wrote that the quickest and most painless death "can be accomplished by the use of electricity, and the most suitable apparatus for the purpose is that class of dynamo-electric machine which employs intermittent currents. The most effective of those are known as 'alternating machines,' manufactured principally in this country by Geo. Westinghouse." Suggested names for the new procedure ranged from "electromort" to "electricide." Edison is said to have recommended "Westinghoused."[41]

Having been rejected and challenged, Westinghouse responded initially with a letter to New York officials. If the issue was safety, he declared that no Westinghouse central station had suffered "a single case of fire of any description from the use of our system." He went on to attack Edison's safety record. "Of the 125 central stations of the leading direct current company [Edison's] there were numerous cases of fire, in three of which cases the central station itself was entirely destroyed, the most recent being the destruction of the Boston station; while among the almost innumerable fires caused by this system, among the users, may be mentioned the total destruction of a large theater at Philadelphia."[42] Westinghouse's defense was joined quietly by Charles Coffin of the Thomson-Houston firm, which also installed AC units.

Edison, however, displayed more drama. An engineer associated with the inventor in July 1888 orchestrated a public demonstration in which he placed wires on a sixty-seven-pound dog described as vicious. The direct current, even at varying voltages, did little to the black retriever, but the alternating current killed it immediately. According to one journalist, "Many of the spectators left the room unable to endure the revolting exhibition."[43] The engineer conducted the same "experiment" on some fifty other dogs, cats, calves, and horses in order to portray AC as the perfect medium for electrocution. Neighbors of Edison's New Jersey lab may have complained about the unexplained disappearances of pets and farm animals, but the gruesome tactics worked. After a reporter witnessed 700 volts of AC kill a 1,230-pound horse, the *New York Times* declared, "The experiments proved the alternating current to be the most deadly force known to science, and that less than half the pressure used in this city for electric [arc] lighting by this [AC] system is sufficient to cause instant death. After

Jan. 1, the alternating current will undoubtedly drive the hangman out of business in this State."[44]

Edison and his lobbyists convinced New York State to install a secondhand Westinghouse generator (Westinghouse refused to sell one) and electric chair at the Auburn State Prison. The first electrocution—on August 6, 1890, of William Kemmler, who had murdered his wife with an ax—was described as "an awful spectacle, far worse than hanging," with witnesses reporting that Kemmler's spinal cord exploded into flames. In fact, the first jolt of AC caused Kemmler to go limp, but he continued to breathe and he oozed a sickly foam from his masked mouth hole. One witness screamed "For God's sake, kill him and have it over!" A second jolt caused Kemmler to go rigid and his clothes to catch on fire. According to the *New York Times*, "The stench was unbearable."[45]

Edison continued to use electrocution to lobby against AC, asking, "Do you want the executioner's current in your home and running through the streets?" Despite such gory questions, many communities sided with AC's economics, and sales of Westinghouse systems rose. Also lobbying for AC were the hundreds of arc light companies that depended on high voltage. Even some of Edison's own employees were asking for AC so they could expand their service territories. At the 1889 meeting of the Edison Illuminating Companies, Detroit Edison's station manager successfully advanced a resolution asking the parent company to provide "a flexible method of enlarging the territory which can be profitably covered from their stations for domestic lighting by higher pressures and consequently less outlay of copper."[46]

The wizard of Menlo Park may have won the debate on electrocution, but he lost the war of the currents to the AC units that could deliver power over longer distances. Perhaps more frustrating, he also was losing Wall Street struggles for control of his own company.

Edison certainly understood the world of finance. In 1890, he and Henry Villard, a savvy investor and the force behind the Union Pacific Railroad, reorganized and capitalized at $12 million the innovator's various companies into Edison General Electric. Yet the increasingly proud Edison would not consider merging with another firm, particularly Thomson-Houston, which he claimed to have "boldly appropriated and infringed every patent we use."[47] Villard, however, favored a consolidation in order to eliminate the sixty patent battles then in the courts and to obtain access to Thomson-Houston's AC lighting systems. Although Thomson-Houston's

Charles Coffin was willing to negotiate, such a merger would not occur without the support of Wall Street's major banker, J. P. Morgan, who in February 1891 could see no gain from a consolidation. A year later, however, Morgan changed his mind.

While Edison thrived on competition, Morgan felt too much battling among companies was "ruinous" and resulted in low profits. He concocted scores of backroom deals and eventually outmaneuvered Edison. The inventor's vulnerability long had been financing, which he often struggled to obtain. During a period when Edison-company sales were stagnant, the innovator lamented, "I do not know just how we are going to live. I think I could go back and earn my living as a telegraph operator."[48] Later, said Edison, when "our orders were far in excess of our capital to handle the business, both Mr. Insull and I were afraid we might get in trouble for lack of money."[49]

Morgan for many years had recognized the profit potential in Edison's genius, but he kept his eyes ever alert to other opportunities. While the New York banker was installing Edison equipment in his Manhattan mansion, for instance, he quietly invested in the Thomson-Houston Electric Company of Lynn, Massachusetts, which had some patents for power plants of its own and some it had pirated from Westinghouse and Edison. To give a sense of the fast pace of the electrical industry's development, consider that only a decade after Morgan turned the switch in his own home did he cleverly arrange for the lesser-known Thomson-Houston to absorb Edison's companies. Both firms enjoyed annual sales of approximately $10 million, but Thomson-Houston was more profitable, with a 26-percent return compared to Edison's 11 percent. Thomson-Houston also was sitting on substantial cash reserves, while Edison's resources were tied up in the stock of local companies marketing electricity.

According to the understated Insull, merger negotiations "were not particularly pleasant."[50] Edison stockholders obtained only $15 million of the new company's stock, compared to $18 million for Thomson-Houston's investors. Morgan largely excluded directors of the Edison companies from the new board. Edison himself, frustrated by the financial machinations and wanting to focus on other inventions, surrendered his patent rights for about $1.75 million in cash and stock, about $1 million of which went to his associates. Although free to launch other ventures, Edison was particularly bitter that the new corporation would not bear his name. General Electric became the industry's dominant firm, controlling three-quarters of the nation's electrical business. Its major remaining competitor was the Westinghouse Company.

WESTINGHOUSE

Unlike Edison, George Westinghouse virtually ignored public relations and posterity. He delivered few speeches and wrote almost no articles, journals, or even private letters. "If my face becomes too familiar to the public," the entrepreneur stated, "every bore or crazy schemer will insist on buttonholing me."[51] While his name still graces a giant corporation, Westinghouse never obtained Edison's mythic status of folk hero. It didn't help his reputation that Westinghouse's early inventions related to railroad brakes while Edison devised the more glamorous phonograph and motion picture. Still, both men played seminal roles in the electricity industry's development.

George Westinghouse. Courtesy of the George Westinghouse Museum.

Edison and Westinghouse invented prolifically. Westinghouse obtained some 400 patents, averaging almost one and a half for every month of the forty-eight years of his working life. Both men inspired teams of creative assistants, yet Westinghouse lacked Edison's giant ego and was more willing to appreciate the genius of other inventors. Westinghouse, in fact, proved to be a resourceful financier of diverse experimenters and he integrated their work into his larger vision for generating and delivering electricity. Both Edison and Westinghouse eventually lost control of their companies to deep-pocketed bankers, but it was their competition—and the eventual success of Westinghouse's AC model—that enabled the electricity industry's expansion and monopolization.

Westinghouse, born the same year as Edison, learned his inventing skills at his father's shop in Schenectady, New York. George Westinghouse, Sr., opened that facility in 1856 to build small steam engines, farm machines, and mill works, and the ingenious mechanic eventually acquired seven patents for sewing machines, thrashers, and winnowers. There's some irony that Edison eventually opened his Schenectady production works near the factory labeled "G. Westinghouse & Co."

Although quiet in public, Westinghouse was engaging and even charismatic. A solid man of six feet, with thick sideburns and a handlebar mustache, he appeared to be both intense and genial. According to a biographer, "With his soft voice, his kind eyes, and his gentle smile, he could charm a bird out of a tree. It is related that in a knotty negotiation it was suggested to the late Jacob H. Schiff, then the head of a great banking house, that he should meet Westinghouse. 'No,' said the astute old Jew, 'I do not wish to see Mr. Westinghouse; he would persuade me.' "[52]

Westinghouse sketched and dictated constantly. At home, he designed on a billiards table, and his car served as a roving office. Each morning Westinghouse delivered reams of sketches and directives to his teams, and he demanded fast action. Throughout the afternoons, he dogged the engineers and workers, listening carefully to their concerns and suggestions and using the corner of virtually any table to sketch alternative approaches.

Westinghouse was a wealthy and successful inventor before he turned his attentions toward electricity. He was most known for his work on railroads. That he survived the ruthless world of railroad conglomerates testifies to his business skills and persistence. He learned painful lessons early when he licensed his first invention—a "car replacer" that moved derailed trains back onto the tracks—to railroad companies, which quickly made slight "improvements" to the device and claimed the patents and profits for their own.

Westinghouse's focus on railroad brakes began in 1866 after two trains traveling between Schenectady and Troy suffered a head-on collision, a tragic accident that could have been avoided if the trains had been able to stop quickly. Existing technology, known by trainmen as the "arm-strong brake," could barely halt a 30-mile-per-hour train within 1,600 feet. Westinghouse's initial air brakes cut that distance to 500 feet. His refinements—which included 103 patents—reduced the distance further, while also curtailing shocks and equipment damage.

Wiser this time around, Westinghouse refused to provide brake licenses to the railroads, deciding instead to manufacture the equipment at his own small factories in Pittsburgh. Still, like Edison, Westinghouse needed lawyers to protect his patents since numerous competitors challenged his claims, arguing that their devices preceded his or that theirs were more comprehensive or effective. Various litigants filed thousands of papers to prove their points. Several of those suits were combined in 1875 and threatened the very foundation of Westinghouse's efforts and business. A Cleveland-based judge agreed that "Westinghouse was not the first to conceive the idea of operating railway brakes by air pressure" and that he "was not the inventor of the larger part of the devices employed for such purposes." Yet the judge concluded that Westinghouse "was the first, so far as appears in the record and proofs, to put an air brake into successful actual use. . . . There are essential differences between these prior patents and the Westinghouse apparatus."[53]

Westinghouse, unlike Edison, willingly considered the inventions of others, and he frequently bought promising patents. For instance, he paid $50,000 to the Swan Incandescent Electric Light Company for William Stanley's designs associated with a carbonized silk filament and a self-regulating DC dynamo. Westinghouse even hired Stanley, at a substantial $5,000-per-year salary, to advance his electrical efforts. After reading in an English journal about a "secondary generator" (now known as a transformer)—which reduced higher voltages to a level at which they could power an incandescent lamp—he sent a representative to Turin in order to negotiate patent rights with the inventors Lucien Gaulard and John Gibbs.

No doubt Westinghouse's electricity work followed Edison's. While the Menlo Park team opened the Pearl Street Station in 1882, Westinghouse's first major lighting projects—the Windsor Hotel in New York and the

Monongahela Hotel in Pittsburgh—started operations in 1886. Later that year, he installed in Trenton his first major "centralized" power station, composed of six 100-volt, DC dynamos, each of which could power 300 lamps. Yet Westinghouse expanded rapidly. Within three years, the Westinghouse Electric Company had placed generators powering more than 350,000 incandescent lights, most of which ran on AC.

Westinghouse turned to AC in response to the laws of science and the costs of transmission lines, otherwise known as the conductors of electricity. The amount of electric power that a conductor can carry depends upon the power's pressure, or voltage, and the size of the conductor. If the voltage is low, as it is from the DC generators that Edison favored, the conductor or transmission line must be large (and expensive) when the power is to be sent a considerable distance. However, a conductor's cost can be minimized if the voltage is increased. Westinghouse realized that AC allows that pressure to be "stepped up" by a transformer, sent long distances through the wires at a high voltage, and then "stepped down" by another transformer near where the electricity is delivered to lights and machines.

The introduction of AC into a U.S. community was done quietly and without fanfare at a small town in rural Massachusetts. Twenty-eight-year-old William Stanley, whom Westinghouse sent from Pittsburgh's smoky factories to the pleasant tranquility of Great Barrington, established a laboratory in an old barn on Main Street. There in March 1886, a 25-horsepower, coal-fueled steam engine sent 500 volts of AC electricity across copper wires. Outside several stores, Stanley placed step-down transformers that delivered 100 volts to scores of incandescent lamps. Over the next several weeks, he added a restaurant, post office, billiards parlor, and dozens of other customers. Not constrained by distance because of the high-voltage AC, Stanley quickly wired the town and surrounding homes.

With success at Great Barrington, Westinghouse decided to take a high-profile gamble with the lighting of Chicago's Columbian Exposition in 1893. Hundreds of thousands would attend the international event, and Chicago leaders viewed the fair as the means to highlight their city and advertise broadly the growing metropolis's energy and inventiveness. National politicians wanted the event to declare American engineering superiority. What they needed were the new-fangled artificial lights . . . and lots of them.

Westinghouse's bid was only half of General Electric's $1.7-million quote. Yet he needed to produce 250,000 lamps within just a few months, and General Electric was threatening patent-infringement lawsuits if Westinghouse used, or developed something close to, the Edison lamp. According to the GE's hard-charging Charles Coffin, a successful lawsuit would place Westinghouse "entirely in our power. He will not be able to make his own lamps, and he can only buy from us."[54]

Westinghouse pushed his team aggressively to create a unique two-piece lamp, on which a "stopper" could be removed in order to replace burned-out filaments. Other inventors had tried the approach and failed, primarily because the design couldn't seem to hold a vacuum, without which the filament would burn out quickly. Westinghouse sketched scores of alternative designs but for weeks nothing seemed to work. With little time remaining before the exposition, Westinghouse settled on his most-reliable option, even though its filaments promised to expire relatively quickly and require replacements. A court eventually upheld the Edison patent, yet Westinghouse converted a warehouse into a glass factory that churned out thousands of stopper lamps, and he arranged for trains every night of the fair to transport damaged lights from Chicago to Pittsburgh and to return the next day with repaired supplies.

General Electric continued to press its case, arguing that even the "stopper" bulb infringed on Edison's now-upheld patent. On the morning of Christmas Eve, GE lawyers sought an immediate restraining order, knowing that any delay would sabotage Westinghouse's Columbian Exposition contract. The judge, however, was not about to rush such a significant decision, and several weeks later he ruled that the Westinghouse bulb posed "no infringement of the Edison lamp patent."[55]

Westinghouse appreciated that he might lose money on the Columbian Exposition, yet he maintained a long-term perspective. "There is not much money in the work at the figures I have made," he stated, "but the advertisement will be a valuable one and I want it."[56] Another major project—to capture and deliver power from Niagara Falls—was pending, and the selection committee of eminent engineers needed proof that Westinghouse's AC system would work.

In addition to the 250,000 lamps, Westinghouse needed advanced motors, more effective transformers, and 1,000-horsepower generators. When he acquired Tesla's primitive AC motor in 1888, it could barely drive a ten-inch ventilating fan. Existing transformers could supply only a few incandescent lamps, and they lost a lot of energy in the process. The prospect of delivering thousands of horsepower at high efficiency seemed little more than an optimist's dream. Thus, on a far grander scale than Edison's Pearl Street Station, Westinghouse needed to upgrade the array of systems required to produce a central power station that could deliver a steady and substantial stream of electricity. He assembled in Chicago the world's largest AC power station, producing the greatest concentration of artificial light, yet his 1,000-square-foot switchboard required only one engineer to operate the forty circuits that delivered power throughout the fairground.

The effect was staggering—on wide-eyed exposition participants as well as skeptical engineers—when President Grover Cleveland pushed a button and caused the fairgrounds to burst into light. Cannons blared, an orchestra and choir performed Handel's "Hallelujah Chorus," and elaborate fountains shot water a hundred feet into the air. Noting that electricity powered far more than lamps, the fair's chief electrician boasted, "The Columbian Exposition is a magnificent triumph of the age of electricity. . . . All the exhibits in all the buildings are operated by electrical transmission (as well as) the Intramural Elevated Railway, the launches that ply the Lagoons, the Sliding Railway on the thousand-foot pier, the great Ferris Wheel (rising 250 feet), and the machinery of the Libby Glass Company on the Midway."[57] The exposition, in fact, generated and consumed three times more electricity than did the entire city of Chicago.

The chairman of the International Niagara Commission, Sir William Thomson (later Lord Kelvin), witnessed the event and dropped his opposition to AC. Westinghouse proved his point, won new contracts, and even forced the General Electric Company to secure a license for the use of Tesla's AC patents. More importantly, he demonstrated the primacy of alternating current and set the stage for centralized power plants and utility monopolies.

Despite that success, Westinghouse and most other businessmen faced severe financial challenges. Three days before the exposition's gala opening, the Philadelphia & Reading Railroad failed, and Wall Street suffered a panic known as "Industrial Black Friday." Five days later, Chicago's Chemical National Bank closed abruptly, and the Panic of 1893 eventually sent 16,000 businesses, 500 banks, and 150 railroads into bankruptcy. The Westinghouse Company almost became one of those casualties.

Electricity companies were particularly vulnerable because they depended heavily upon capital in order to expand. Westinghouse's short-term liabilities exceeded his assets by $500,000, and the umbrella-totting entrepreneur headed to New York in search of cash, which was hard to come by in a depression. Bankers concluded that Westinghouse had mismanaged his company and been too generous, paying, for example, $70,000 (as well as lucrative royalties) to Tesla for patents to an AC induction motor. The *New York Times* reported that "financiers and stockholders now favor the appointment of a receiver for the Westinghouse Electric Company."[58]

The idealistic Tesla, however, proved to be Westinghouse's savior. In a letter, Tesla declared: "Mr. Westinghouse, you have been my friend, you believed in me when others had no faith; you were brave enough to go ahead and pay me . . . when others lacked courage; you supported me when even your own engineers lacked vision to see the big things ahead that you and I saw; you have stood by me as a friend. The benefits that will come to civilization from my polyphase system mean more to me than the money involved. Mr. Westinghouse, you will save your company so that you can develop my inventions. Here is your contract and here is my contract—I will tear both of them to pieces and you will no longer have any troubles from my royalties. Is that sufficient?"[59] That action and other efforts initially allowed Westinghouse to maintain control of his company. According to Tesla's long-time friend and biographer, the eccentric inventor's sacrifice cost him a princely $17.5 million in royalties.[60]

TESLA

Nikola Tesla may be history's most overlooked electrical genius. Odd idiosyncrasies, fanciful predictions, and failures to capitalize on patents contributed to his low profile, particularly in comparison with Thomas Edison, the American-born icon. Yet the *New York Times* in 1895 declared: "Perhaps the most romantic part of the story of this great enterprise (of capturing and delivering electricity) would be the history of the career of the man above all men who made it possible . . . a man of humble birth, who has risen almost before he reached the fullness of manhood to a place in the first rank of the world's great scientists and discoverers—Nikola Tesla."[61]

Tesla was born in 1856 in a part of the Austro-Hungarian Empire that is now Croatia, the youngest child of a parish priest and an inventive mother who created a mechanical eggbeater and other practical appliances. The entire family demonstrated remarkable skills, and young "Niko" managed at the age of six to show frustrated town officials how to operate their new fire engine. He graduated in 1873 from Austria's Real Gymna-

Nikola Tesla. Courtesy of the Tesla Memorial Society of New York.

sium at Carlstadt and soon obtained a job with Edison's European-based company, where he designed a creative repeater that foreshadowed the loudspeaker. When Tesla decided to seek opportunities in the United States, Charles Batchelor, manager of the Continental Edison Company, wrote a glowing letter of introduction.

Tesla's first meeting with Edison (like Edison's later meeting with Samuel Insull, which is described in the next chapter) illustrated a clash of cultures and personalities. Although almost penniless, Tesla wore an immaculate bowler hat and white gloves. At more than six feet tall, with a slim build and piercing eyes, he appeared to be a worldly gentleman who spoke fluent English, Serbian, German, French, and Italian. Edison, in contrast, was frumpy and grumpy, and his English, muddled by chewing tobacco, reflected a midwestern drawl. Despite their differences and awkward exchanges, the U.S. inventor desperately needed engineers and asked Tesla if he could fix a lighting system on the SS *Oregon*, whose wealthy owner was growing increasingly angry at the delays. Tesla completed the electrical repairs within twenty-four hours and was offered a job, yet at only $18 per week.

Both Tesla and Edison thrived on work, often staying up all night to test different approaches or materials. Yet Tesla maintained an excessive cleanliness, actually demonstrating a compulsive fear of germs, while Edison, according to Tesla, "lived in utter disregard of the most elementary rules of hygiene."[62] Both men, moreover, had high opinions of their own abilities and did not take kindly to other egocentrics.

Tesla tried to convince Edison of AC's advantages, suggesting that it would liberate the Edison systems from the shackle of their one-mile-radius limitation. According to Tesla, Edison responded "very bluntly that he was not interested in alternating current; there was no future to it and anyone who dabbled in that field was wasting his time; and besides, it was a deadly current whereas direct current was safe."[63]

Edison's engineers had developed a score of inventive dynamos and machines, yet Tesla boldly declared he could increase their efficiency dramatically. Edison remained skeptical, but, according to Tesla, promised $50,000 for success. After months of hard work and remarkable progress, Tesla asked to be paid. Edison expressed astonishment at the request and, according to Tesla's later account, stated that his monetary offer had been made in jest: "When you become a full-fledged American you will appreciate an American joke."[64] Tesla did not laugh, and despite Edison's offer of a $10-per-week raise, the immigrant left and spent the next several months working odd jobs and digging ditches on New York City's streets. Word of the brilliant Serbian, however, passed among various financiers, several of whom helped form the Tesla Electric Light Company in order to improve arc lighting for urban streets and to design an AC motor.

Tesla, who admitted to being extremely sensitive to sound and light, was able to visualize electrical processes vividly. When walking as a student in a Budapest park and quoting Goethe's *Faust*, the inventor claimed to have grabbed a stick and drew in the dirt a diagram of the rotating magnetic field and a motor that could capture its energy. Expanding on discoveries by Michael Faraday, Tesla envisioned how a magnetic field would build at right angles to a copper wire carrying electricity and, at the same time, how the field's flux lines would cut through a parallel wire and create momentary flows in the opposite direction. He saw that by varying the current in the first wire the magnetic field would rise and fall and a continuous, varying current would flow in the second wire. Some six years after his initial drawing, Tesla and his Electric Light Company filed seven

U.S. patents for a complete system of AC generators, transformers, transmission wires, motors, and lights. In 1888, at the age of thirty-one, he delivered a major speech that outlined the potential of AC, startling and amazing the American Institute of Electrical Engineers assembled at Columbia University. The outline did not become a reality, however, for another four years, when Tesla devised a 100-horsepower motor that he sold to the Gold King Mine high in Colorado's San Juan Mountains.

The ever-dreamy Tesla portrayed his discoveries with broad strokes and envisioned contributing his inventions to the world: "No more will men be slaves to hard tasks. My motor will set them free, it will do the work of the world."[65] Tesla also demonstrated a flare for public relations, as evidenced by his dramatic and engaging photographs of himself holding and pondering a glowing globe without any wires. The eccentric scientist even punctuated his lectures with electrical flames leaping from his body as he held a line carrying thousands of volts.

Westinghouse, although wealthy from his railroad inventions, was a struggling electrical engineer when he recognized Tesla as "an inspired genius, into whose mind inventions sprang."[66] He also understood that Tesla's induction motor and polyphase system could enable Westinghouse companies to deliver electricity efficiently to an array of factories and appliances. He offered $70,000 for Tesla's patents, as well as royalties of $2.50 for every horsepower of electrical capacity that the Westinghouse Company sold. That later provision would make Tesla, at least temporarily, a wealthy man.

Tesla also proved to be a dapper and socially connected scientist. Erudite, erect, and handsome, with jet-black hair parted in the middle, he was often invited to dinner parties at some of New York City's most prominent houses. Yet the inventor also possessed his quirks, including a deep fear of germs. Recognizing his need to wash, hotels supplied him with at least eighteen clean towels daily. The scientist particularly abhorred any contact with hair, and he claimed to have "a violent aversion against the earrings of women."[67] Peaches, even thoughts of the fruit, would bring on a fever. He also displayed a phobia for the number "three," requiring that his footsteps in walks around the block be divisible by three, and he would not sleep in a hotel room unless its number was so divisible. Tesla's joy came from reciting from memory long poems by Goethe or Serbian authors. Not surprisingly, the suave and successful scientist remained a bachelor. While ignoring Edison and Westinghouse, Tesla justified his choice by declaring, "I do not think you can name many great inventions that have been made by married men."[68]

Tesla's designs allowed Westinghouse to succeed at Chicago's Columbian Exposition and the Niagara Falls Power Project. His motivation was idealism, as reflected by his conclusion that Niagara "signifies the subjugation of natural forces to the service of man, the discontinuance of barbaric methods, the relieving of millions from want and suffering." His idealism, in fact, caused a rupture with the more pragmatic and profit-motivated Westinghouse. In remarks for a dinner speech to Niagara's celebrating developers, Tesla wrote of his intention to make the project's power lines obsolete. He expressed hope that "I shall see fulfillment of one of my fondest dreams, namely, the wireless transmission of energy."[69] Having read the speech beforehand, Westinghouse's colleagues abruptly excised comments that challenged their investments.

That episode symbolized much of Tesla's later achievements and predictions—brilliant, but unappreciated and often unrealized. Tesla, in fact, viewed himself as a discoverer rather than an inventor of useful and profitable devices.

He filed the first basic radio patent in September 1897, more than three years before Guglielmo Marconi. Patent authorities, in fact, initially rejected Marconi's application for wireless transmission, citing the priority of Tesla's experiments. Yet Marconi, not unlike Edison, was a consummate promoter who attracted investments from Andrew Carnegie, J. P. Morgan, and other influential backers. Perhaps because of that influence, the U.S. Patent Office abruptly reversed its decision in 1904 and granted a patent to Marconi, allowing his company (which later became RCA), as well as his name, to flourish. After Marconi won the Nobel Prize in 1911, a bitter Tesla sued, but by then he lacked the financial resources to challenge a major corporation. Ironically, in 1943, a few months after Tesla died, the Supreme Court, responding to a Marconi lawsuit against the U.S. military, declared that Tesla, in fact, was the radio's inventor and that his patent had anticipated those of Marconi and all other contenders.

Despite the brilliant ideas, Tesla faced persistent financial problems, and he increasingly focused on projects that failed to demonstrate near-term, practical results. Tesla's rudimentary radio telescope, for instance, captured the first sounds from space, but his claim that the noises came from life on Mars elicited much ridicule. Another expensive and result-poor experiment was a 187-foot transmission tower topped with a 55-ton sphere. Sixteen iron pipes extended some 420 feet into the ground, where the unit's electrical currents were to take advantage of the Earth's magnetic fields and transmit wireless signals to all parts of the world, using the planet as a natural conductor. The effort—located at Wardenclyffe, some 60 miles from New York City on Long Island—was soon abandoned, and the inventor eventually declared bankruptcy.

Tesla, who never worked well with others, increasingly became a recluse and an unappreciated prophet. He developed the first remote-controlled vessel and extremely accurate clocks, yet no one paid any notice. He foresaw automation in which "a race of robots, mechanical men, will do the laborious work of the human race,"[70] yet his notions proved to be decades ahead of his time. He envisioned the harnessing of energy from the sun, foresaw machines that could think, and outlined the technical concepts for radar.[71] Even at age 72, Tesla filed a patent for a flying machine that mixed attributes of an airplane and a helicopter. Yet some of his predictions were simply wild visions. Tesla, for instance, foresaw individuals taking dry baths with the "cold fire" of millions of volts of electricity that would throw off dirt and dead skin.

Edison and Westinghouse certainly became more famous, in part because their efforts built substantial corporations that still flourish. Yet Tesla, despite his idiosyncrasies and bizarre predictions, proved to be a genius who advanced the electrical age. According to the American Institute of Electrical Engineers: "Were we to seize and eliminate from our industrial world the results of Mr. Tesla's work, the wheels of industry would cease to turn, our electric cars and trains would stop, our towns would be dark, our mills would be dead and idle."[72]

NIAGARA

Tapping the 164-foot torrent at Niagara Falls had been an engineer's dream since the first sawmill was constructed there in 1725. More than seventeen firms had submitted hydroelectric plans by 1891, but the high-profile Niagara Falls Commission rejected them all. Westinghouse finally obtained the contract in 1893 with a bold plan that called for an elaborate system of canals and tunnels through which a diverted Niagara River would turn 29-ton turbines. Ten Tesla-designed generators, as well as transformers and transmission lines, would send alternating current over the 22 miles to Buffalo.

Westinghouse's plan marked a dynamic shift from a mechanical era to the age of electricity. While rejected conceptions called for 238 water wheels attached to shafts and pulleys and placed along a long intake canal, Westinghouse and the Niagara Commission gambled that a series of new electric technologies could generate and transmit 100,000 horsepower, more than was then provided by all existing U.S. central power stations. To deliver the electricity from Niagara Falls to Buffalo's population center, the power was to be stepped up by transformers from 2,000 to 10,000 volts, sent across copper wires attached to wood poles, and then stepped down at the Buffalo substation to 2,000 volts by a second set of transformers. Commission executives later admitted that their decision to use AC was based on "faith and hope." According to Westinghouse, "The conditions of the problems presented, especially as regards the amount of power to be dealt with, have been so far beyond all precedent that it has been necessary to devise a considerable amount of new apparatus. . . . Nearly every device used differs from what has hitherto been our standard practice."[73]

The Niagara Falls project was not the world's first demonstration of long-distance electricity transmission. German engineers previously had powered a small 100-horsepower motor at the Frankfort Exhibition with electricity generated in Lauffen, 108 miles away. Tesla himself in 1881 helped send hydropower from Telluride, Colorado, to high-altitude mines desperate for power. In 1886, William Stanley, with backing from Westinghouse, had demonstrated a modest AC generator in Great Barrington, Massachusetts, that provided lighting to thirteen stores, two hotels, and a post office. Yet these early efforts were limited in scope, while Niagara Falls demanded an engineering feat on a grand scale. The *New York Times* referred to it as "the unrivaled engineering triumph of the nineteenth century."[74]

The site's scale overwhelmed observers. The water tunnel was 1,500 feet long and 500 feet wide, dug out by 1,300 workmen. The 29-ton turbines were then the world's largest. According to author H. G. Wells, "These are altogether noble masses of machinery, huge black slumbering monsters, great sleeping tops that engineer irresistible forces in their sleep. . . . I fell into a daydream of the coming power of men, and how that power may be used by them."[75]

Buffalo's street railway company obtained Niagara's first 1,000 horsepower on November 16, 1896. The date was postponed by a day because the unit's chief engineer promised his father, an Episcopal minister, not to work on the Sabbath. When the three switches were thrown, a delighted mayor declared, "The power is here!"[76] The abundant electricity eventually attracted to the Buffalo/Niagara region the world's largest concentration of electrochemical companies as well as the firm that became the Aluminum Company of America. Electricity from the falls soon traveled all the way to New York City, where it helped light Broadway and power new subways.

The AC system envisioned by Tesla and produced by Westinghouse revolutionized the power industry, allowing the construction of large generating plants far away from a central city and its demand for electricity. High-voltage transmission lines and giant generators also concentrated power companies, allowing Samuel Insull and others to create the regulated utility monopolies that have dominated the U.S. electricity market for almost nine decades.

3

Monopolists

Prospects for the electricity industry flickered at the dawn of the twentieth century, despite Edison's optimistic predictions. Motors electrified only one factory in thirteen since manufacturers were reluctant to abandon their steam-powered, belt-driven systems for unreliable generators. Incandescent bulbs illuminated only one lamp in twenty as most homeowners favored the less expensive and more pleasant glow of gas lamps. In 1907, electricity served only 8 percent of American homes.

Chaos reigned on the wires. Different electric systems in the same city were based on patents by Edison, Sawyer, Maxim, Westinghouse, or Brush. Some DC operations offered power at 100, 110, 220, or 600 volts; AC firms provided frequencies of 40, 60, 66, 125, or 133 cycles. A customer moving across the street often found his lamps and electrical appliances did not work in his new home or office.

Even most power entrepreneurs believed electricity would remain a luxury item. Additional customers, they feared, would only require the borrowing of more money and the construction of expensive generators and distribution lines, which would increase costs and decrease profits. The favored business plan was to grow slowly by encouraging a niche market of wealthy consumers to employ more light bulbs.

Smart money also supported small and dispersed generators over central power stations. Even with the advance of AC and the ability to construct large plants that transmitted electricity over long distances, banker J. P. Morgan and his General Electric Company preferred the immediate profits of selling isolated generators rather than the uncertainties of marketing electricity from centralized generators. He and other investors thought the best way to make money was to mass produce small-scale, generate-your-own-power systems for factories and office buildings. Morgan's Manhattan mansion and Henry Villard's steamship sported small generators, two of the 150 operating before Edison's Pearl Street Station even opened. Morgan, in fact, had General Electric charge inflated prices for its central-station equipment in order to protect the manufacturing firm's profits from small-scale generators.

The prospect of utilities selling electricity from large power plants seemed dim. By the spring of 1883, Pearl Street remained the only central (yet still small) generator, while 334 isolated Edison plants operated. Although several towns slowly adopted Pearl Street-sized systems, Edison's focus was on hustling units to hotels, banks, mills, ironworks, and theaters across the country, and George Westinghouse was winning high-profile contracts to provide small generators for the St. Louis post office, the New York State Capitol building, and the Pennsylvania Railroad's eight Hudson River ferries.

Samuel Insull developed a different vision. Edison's personal assistant had spent several years convincing communities around the country to build centralized power plants that employed Edison equipment. Before J. P. Morgan grabbed control of Edison's company, Insull lined up contracts in Harrisburg, Pennsylvania; Newburgh, New York; Tiffin, Ohio; and two dozen other towns. He recognized a marketing potential.

Since Wall Street financiers favored building-specific power plants, Insull decided to strike out on his own. The brilliant promoter realized that AC enabled larger generators, and he envisioned creating giant monopolies. In 1892, Insull rejected General Electric's $36,000-per-year job in favor of a $12,000-per-year position managing the Chicago Edison Company, one of many struggling electricity-generating firms in the Windy City. He decided to move from managing GE's Schenectady Works and its 6,000 employees to running a small Chicago firm that employed only 300 men. At his farewell dinner from New York at Delmonico's Restaurant, Insull brashly predicted his new company soon would be bigger than General Electric, which then held twenty times more assets. That remark, according to Insull, "caused a great deal of amusement." Yet few in the audience realized how quickly the consummate hustler could create an empire.

INSULL'S GENIUS

Chicago Edison Company appeared fragile when Samuel Insull arrived in 1892. It served only a fraction of the present-day Loop, and it had built its only power plant just four years before. More than forty other firms generated electricity within the city limits.

Traction companies produced most of the town's power. Electric streetcars, a relatively new urban feature, first appeared at the Berlin Industrial Exhibition of 1879. Six years later, New Orleans, South Bend, and Minneapolis installed systems, and Chicago and most other U.S. cities quickly joined the rush to replace horse-drawn public transportation with one or several traction companies. Those firms devoured electricity in quantities that overshadowed the demand from electric lights, and they owned their own generators in order to obtain cheaper power than was provided by the few centralized stations. In fact, on-site generators—operated by streetcar companies, commercial building managers, and industrialists—supplied two-thirds of the nation's electricity in the late nineteenth century.

Insull understood that if Chicago Edison was to grow it needed to integrate and optimize the demands of streetcar companies and disparate electricity consumers. The traction firms ran their trams mostly during the morning and evening commutes, leaving their generators virtually idle most other hours. Large office buildings employed illuminated lights during the day, but demanded little electricity at night. Street lighting companies, in contrast, needed power at night but not throughout the day. Translated into engineering terms, these isolated generators suffered low load factors, and electricity remained relatively expensive.

Insull saw the potential for interconnecting different loads and enhancing the efficiency of centralized power plants. He shut down the isolated street-lighting generators and obtained night-time demand. He bribed the streetcar companies to purchase rather than generate power and gained a large load during the morning and early evening. (To ensure his success, Insull also persuaded Chicago's politicians, to whom he was a large contributor, to designate his company as the sole supplier of power to traction firms, thus doubling his sales.) By marketing special rates to large office buildings and industries, Insull also sold electricity through-out the day. His centralized power plants, as a result, operated regularly, thus reducing his costs and rates, which only increased the demand for his electricity. According to Insull, "Every home, every factory, and every transportation line will obtain its energy from one common source, for the simple reason that that will be the cheapest way to produce and distribute it."[1]

Most utility executives were engineers who felt they simply needed to construct enough generators and power lines to meet the peak demand during early evening hours when consumers rode trolleys and turned on their home lamps. They cared little if their equipment laid idle most of the rest of the day and night. Insull, in contrast, realized that his profits would be determined primarily by the percentage of time his power plants operated. Since his goal became running those generators as consistently as possible, he fervently sought customers.

Insull inverted contemporary thinking that electricity was a high-priced luxury item. Noting that electric rates at the turn of the century were uncompetitive, almost 50 percent greater than gas, he cut prices from 20 cents per kilowatt-hour to 10 cents by 1897, and he proceeded every year or two to impose an additional 1-cent drop until prices reached 2½ cents per kilowatt-hour in 1909. As a result, the number of Chicago Edison customers soared from 5,000 in 1892, to 50,000 in 1906, to 200,000 in 1913.

A less charitable view of Insull's motives would highlight his passion against competition. Although Edison needed competition to invent, his former secretary declared it to be "economically wrong." Insull consistently directed his salesmen to "sell your product at a price which will enable you to get a monopoly."[2] He also did his best to block new competitors. When Westinghouse tried to obtain a midwestern foothold, Insull quickly surrounded the small power plant in Evanston, Illinois, with his own electric facilities. Westinghouse soon realized he could not expand and abandoned the effort.

Insull acquired coal mines and railroads in order to reduce his supply costs, and then he targeted Chicago's other power companies. Over lunch with the president of Chicago Arc Light and Power, for instance, Insull announced his intention to purchase the firm. The executive laughed at the absurd suggestion since his own firm was then much larger. According to Insull, in his typical English understatement, "Relations at the end of the lunch were not quite as cordial as they were at the start." But the discussion did open a negotiation, and Insull, ever the aggressive dealer and financier, issued almost $2.3 million of debentures in order to buy his competitor's stock.

The Chicago Edison Company's board of directors sometimes had to be dragged into Insull's expansionist vision. During one meeting at which the executive argued aggressively for a $25-million mortgage in order to buy more power systems, the more cautious directors would agree to no more than $6 million. Still, Insull continued to take over small suburban generators, increasing his control of the region's electricity market.

The utility executive's vision of conglomerates was not unique. The late nineteenth and early twentieth centuries were times of rapid corporate consolidation. More than 3,000 industrial firms disappeared into mergers, and several corporate giants—including U.S. Steel, American Tobacco, International Harvester, DuPont, Anaconda Copper—formed through the coalition of smaller companies.

Insull also targeted the isolated power stations owned by individual consumers. To describe the disadvantages of small, on-site generators, the promoter often discussed the economics of powering a block of northside Chicago homes. The 189 apartments, he explained to whomever would listen, used a total of 68.5 kilowatts of electricity for lighting. But because the lamps were lit at different times in different apartments, the block's maximum demand for power at any single moment was only 20 kilowatts. Therefore, Insull reasoned, a central power station providing 20 kilowatts would be more efficient and economical than a series of separate generating plants in each apartment with an aggregate capacity of 68.5 kilowatts. Of course, a single power plant supplying several users also promised lower costs and higher returns for Insull's electric company. (These economics, as will be explained in later chapters, have changed since apartments and other consumers now are connected to an integrated electricity grid, allowing isolated power stations the chance to sell and buy power efficiently.)

Selling was Insull's passion. He created a twenty-five-person sales force and ordered them to offer service for less than gas. He provided "ridiculously low" rates to encourage the use of electricity by new enterprises, such as the Great Northern luxury hotel. Insull also established an advertising department, published *Electric City* magazine, and provided free electricity to Chicago stores that would highlight his display racks. Insull admitted to a circus-like hucksterism: "I have always said that Mr. Edison taught me all that I know about electricity, but I owe to one of Mr. Barnum's men all that I know about publicity."[3]

Insull even advertised to children. Recognizing that kids would "be the customers, the investors, the voters, and the lawmakers of the future," he provided schools with a thirty-two-page, color brochure entitled *The Ohm Queen* that praised electricity's benefits.[4]

Trying to increase home energy use, Insull stressed the advantages of refrigerators, cookers, and water heaters—all new appliances that devoured electricity. The utility executive told his sales force that these "long-hour 'automatic' electric services would roll up the kilowatt-hours in volumes sufficient to make possible lower average rates."[5]

For those homes and offices that already enjoyed electric lights, Insull emphasized increasing the intensity of existing illumination. He waged an aggressive campaign in schools under the slogan "Better Light—Better Sight."

Insull paid particular attention to commercial and industrial customers that could consume lots of power. To secure this business, rates had to be very low. So in 1912, the executive began selling off-peak industrial power at a half-cent per kilowatt-hour.

Setting the rate for electricity was an uncertain exercise. Edison had wanted to charge for illumination, so he favored a set price per light bulb no matter how often it was illuminated. Insull, in contrast, felt profits were to be made in marketing power rather than fixtures, so he decided to charge according to the amount of electricity consumed (measured in kilowatts) over an hour (thus, kilowatt-hours). This shift from selling lighting and other services to marketing electricity marked a significant transformation in the power industry, and it reinforced Insull's "grow and build" strategy.

Insull even devised a dual-rate structure to encourage more electricity consumption. In order to recoup his investment in generators, distribution lines, transformers, and meters, the promoter imposed a basic charge for the first several hours of electricity use, and he offered a progressively lower rate for additional demand. Insull realized that the more consumers used, the more he gained.

Insull's product, of course, became more attractive as technologies advanced. The tungsten-filament lamp created a widespread market for electric illumination, and enhanced motors allowed industrialists to increase their factory's productivity substantially. More efficient generators and higher-capacity transmission lines enabled residential electricity costs to fall consistently. Not surprisingly, electricity sales grew over the twentieth century's first two decades at a rapid 12-percent annual rate.

Insull also marketed his company as a wise investment to the general public. Long skeptical of Wall Street bankers, he launched "customer ownership" drives and retailed his corporate bonds to the masses. His sales pitch—"If the light shines, you know your money is safe"—increased the number of investors from 6,000 in 1921 to more than 1 million in 1930. Although originally designed to obtain political support from customers who became shareholders and bondholders, the public relations effort also represented a major innovation in corporate finance and weakened the stranglehold of New York bankers. Insull and his colleagues became a new managerial class running giant corporations that were owned by thousands of investors. Their efforts, however, raised the ire of Wall Street financiers, who vowed (and eventually would obtain) revenge.

FROM LONDON TO NEW YORK TO CHICAGO

Born into a lower-middle-class English family, Insull attended primary school but couldn't afford further education. Short and skinny, with protruding and intense eyes, he began working as an office boy at the age of fourteen, but earned less than the cost of railway fare and lunch. The bright and ambitious Insull learned shorthand and became the evening stenographer at *Vanity Fair*, the successful weekly journal on politics and fashion, where he gained an appreciation for both political affairs and the printed word's power. After losing that job to a former clerk who volunteered to work at the magazine without pay, Insull taught himself bookkeeping and answered a classified job advertisement in *The Times* to be the personal secretary to an American gentleman. Insull didn't know it when he interviewed, but Colonel George Gouraud was Thomas Edison's London representative. Since Edison was launching a telephone business in the city, young Insull got to sit in on meetings with bankers and technical experts. His hard work and growing knowledge of the Edison businesses impressed senior executives. When Edison's personal secretary resigned, Insull was beckoned.

Insull's family thought he was making a mistake to leave the security of his London employment for the uncertainties of America. There was no

Samuel Insull. Courtesy of the Loyola University of
Chicago Archives, Samuel Insull Papers.

way they could imagine the wild ride he would face—that forty years later
he would be the emperor of America's largest electricity monopoly, or that
thirteen years after that he would be a prisoner charged with embezzlement and fraud.

Insull arrived in New York City in February 1881 aboard the steamer
SS *City of Chester*. He was whisked off to meet the great inventor at the
Edison Electric Light Company's new offices at 65 Fifth Avenue. The in-
troductory session disappointed both men and revealed their stark con-
trasts. The twenty-one-year-old Insull possessed a formal English manner,
slicked-down hair, and boyish appearance. Edison, in contrast, looked
dowdy, ill-shaven, and was clothed in a seedy black coat, rumpled trousers,
and dirty white shirt. Insull, a status-conscious Brit, later wrote, Edison's
"appearance, as a whole, was not what you would call 'slovenly;' it is best
expressed by the word 'careless.' "[6] Insull, with a high-pitched Cockney
tone, and Edison, with a mouth full of tobacco and a strong midwestern
accent, even had difficulty understanding each other.

The two men's temperaments also clashed. According to Insull, Edison had an "almost pathological hostility to any form of system, order, or discipline imposed from without." Insull, in contrast, possessed a computer-like memory for detail and a craving for organization. Edison enjoyed cigars and stiff drinks, but Insull had promised his mother never to consume any liquor throughout his entire life. Still, each was exactly what the other needed. Insull rationalized Edison's businesses, while Edison introduced Insull to the wonders of engineering.

Insull worked with Edison that first night until four or five o'clock in the morning. Despite their differences, he quickly fell victim to "Mr. Edison's peculiar gift of magnetism." What struck Insull was Edison's "wonderful intelligence, the magnetism of his expression, and the extreme brightness of his eyes." The young secretary concluded that he had met "one of the great masterminds of the world."[7]

Throughout his twelve years with Edison, Insull performed myriad tasks, initially organizing Edison's office, answering his mail, and buying his clothes. As he gained experience, Insull arranged financing for the Pearl Street Station, sold central power plants to several cities across the country, and quadrupled sales at Edison's main factory in Schenectady, New York.

Each of these tasks demonstrated Insull's unique skills. According to Edison, his secretary had "a positive gift for borrowing money" and building businesses. Insull's salesmanship was unparalleled and included bribing and cajoling numerous city councils for the necessary permits to build plants and string wires. His business acumen—in his words, "to develop manufacturing methods of the most economical character"—enabled the Schenectady plant to increase its payroll within only six years from 200 to 6,000.[8]

As Insull became more independent, he became more frustrated by Edison's business bungles and intrusive oversight. In April 1892, when he was trying to increase productivity at the Phonograph Works, Edison abruptly decided to fire all the workers and close the factory. The order-conscious Insull also complained that "Edison's whole method of work would upset the system of any business office."[9] Such moves and complaints, as well as Insull's outrage at the role of New York bankers in the newly merged General Electric, led the young executive to explore other opportunities, including one at the struggling Chicago Edison Company.

When accepting the utility's offer late in 1892, the thirty-two-year-old Insull demanded free rein to run the business as well as promises that

Chicago Edison's rich directors would raise money for a new power station. Marshall Field, who owned the city's major department store, agreed and even provided a $250,000 loan so the new executive could acquire shares in the power company's stock.

The Windy City was a rough and vigorous metropolis, filled with opportunities as well as racketeers, corrupt politicians, and larger-than-life entrepreneurs. Al Capone was organizing a crime syndicate, and many city officials were on the take. George Pullman with railroad cars, Cyrus McCormack with farm equipment, and Philip Armour with meat packaging were building giant corporations. Insull saw similar openings for the electricity business. Chicago, as the midwestern transportation hub, promised tremendous industrial expansion, and 99.5 percent of the city's residences still didn't use electric lamps. Even Edison saw the potential, stating, "You know Sammy, this is one of the best cities in the world for our line of business."[10]

The transplanted Englishman became a U.S. citizen in 1896 and a committed Chicago booster, realizing that the metropolis's progress would translate into his own profits. Yet the executive also featured a populist streak when it came to his adopted community. Insull's charitable contributions—to the Chinese YMCA, recreational facilities for Chicago's minorities, and local hospitals—often exceeded his salary, and he built a grand auditorium for the Chicago Civic Opera without the prominent box seats desired by the rich and famous in order to bring high culture to the common man.

THE CHIEF

Chicago, however, wasn't big enough for Insull's ambitions. At his very first board meeting, the young executive announced plans to purchase the Indiana-based Fort Wayne Electric Company, and he subsequently acquired power-and-light businesses in Rockford, Illinois, and New Albany and Jeffersonville, Indiana. Since financing these operations taxed Chicago Edison's resources, he formed Middle West Utilities; convinced wealthy friends in London, Chicago, and New York to purchase stock in the holding company; and then used that capital to acquire additional properties. The holding company remained largely an Insull family affair, with brother Martin as vice president and son Samuel III eventually appointed vice chairman.

Insull's electric empire grew quickly. By 1912, it encompassed 400 communities throughout thirteen states, and it eventually served more than 4 million customers, spanned thirty-two states, and produced one-eighth of the nation's electricity. Executives with these far-flung subsidiaries met with "The Chief," as they called Insull, every Monday morning at 9:00 A.M. to plot strategies and review operations.

Insull wasn't the only electricity emperor, although he was for several years the largest and most influential. The pipe-smoking John Barnes Miller merged many community power companies into Southern California Edison, which brought light and power to much of the West. Another advertising genius, Miller hired "cooking experts" to tour communities and demonstrate the glories of electric ranges, and he offered floodlights, or what he called "artificial daylight," to the burgeoning motion picture industry. Alex Dow controlled service across Detroit and eastern Michigan. Wilbur Foshay expended his power trust into thirteen states, Alaska, Canada, and Central America. J. P. Morgan's United Corporation managed most choice utilities throughout New York, New England, and the Southeast. By the late-1920s, ten holding companies dominated more than three-fourths of the privately owned electricity industry.

Such corporate consolidations accompanied a move to larger power plants. As Insull integrated the demands of disparate customers and networked his expanding empire with high-voltage transmission lines, he convinced General Electric to build new generating technologies that would replace the size-limited, gasoline-powered, piston-driven engines. In October 1903, General Electric and Chicago Edison opened the Fisk Street Turbine Station, which was powered from water boiled by burning coal and provided a then-remarkable five megawatts of electricity. Since its shaft could attach to a generator's rotor, the turbine eliminated the need for belts and gears, thereby requiring about a tenth the space and a third the cost of traditional engines. The turbine proved to be an engineering wonder since its blades were the first human-made devices to travel faster than the speed of sound. The turbine's hardened metal also maintained its shape despite being blasted by high-temperature steam, and the unit operated under these red-hot conditions consistently for twenty-four hours a day. By 1911, Insull added ten 12-megawatt turbines at the same site. By the mid-1920s, a single turbine was producing 175 megawatts, enough to power a small city. The introduction of metal alloys and high-temperature and high-pressure steam turbines increased a power plant's thermal efficiency from about 4 percent in 1890 to almost 10 percent in 1913. Put another way, the amount of coal needed to generate 1 kilowatt-hour of electricity fell from 7.3 pounds in 1902 to 1.5 pounds in 1932.

Insull and his colleagues also embraced new transmission technologies, reflecting a rapid transition from a copper wire strung along short wooden poles to compound lines attached to tall steel towers. The Niagara Falls line in 1895 seemed extraordinary with 10,000 volts. By 1901, a 60,000-volt wire ran 142 miles from California's Yuba River to Oakland. Seven years later, a Michigan line carried 110,000 volts. By the late 1920s, wires were transmitting a staggering 220,000 volts of electricity.

The growing size of generators and lines led to a mass of mergers since only large companies could afford the new equipment and provide the needed demand for power. The corporate size concerned many reformers, who argued that an important product like electricity should be controlled by public rather than private enterprises. Municipal governments, in fact, were using their ability to obtain low-cost financing through tax-exempt bonds in order to buy up power companies. Munis were expanding in the early twentieth century at twice the rate of private electric firms, growing from 400 in 1896 to more than 1,250 a decade later. Even those municipalities not interested in public ownership tried to impose restrictions on investor-owned utilities.

Like his mentor Edison, Insull understood firsthand the corruption of many municipal politicians. Chicago officials, practiced in extracting payments from executives wanting to do business in their city, thought they could squeeze $1 million from Insull for an electricity franchise. When Insull didn't contribute immediately, they conferred upon a dummy corporation the right to operate in Chicago for fifty years. Yet Insull enjoyed an economic advantage. Having obtained the exclusive regional rights to buy electrical equipment from General Electric and other suppliers, Insull ensured that the politicians' Commonwealth Electric Company remained an empty shell unable to generate or deliver power. He eventually purchased the name-only corporation—and its valuable franchise—for only $50,000, which a frustrated local official described as "one of the greatest bargains since the Russians stole Alaska."[11] In 1907, Insull renamed his company Commonwealth Edison, which was sixty times larger than when he arrived in Chicago just fifteen years earlier. Edison's former secretary had quickly become one of Chicago's elite business titans.

Insull was one of the few business leaders to join Robert LaFollette and other progressive politicians to oppose municipal corruption, to advance "scientific" approaches for managing government and business, and to argue that electricity companies constituted natural monopolies that required public oversight. The executive and the reformers declared that state oversight would take politics out of the electricity business, obtain uniform accounting standards, and achieve the lowest cost for consumers. In 1907, Wisconsin enacted the first power-company-regulation statute, which established a commission to set rates for privately owned utilities. Massachusetts and New York quickly followed, and within nine years thirty more states had joined the utility regulatory bandwagon.

Insull's less vocalized motivation was a desire to deal with only one state agency rather than hundreds of city councils with whom his expanding empire was doing business. In his presidential speech to the National Electric Light Association in 1898, the executive called for state regulation of privately owned utility monopolies. "While it is not supposed to be popular to speak of exclusive franchises," he stated, "it should be recognized that the best service at the lowest possible price can only be obtained, certainly in connection with the industry with which we are identified, by exclusive control of a given territory being placed in the hands of one undertaking."[12]

Although criticized by many of his utility colleagues who wanted no government intervention, Insull became the chief proponent of regulation and monopoly. He understood that public oversight meant utilities would gain protection from competitors as well as the right of eminent domain, which previously was reserved for the state. Regulation also enabled Insull and his colleagues to obtain the government's sanction for their monopolies, something John D. Rockefeller and other oil giants could acquire only through marketplace warfare, secret deals, and attrition. As Insull declared, "There is one great advantage that must follow regulation, and that advantage is protection."[13]

This regulated-monopoly approach also promised to convince the investment community that utilities would receive sufficient revenues from their customers in order to remain financially solvent. In keeping with Supreme Court decisions associated with railroads, regulators allowed utilities to earn fair returns on their investments. In practice, this legal doctrine encouraged power companies to build more and more generators and transmission lines. It meshed well with Insull's expansionistic plans, and expand the utility industry did, with construction projects rising from about $500 million in 1902, to more than $1 billion in 1907, and to almost $2 billion in 1912.[14]

State commissions essentially transformed the electricity industry from a hodgepodge of competitive businesses into centralized utility monopolies. They allowed power companies to eliminate the clutter and expense of duplicative transmission and distribution wires, as well as to take advantage of the economies of scale then available from larger power plants.

Understanding the danger of public hostility to monopolies, Insull mastered the art of public relations. "Unless you can so conduct your business as to get the good will of the community in which you are working," he warned his colleagues, "you might just as well shut up shop and move away."[15] Insull contributed heavily to local causes and nonprofit institutions. He encouraged employees to join civic organizations in order to make political contacts and advance the causes of electricity and Commonwealth Edison. To gain cooperation from the miners who dug his coal, he promoted mine safety laws. To ensure a neutral stance from social reformers on public power, he organized the National Civic Federation and attacked urban corruption. Unique for his time, he hired minorities and women and offered all employees relatively generous fringe benefits.

The empires created by Insull and other monopolists sparked the growth of several other institutions, including engineering colleges, multipurpose consulting and construction firms, and regional power pools. The Massachusetts Institute of Technology (MIT) launched the first program to train electrical engineers in 1890, and several other colleges soon followed suit in order to meet the power industry's growing demand for experts and research on innovative technologies. Charles Stone and Edwin Webster, two years after graduating from MIT, started a business to design and build power plants for utilities unwilling to assume the construction headaches, and they soon faced competition from Bechtel, Brown & Root, Combustion Engineering, and several other consultants. President Woodrow Wilson during World War I created a War Industries Board that ordered private utilities to interconnect with each other in order to use electricity more efficiently, and Pennsylvania and New Jersey subsequently developed the first regional power pool to share diverse loads and satisfy different consumer demands with fewer power plants and much less investment. The expansion of holding companies and power pools demanded an increasingly sophisticated and costly transmission system, complete with steel towers, copper or aluminum lines, insulators, lightning protection equipment, circuit breakers, switches, and huge transformers. According to one estimate, utilities during the 1920s invested more money in equipment than did the transcontinental railroads during the decade of their most rapid expansion.

SCANDAL

Insull's expanding empire and outspoken advocacy prompted increased scrutiny of his political activities, and in 1925 his aggressiveness sparked a scandal. Insull long had given judicious and small contributions to most political candidates in areas where his companies supplied electricity. Yet he personally abhorred Illinois senator (and future president) William McKinley, who had refused to sell to Insull his streetcar companies and utility franchises in southern Illinois communities. When Frank Smith declared he would run against McKinley, Insull opened up his pocketbook and provided more than $125,000, a substantial sum in the 1920s. The problem was that Smith had been head of the Illinois Commerce Commission, the agency that regulated Insull's state-based companies. A U.S. Senate committee held hearings and highlighted the conflicts of interest, labeling Insull "brazen" and "arrogant" for his contributions. The executive tried to ignore the inquiries and refused to testify, but this tactic led to him being cited for contempt. Only years later did Insull admit having been "foolish to allow my personal feelings [against McKinley] to govern me."

Insull increasingly became a political target. A Federal Trade Commission (FTC) investigation criticized utilities for "buying" elections and spending enormous sums, surpassing $30 million annually, on advertising campaigns to sway public opinion. Perhaps more damaging, the FTC concluded that 75 percent of power companies inflated their assets and profits and that holding companies often claimed fictitious income when selling power plants at high prices to their own subsidiaries in exchange for stock in those subsidiaries. New York Governor Franklin Roosevelt blasted Insull's network as "a kind of private empire within the nation." FDR suggested utility holding companies were "challenging in their power the very government itself," and that they represented a menace "of such a highly centralized industrial control that we may have to bring forth a new declaration of independence." Roosevelt even attacked Insull's public relations machine, denouncing utility advertisements as "a systematic, subtle, deliberate, and unprincipled campaign of misinformation, of propaganda, and, if I may use the words, of lies and falsehoods."[16]

Although most Americans in the 1920s admired self-made tycoons such as Samuel Insull and John D. Rockefeller, a growing chorus of reformers and muckrackers criticized the nation's largest corporations and monopolies. Ida Tarbell exposed Rockefeller's manipulation of petroleum markets. Upton Sinclair vividly described the jungle within Chicago's meat-packing houses. Senator George Norris, a Republican from Nebraska, focused on utility "power trusts" and protested that "practically everything in the electric world is controlled either directly or indirectly by some part of this gigantic trust." Norris declared that state regulatory commissions "can no more contest with this gigantic octopus than a fly could interfere with the onward march of an elephant."[17]

Insull also became a financial target. Cyrus Eaton of Cleveland quietly began buying large blocks of shares in Middle West Utilities. Fearful of a raid, Insull, ignoring his instinct against New York financiers, took out large loans from J. P. Morgan and formed a new investment trust, Insull Utility Investments, in order to protect his holding companies.

This corporate pyramiding proved extremely popular among investors, who in the giddy days of the late 1920s drove the price of Insull Utility Investments up from $12 to $150 a share. According to one calculation, the securities "appreciated at an around-the-clock rate of $7,000 per minute, for a total rise of more than one-half billion dollars."[18] Insull later commented on the public's willingness to invest in utilities: "If we issued a piece of brown paper with a signature on it we could raise all the money we wanted to."[19]

Even after October 19, 1929—Black Friday—utility companies remained islands of solidity in a sea of stock-price disasters. The troubled industrial sector certainly cut back its electricity consumption, yet household demand continued to rise as more consumers embraced electricity's versatility and convenience. During the Great Depression's first two years, homeowners purchased more than 2.3 million refrigerators, virtually doubling the residential energy load.

Insull accepted Herbert Hoover's invitation to attend a White House conference on the economy and was convinced by the president's assurances that the depression would be short lived. Adhering to Hoover's call for executives to "go home and conduct their business as usual and proceed with their expansion plans just as if nothing had happened," Insull continued to spend and invest.[20] He even advanced the cash necessary for his employees to cover their margin brokerage accounts, and he purchased $197 million of utility equipment in 1930. Insull bought up municipal power plants in North Carolina and purchased Cyrus Eaton's holdings for $6 million above their market value. Because investment capital was drying up, he had to ask the Morgan group and other New York bankers for ever-larger loans, using his utility properties as collateral. Years later Insull would reflect, "I—my companies—spent money as though things were all right. We increased our floating debt and this eventually brought about our bankruptcy."[21]

The power company executive had good reasons to be optimistic in 1931. Earnings for his firms rose 15 percent in 1930, and total sales of electricity for the first six months of 1931 set an all-time record. Yet some of the good news resulted from deception. According to a subsequent Federal Power Commission report, utility executives often inflated their assets and earnings in an "apparently flagrant lack of compliance with the law."[22]

The utility industry, in fact, was a fragile house of cards when England abandoned the gold standard in September 1931. U.S. investors panicked on the British news, and as stock prices plummeted further, highly leveraged utility empires teetered, particularly as banks began to call in their loans. Although many of the single-state utilities held up well during the depression, enjoying increased demand for electricity, holding companies withered under the financial strain. The value of Insull's securities fell $150 million in one week, with a share of Middle West Utilities eventually plummeting from $570 to only $1.25. Insull's empire was not alone. Shares in Central Public Service dropped from $80 to only 25 cents. Tri-Utilities Corporation went bankrupt, offering only 30 cents on a $1,000 debenture to bondholders and absolutely nothing to stockholders. One power tycoon left just a thirty-two-story monument in Minneapolis that carried the ironic inscription: "All Your Money—All the Time—On Time."

J. P. Morgan, to whom Insull had gone for loans, saw an opportunity in the chaos to gain control of midwestern power assets. In order to tarnish Insull's public image, he arranged an audit of the utility's investment trust and accused the executive of embezzlement, a charge that was never proven. Morgan backed Insull into a corner by calling in his loans early and blocking other bankers from covering a $20-million note. Repeating tactics he used against Edison, the banker maneuvered to oust the chief.

Commonwealth Edison and most of Insull's individual utilities remained solvent throughout the depression, largely because the rigidity of Insull-inspired rate structures provided some stability to utility operating revenues. Power company revenues shrank only 6 percent, far less than the 63-percent plummet for manufacturing firms. Yet fragile pyramiding, inflated assets, and questionable accounting destroyed the utility empires. Investors in Insull's holding companies lost between $500 million and $3 billion, depending upon how unrealized paper profits were tabulated. A federal official involved in these receiverships labeled Insull's financial failure as "the tragedy of the century." He described the individual investor's blight: "One day I stood and watched those holding securities and obligations of these companies coming in and filing them [to receive a refund]. They were just the average run of people—clerks and schoolteachers there in Chicago, small shopkeepers in Illinois, farmers from Wisconsin—and what they brought in, of course, was worth nothing. They had lost every penny."[23]

Subsequent investigations offered little solace to investors as the Securities and Exchange Commission charged holding companies with "stock watering and capital inflation, manipulation of subsidies, and improper accounting practices." The Federal Trade Commission's general counsel argued that "words such as fraud, deceit, misrepresentation, dishonesty, breach of trust, and oppression are the only suitable terms to apply."[24]

Having lost his companies and much of his own money, the seventy-one-year-old Insull, exhausted and disheartened, set sail for Europe. In his absence, politicians began to demonize the executive, portraying him as an example of the corporate greed that had led to the stock market's collapse.

Insull spent several months relaxing in Paris. When he heard that a Cook County Grand Jury was about to indict him, the former executive, not wanting to put "my head in the lion's mouth," moved to Italy and then to Greece, where he stayed for eighteen months. U.S. reporters trailed and hounded Insull. Greek police detained him for thirty-six hours and put him on trial, but the jury could not find him guilty of an offense punishable under Greek law. Greek officials subsequently arrested him a second time, yet again failed to win a conviction. Pressured by the U.S. Embassy, the Greek government canceled Insull's visa and ordered him to leave the country.

Although claiming not to be a fugitive from justice, Insull set sail from Athens under disguise—with darkened hair and mustache and without his glasses—"in such a manner as to avoid publicity."[25] Hoping that his friends would identify some safe place for him to reside, he and his chartered Greek steamer—the SS *Maiotis*—wandered the Mediterranean Sea for ten days. Inspired by a U.S.-government bounty of $200,000, or four times that offered for Al Capone, Turkish authorities boarded the ship, although in international waters, and arrested the former tycoon. They transferred Insull to a U.S. vessel bound for New York, and, fearing suicide, took away his knives and razors. Insull, however, displayed a surprisingly jolly mood, as attested to by several newspapermen who joined the Atlantic crossing and enjoyed tea and lengthy off-the-record remembrances of the electricity industry's early days.

When the former utility executive arrived at New York harbor in May 1934, his son and lawyers greeted him with a prepared statement that Insull read to the assembled media: "I have erred, but my greatest error was in underestimating the effect of the financial panic on American securities and particularly on the companies I was working so hard to build. I worked with all my energy to save those companies. I made mistakes, but they were honest mistakes. They were errors in judgment, but not dishonest manipulation."[26]

Insull spent one night in a Chicago jail before being transferred, because of his ailing heart and diabetes, to a local hotel, where he devoted the summer to writing his memoirs and preparing his legal defense. The subsequent trial began in October 1934, lasted eight weeks, and focused mainly on mail fraud charges but ranged over Insull's entire life. It became a media circus, with journalists from around the world reporting from the Chicago courthouse. One writer suggested that prosecutors and politicians "needed a scapegoat for the sins of capitalism." Despite health problems, the ruddy-faced, white-mustached Insull took the stand for three hours on his own behalf and suggested he was a public benefactor who was being persecuted for the greed of an entire generation. The banner story in Chicago's *Herald Examiner* declared: "Insull . . . Puts Courtroom in Tears!" A spectator was quoted as saying, "The old man is selling himself. I bet he could sell the jury Corporation Securities right now."[27]

The jury sided with the executive, declaring him innocent of all charges. It deliberated for only five minutes, but dawdled for two hours to celebrate a member's birthday and to not appear bribed.

Edison once told his secretary, "Whatever you do, Sammy, make either a brilliant success of it, or a brilliant failure." Insull met both prophecies as he journeyed from shop clerk to utility chief to accused criminal. He transformed small and struggling electric firms into successful utility empires and then into despised corporate monopolies. According to one commentator, Insull was the most powerful businessman of the 1920s and the most notorious business villain of the 1930s.

Insull, feeling vindicated by the jury, moved to Paris, where, with his pension restored, he lived a quiet existence. He died of a heart attack there in 1938 and was buried in London, the city of his birth. Within only three decades, Insull and a few other utility emperors had revolutionized the electricity business. They had ordered larger and more efficient generators, strung long-distance transmission lines across the countryside, and marketed an array of power-gobbling and burden-reducing appliances. They had driven down the average cost of electricity, enabling 13 million Americans to consider electric power a "necessity of life." They had raised more than $8 billion from 5 million individual investors, temporarily breaking the financial control of New York investment banks. They also had eliminated competition, advanced state regulatory commissions, and established monopolistic empires, the three largest of which in 1930 controlled 40 percent of the nation's electricity.

These corporate giants became both admired and vilified. On one hand, they supplied the power that reduced life's drudgeries, and their companies provided a steady income for individual investors. Yet their backdoor campaign contributions, deceptive accounting, and manipulative advertising prompted scorn. Despite the not-guilty verdict, Insull remained a symbol of corrupt corporate excess. General Electric quietly expunged all record of Insull from its official history, while President Franklin Roosevelt and Senator George Norris quickly passed a series of bills to limit private power companies and increase government control of utility assets.

ENTER THE POLITICIANS

Sam Insull thought George Norris was little more than an "agitator." Norris found Insull to be deceitful and dangerous. Yet the conservative power tycoon and the progressive Nebraska senator agreed on two points—that electricity fostered prosperity, and that this energy source must be controlled by a monopoly. Insull, as noted earlier, felt competition was "economically wrong." Norris reached the same conclusion, arguing that only large enterprises unburdened by market forces could finance and operate the large power plants needed to meet the diverse demands of a growing economy. "Some kind of monopoly is necessary to get the most out of [electricity]," the senator declared, "a gigantic monopoly, bigger than any we've ever known."[28]

Whether that monopoly should be owned by a private corporation or a government agency, however, split the two men. Insull equated public power with "socialism." Norris felt privately owned monopolies would "eventually . . . come to tyranny."[29]

Norris would seem to have had the advantage after the Federal Trade Commission revealed utility abuses, Roosevelt railed against power pyramids, and the collapse of energy empires hurt millions of investors. No doubt Norris and FDR created giant government agencies and clipped the wings of holding companies. As public opinion turned against private utilities, the industry's very structure could have changed dramatically, with the federal government or municipalities poised to appropriate power companies. That the private utility industry survived is testimony to its political clout and public relations mastery.

Norris worried particularly about power trusts gaining control of the Tennessee, Columbia, and other mighty rivers on which utility engineers longed to place hydroelectric dams. As early as 1907, President Teddy Roosevelt's Inland Waterways Commission concluded that "streams of the country (are) an asset of the people" that should be protected from the power trusts.[30] In 1917, President Woodrow Wilson proposed that a federal commission administer those prime water-power sites and reserve the electricity for government agencies. Contemporary public opinion would not support such a substantial expansion of the federal government into private enterprise, but the military requirements of World War I opened the door a bit for public power proponents.

The battle lines were drawn near the town of Sheffield in northern Alabama. Not far away, at Muscle Shoals, the Tennessee River narrows and accelerates. At this prime hydroelectric site, argued President Wilson, the government should build a dam to power an air nitrate factory that would make munitions for the army during the war and fertilizer for farmers after the conflict. Because German submarines and "surface raiders" were blocking shipments of nitrate from Chile, the War Department quickly built a small coal-fired power plant and a nitrate factory at Muscle Shoals. Yet by the 1918 armistice, Wilson's 100-foot-high, mile-long dam was only half complete. An array of luminaries—including Henry Ford, Thomas Edison, Wendell Wilkie, George Norris, and Franklin Roosevelt—would battle over the next fifteen years for control of the site's electricity production.

The power trusts appeared to have the upper hand with the 1920 election of Warren Harding, who brought in pro-businessmen Andrew Mellon as secretary of the Treasury and Herbert Hoover as secretary of Commerce. With an administration motto of "Less Government in Business," Harding decided to offer the dam and nitrate plant to the highest bidder.

The inside track initially belonged to Alabama Power, part of the Commonwealth and Southern holding company, which was led by Wendell Wilkie, the frequent Republican presidential candidate. Believing that his only opposition might come from public power advocates, Wilkie dismissed them as "socialists" and aggressively declared, "They shall not pass."[31] The utility executive, therefore, was shocked in July 1921 when Henry Ford unexpectedly threw his hat into the ring.

Ford's entry shouldn't have been a total surprise since the automobile pioneer had a long-standing interest in the electricity industry, beginning with his first job as an engineer at a Detroit Edison power plant. He had befriended Thomas Edison, and the two of them often took camping trips together and commiserated about the critical role of electricity in industrial expansion.

Ford and his Model T's were American legends, and his proposal to use the Muscle Shoals facilities to spark the creation of 1 million manufacturing jobs in the Tennessee valley ignited immediate interest. The automobile executive flamed that interest with an impressive public relations campaign, complete with a well-publicized Muscle Shoals visit by Edison, who proclaimed the importance of electricity development. Ford also promised to use the nitrate plant to provide fertilizer to farmers at half the government's rate. He even successfully lobbied the Nebraska legislature to endorse his proposal in order to put pressure on the skeptical Senator Norris, who was strategically positioned as chairman of the agriculture committee responsible for the project's oversight.

The auto executive, however, alienated government auditors. Their review of Ford's proposal revealed that he wanted to pay less than 5 percent of what Washington had spent to build the nitrate facility. For the hydroelectric dam, Ford proposed a 100-year lease (twice the fifty-year limitation allowed by the Federal Power Act) at less than 10 percent of what the government would spend simply to complete the half-finished dam. Moreover, he wanted Washington to finance his venture with a loan at less than 4-percent interest.

Ford also frightened the power trusts, which worried the industrialist would build competing transmission lines and challenge their empires. Twelve days after Ford made his proposal, Alabama Power Company, realizing it faced serious competition, upped its offer to $5 million for a fifty-year lease of the dam.

George Norris organized Senate hearings to compare the proposals, and he found fault with both. Ford, he concluded, couldn't be trusted because he was promising to provide cheap fertilizer with an expensive and outmoded air nitrate process. Alabama Power's $5-million offer, moreover, was well below the property's $100-million value. Fearful of the utility empires being built by Wilkie and Insull, the senator introduced a separate proposal to have the government own and operate the project.

Norris's motivation was more than simply government management of electricity. "I, at least, have always believed," he wrote, "that the first and most important objective was the control of the flood waters of a great river."[32] The Tennessee's periodic torrents washed away farms and valuable soil, clogged the river with sediments, and prevented water-borne commerce. Yet if flood-control dams were to be built, argued Norris, it would be relatively cheap to add turbines that supplied electricity to impoverished communities. Congress, at least partially swayed by his arguments and constant appeals, continued to provide funds for the War Department to construct the dam and hydroelectric facility.

During the construction period, conservative politicians and private-sector businesses lost political credibility when members of the Harding administration were exposed for secretly leasing federal oil fields at Wyoming's Teapot Dome to corporations in exchange for political contributions. Some politicians suggested that awarding the Muscle Shoals properties to Ford or Alabama Power would "make Teapot Dome look like bagatelle."[33]

Yet Norris and public power advocates had their own critics. The American Farm Bureau and most southern farmers favored Ford's proposal and its promise of cheap fertilizer. Residents of Sheffield and the surrounding area believed Ford would bring jobs and prosperity. Hundreds of investors from around the country bought nearby property with the expectation that their investments would grow. Angry at critics of Ford or Alabama Power, several communities burned Norris's effigy. A few individuals issued threats against the senator's life.

The House of Representatives, with strong support from southern lawmakers, ignored the Teapot Dome analogy and eventually approved Ford's proposal. Yet the auto industrialist, weary of the debate and nervous about facing Norris in the Senate, backed down and withdrew his offer.

Alabama Power Company and its allies immediately went on the offensive against the Nebraska Republican. The utility trade association labeled Norris's efforts as "unwarranted and unfair, originating with predatory politicians and demagogues." The conservative *New York Commercial* argued that Norris received his "inspiration from the teachings of Marx."[34]

Norris and his supporters struck back. "The people own the resources," asserted the senator. "They should get the full benefit from them without any corporation reaping a profit."[35] Franklin Roosevelt, then governor of New York, added, "We have permitted private corporations to monopolize the electrical industry and sell electricity at the highest rates they could obtain."[36] Declaring that consumers deserved more power for their money, FDR launched a "waffle iron campaign" and argued that government-owned rather than privately owned utilities would provide the lower rates needed for more Americans to enjoy washing machines, vacuum cleaners, and even waffle irons.

Controversies accelerated in September 1925 when the War Department finally completed the hydroelectric facility, which was named the Wilson Dam. Although the federal government generated the electricity, it could sell its power only to the Alabama Power Company, which owned the sole transmission line out of Muscle Shoals. The War Department was forced to offer its energy at just two-tenths of a cent per kilowatt-hour, while Alabama Power marketed that same electricity to nearby residents for ten cents per kilowatt-hour. Highlighting such inequities, Norris obtained congressional resolutions favoring government control of the Wilson Dam, but President Calvin Coolidge, another supporter of big business, vetoed them.

By the mid-1920s, the muckraking media began to focus on power trusts, their high rates, and their bribes to politicians and academics in order to manipulate public opinion and bolster their monopolies. The Hearst newspapers branded Insull as "the embodiment of avarice, the fat plutocrat of capitalism defiled, who had ruined the innocent and smeared the image of holy free enterprise."[37]

Several lawmakers called for a formal investigation of the power conglomerates. Utilities obviously opposed the effort, but, realizing that they couldn't block it outright, they tried to ensure the inquiry would be tepid. Arguing against a Senate investigation, which would include the aggressive Norris, industry lobbyists proposed a study by "professionals" at the Federal Trade Commission. They also made sure President Coolidge would appoint the investigation's general counsel.

Quite pleased with their maneuvering, the lobbyists had not counted on Robert Healy. Coolidge felt the former lawyer for bankers and member of Vermont's Supreme Court possessed a reliable record of support for business development and free enterprise. Yet the lanky and stubborn Republican also possessed a firm belief that businesses needed to operate according to strict accounting rules if capitalism was to survive.

After a seven-year investigation, Healy and the Federal Trade Commission concluded that utilities employed shadowy and deceitful accounting practices. He found that numerous holding companies, including Insull's, declared dividends from fictitious income, that they sold power plants to their own subsidiaries at inflated prices and received payment only in the subsidiary's worthless stock. "The counting of fictitious profits," wrote Healy, "was a normal feature of [Insull's] Middle West Utilities Company income as counted and reported." Healy's 486-page report also blasted the power industry's efforts "to mold the thoughts and beliefs of the present and future generations in conformity with the utility interests."[38]

The commission document and media attacks began to shift public opinion and embolden politicians. Herbert Hoover's 1928 election, however, meant private utilities still enjoyed the upper hand. The new president previously directed the Northeastern Super Power Committee, which enabled New England's utilities to interconnect their lines and pool their power. When secretary of the Commerce Department, Hoover established a power bureau, and he often spoke before the utilities's trade association. Like Insull, he favored regulation and opposed government ownership.

The public power debate became something of a crusade for both sides. Utility advocates felt Norris was trying to destroy a system that supplied reliable electricity to consumers and solid investments for widows. They portrayed themselves as representatives of the free enterprise system that had made America great, and they viewed government-owned power systems as corrupt and unaccountable. Norris and his supporters, in contrast, felt they were fighting to tame corporate chieftains who had accumulated too much political and economic clout. Theirs was a campaign for democratic reform, cheaper electricity, and financial sanity.

The stock market crash and economic depression changed the debate's dynamics. Since a growing number of Americans perceived Hoover as favoring businesses over workers and as being too cozy with the power trusts, the president's Republican Party in 1930 lost control of the House of Representatives and narrowed their Senate majority to only one vote. Several lawmakers sympathetic to private utilities, including Representative Carroll Reese of Tennessee and Senator Tom Heflin of Alabama, lost reelection to power company critics. The Scripps-Howard newspapers observed that "never in recent years has there been such a strong expression on the subject of power." Although weakened, Hoover continued vetoing Norris's legislation for government control of Tennessee valley power plants. "I am firmly opposed," declared the president, "to the government entering into business the major purpose of which is competition with our citizens." (Noting such opposition to public power, it is ironic that the giant Boulder Dam on the Colorado River was renamed to commemorate President Hoover.) Since the veto override obtained a majority but not the needed two-thirds vote in Congress, Norris and other public power advocates waited hopefully for the 1932 presidential election.[39]

FIGHTING LIBERAL

George Norris was born in 1861, when the Civil War was just beginning, into a twelve-child family living in a ramshackle farm house in the Black Swamp section of Ohio near Sandusky. In his own words, he "lived the hard boyhood of a primitive Ohio farm."[40] When Norris was only three, his father died of pneumonia, having become chilled and exhausted from trying to control a spooked horse. His only brother was killed while fighting in the Union army. Norris's own first child died at birth, and his wife died delivering the couple's third daughter. His second wife gave birth to dead twins.

Norris often recalled his exhaustion from milking cows and performing other farm chores by "the flickering, undependable light of the lantern in the mud and cold rains of the fall, and the snow and icy winds of win-

George Norris. Courtesy of the Nebraska State Historical Society Photograph Collections.

ter." From those experiences, he said, "the possibilities of electricity for lightening the drudgery of farms and urban homes, while revolutionizing factories, fascinated me."[41]

Norris, an obviously bright student, worked his way through Ohio's Baldwin University and Indiana's Valparaiso. He became a teacher in Lucas County, Ohio, and traveled throughout the rural communities as an itinerant instructor. The parents of many of his students had been forced to mortgage their 160 acres in order to buy farm equipment and seeds. Battered by the economy and weather, their surplus harvests in good seasons often fetched low prices, and their crops could be destroyed when hot winds blew up from the South. Indebtedness was a constant fact for farm families.

Following his mother to Nebraska, Norris established a law practice and began to dabble in politics as an "ardent Republican." His electioneering, however, did not come easily, and Norris lost his first race for prosecuting attorney. At the age of thirty-four, he finally won a judgeship, but only by seven votes.

Norris was a proud and staunch conservative who portrayed himself as "breasting the Populist tide." He also was headstrong—"sure of my position, unreasonable in my conviction, and unbending in my opposition to any other political party, or political thought except my own."[42] Norris's conservatism prompted Republican leaders to run him for Congress, which he did in 1902 and won by 200 votes.

Washington changed Norris. The forty-three-year-old idealist was shocked by the capital's petty politics and the power of its party machines. He slowly realized that his Republicans were "guilty of all the evils that I had charged against the opposition." Throwing "off the cloak of bitter partisanship," Norris took on the powerful political operation of Joseph Cannon, arguing that the Republican speaker undemocratically dominated congressional actions by controlling patronage and appropriations. Such a challenge was anything but the norm for a relatively new congressman. His targeted issue may have been fairly arcane—arguing that appointees to investigative committees should be elected by all House members rather than appointed by the speaker—but it was a direct affront to the power of Boss Cannon. Amazingly enough, Norris won, but he soon decided that the better part of political valor would be to leave the House and run for the Senate.

Norris transformed himself from strict conservative to "fighting liberal," as he titled his autobiography. Bucking a pro-business climate, the lawmaker advanced bills to bail out indebted farmers and to restrict the power of corporations. He lamented that "the early 1920s brought the American people to their knees in worship at the shrine of private business and industry."[43]

Norris offered good copy for reporters and political cartoonists, several of whom praised the politician's willingness to take on Boss Cannon as well as the power trusts. With his customary bow tie, neat black suit, and heavy gold-link watch chain, Norris was portrayed as an iconoclast and political dragon slayer.

Remembering the struggles of his early farm life, Norris focused his formidable energies on rural development and electrification. He successfully pushed annual appropriations to complete the Wilson Dam, despite opposition from the power empires, and he organized numerous hearings on the cost discrepancies between private and public utilities. Perhaps his favorite example was the lighting expenses of the International Bridge at Niagara Falls. Government-owned Ontario Hydro Power charged only

$8.43 per month to illuminate the Canadian half of the bridge. The private U.S. corporation, in contrast, billed $43.10 for its half. Norris concluded from these price differentials that "the development and conservation of such resources ought to be under public control, public operation, and public ownership."[44]

THE GOVERNMENT ADVOCATES

Both Norris and Hoover labeled themselves Republicans, but the senator in 1932 broke with the president—whom he described as "the Janus of politics, . . . always two-faced, always equivocal, except when he champions big business"—and endorsed Franklin Roosevelt. While blaming Hoover for the stock market collapse and bread lines, FDR also railed against the "Ishmaels and Insulls whose hand is against every man." The Democratic candidate consistently blasted the power trusts as a menace of "highly centralized industrial control."[45]

Roosevelt's first stop after sweeping the Electoral College was Muscle Shoals, where he met with Norris to discuss the Tennessee valley's needs. The two agreed that the Wilson Dam should be part of a broader initiative to tame the Tennessee River and bring economic development to the impoverished region. Only a month after his inauguration, FDR, building on Norris's previous initiatives, proposed a Tennessee Valley Authority (TVA) to tackle the recurrent floods that washed away farms, to provide navigation on the area's waterways, and to reforest and fertilize the lands. (Electrification was an afterthought, yet TVA now is essentially a power company.) Roosevelt envisioned "a corporation clothed with the power of government but possessed with the flexibility and initiative of a private enterprise." This cornerstone of the New Deal, stated Roosevelt, would be "the widest experiment ever conducted by a government." From Norris's perspective, the presidential proclamation was "an official approval of a 12-year dream that I have had."[46]

FDR gave to the silver-haired Norris the pen with which, on May 18, 1933, he signed the law creating the Tennessee Valley Authority. The president later arranged for the TVA dam built on the Clinch River in east Tennessee to be named after the Nebraska senator.

The already-lengthy TVA political battle, however, was not over. Nineteen private utilities characterized the federal agency as an "unconstitutional competitor with private business" and filed legal challenges all the way to the Supreme Court. TVA survived those initial lawsuits, but wrangles persisted as TVA itself tried to expand its sprawling empire.

TVA won praise for controlling floods, cutting electricity rates, and spurring economic development, but controversies soon erupted within the agency. TVA's first chairman, Dr. Arthur Morgan, was an eminent engineer, but, in Norris's words, he "seemed at times desirous of establishing himself as a dictator in control of every activity of the [three-person] board." Morgan exhibited particular animosity toward David Lilienthal, the brilliant lawyer who had reorganized Wisconsin's Public Utility Commission for progressive Governor Phil LaFollette. After several confrontations between Morgan and Norris, Roosevelt asked for Morgan's resignation and reappointed Lilienthal to the TVA board.

Public power campaigns expanded well beyond the Tennessee valley. Roosevelt signed the Bonneville Project Act in 1937, creating a massive electricity-marketing agency in the Pacific Northwest, and the government-owned Grand Coulee dam, the nation's largest hydroelectric facility, began operating in 1941. Cleveland Mayor Tom Johnson devoted $2 million of public funds to construct a municipal power station, and he cut rates 75 percent below those charged by the private utility. In Los Angeles, the Bureau of Light & Power paid $46 million to purchase the Los Angeles Gas and Electric Company in order to prevent the private Southern California Edison from monopolizing the entire region. In rural South Dakota, Virgil Hanlon outmaneuvered investor-owned utilities, formed the East River Electric Power Cooperative, and built publicly owned dams throughout the Missouri River basin.

Lamenting that only 15 percent of rural Americans enjoyed access to electricity, public power advocates built federal dams along the Columbia and Colorado rivers and brought subsidized power to large parts of the West. FDR also established the Rural Electrification Administration (REA), setting aside $100 million in work relief funds to help farm communities construct generating plants and transmission lines. Despite private utility opposition, REA within 18 months brought electric power and some relief from drudgery to half a million Americans. Numerous farm wives wept openly as work crews strung power lines that finally allowed them to enjoy the lights and appliances that city folk long had taken for granted.

Highlighting the accounting abuses by utilities, FDR and Norris also created the Securities and Exchange Commission to monitor and prosecute deceit within the stock markets. They secured the Public Utilities Holding Company Act (PUHCA) of 1935 in order to prohibit power-company pyramiding. Although that law broke up the electricity trusts, utility industry lobbyists were able to block an amendment that would have converted power lines into "common carriers" required to transmit independently generated electricity.

(These New Deal initiatives remain key components of current power battles, as the Securities and Exchange Commission investigates Enron's abuses, utility lobbyists try to overturn PUHCA, and today's power entrepreneurs seek access to transmission wires.)

Private power companies throughout the late 1930s filed legal challenges to the new laws, and some refused to register with the Securities and Exchange Commission. They also continued to suffer a string of political controversies, including accusations of bribery and price fixing. A 1955 Senate investigation discovered "fairly consistent abuse of the monopoly position which private utilities enjoy." Yet despite the appearance of giant federal utilities and numerous rural coops, the political lobbying, public relations, and deep financial pockets of investor-owned utilities allowed them to maintain control of most of the nation's expanding electricity market. Municipal utilities increased their share of the nation's power from 7 percent in 1939 to only 9 percent in 1984. While contributions from federal power projects rose to 10 percent of U.S. capacity, private firms maintained control of 75 percent of the nation's generators and customers.

The success of private utilities resulted from several factors, including a resurgence of conservative, pro-business values as evidenced by General Dwight Eisenhower's 1952 election. The new president described TVA as "creeping socialism," and he gave the Idaho Power Company three dam sites at the Snake River's Hell Canyon, an area President Truman had reserved for public development. Eisenhower dedicated the McNary Dam on the Columbia River and declared, "The federal government should no more attempt to [supply all the power needs of our people] than it would assume responsibility for supplying all their drinking water, their food, their housing, and their transportation."[47]

Edwin Vennard took advantage of this conservative tide and masterminded an advertising campaign that would have made Sam Insull proud. Vennard actually had been a vice president of Insull's holding company, and he later directed the utility trade association for many years. He un-

Edwin Vennard. Courtesy of the Edison Electric Institute.

derstood well that most Americans, swept up in Cold War fervor, rejected socialism and equated private firms with patriotism.

Utilities, of course, were regulated monopolies that avoided competition and the free enterprise system, but Vennard wrapped them in the American flag while he attacked his public power opponents as socialists. On behalf of the "business-managed, tax-paying" utilities, Vennard regularly published advertisements arguing that "tax money shouldn't be spent on socialistic federal power projects that this country neither wants nor needs."[48] One red-baiting spread in the October 1951 issue of the *Saturday Evening Post* pictured a proud father with his arms around his two children, the clean-cut daughter looking up admiringly at her brother in an army uniform. The father is quoted to say, "Sure, I used to think it wouldn't do any harm to have the government run the electric business. But I've changed my mind. Because when government meddles too much in any business, you get socialism. And who'd want to leave a socialistic U.S.A. to his kids?"

A pioneer in polling and public relations, Vennard hired George Gallup to discover phrases and images that would spur Americans to feel positively about private utilities and negatively about public power. The two discovered that the public preferred the concept of an "investor-owned" company rather than a "privately owned" firm, and they disliked the sound of "government-owned" utilities more than "public power." The marketers devised several hard-hitting ads, including one in the early 1960s that pictured armed guards stopping an old couple from crossing the Berlin Wall to freedom. The headline reads: "Freedom Is Not Lost by Guns Alone," and the text links communist takeovers to public power: "When government owns business, it can control both goods and jobs. It adds economic power to its vast political power. . . . Then freedom has slipped quietly away. A quiet threat can be the deadliest. You may not know it's there until too late."[49]

Such public relations efforts worked extremely well. After Vennard's placement of forty advertisements, support for public power plunged from 70 percent to only 30 percent.

Insull, Norris, and their colleagues powered . . . and changed . . . America. Electric lights, as noted before, extended days; elevators and trolleys altered dramatically the urban landscape; and electric-powered devices enabled mass production. Many of the changes, however, were subtle. Since electric lamps improved illumination, they encouraged reading, so much so that loans from the library in Muncie, Indiana, increased eightfold from 1890 to 1925. Historian David Nye wrote of how electrification adjusted our language and social outlook: "Americans regularly shifted from seeing electricity in terms of technical change to a metaphorical level where it meant novelty, excitement, modernity, and heightened awareness. Anything electric was saturated with energy, and the nation came to admire 'live wires,' 'human dynamos,' and 'electrifying performances.' "[50]

Yet neither Insull nor Norris fully achieved their corporate or political visions. The executive certainly created regulated monopolies, but his electric empire collapsed and was broken apart. The politician built public power agencies, but he couldn't stop the advance of private utilities. Despite their different perspectives on the control of power, both Insull and Norris predicted accurately that consumer demand for electricity in the coming decades would soar dramatically.

4

The Golden Era and Shattered Momentum

The 1940s and 1950s were wonderful years to be in the utility business. Power consumption rose steadily, increasing almost two-and-one-half times faster than the overall economy. Despite a dearth of Edison-style revolutionary inventions, engineers increased the size of the average power station almost sevenfold, and improved transformers and circuit breakers allowed higher voltages of electricity to be transmitted over longer distances.

Such technical achievements enabled utilities to build more and larger generators, meet a rising demand for electricity, and still lower their rates. The amount of coal needed to generate 1 kilowatt-hour of electricity fell more than 25 percent during the 1950s, and the average price per kilowatt-hour dropped by half, from 5.3 cents to 2.5 cents, during the 1940s and 1950s.

The power industry's growth transformed America and the American lifestyle. Consumers lightened their daily burdens with electric-powered vacuum cleaners, clothes dryers, irons, and sewing machines, and they found entertainment from radio, television, and air-conditioned movie theaters. Air conditioners, in fact, enabled a population shift to the humid South and the arid Southwest. Refrigerators broadened a family's food options, allowing New Yorkers to enjoy California oranges in the winter, and they decreased diseases by retarding food spoilage. Electric-powered irrigation opened vast tracts of desert to cultivation, while assembly lines provided more products and less dangerous jobs.

Utilities initially sold appliances directly to their customers, yet equipment manufacturers increasingly improved their products, transformed the refrigerator from a homely box with a hard-to-clean filter to a "quiet marvel of convenience,"[1] and took over that market. They redesigned the heavy and clumsy vacuum cleaner into an attractive unit with a high-speed motor. They regularly introduced new conveniences, such as the electric can opener in 1958. By 1960, the average American home sported a dozen appliances, double the number from a decade before. More than 50 million refrigerators, radios, televisions, and electric washers devoured a rising amount of power.

Charles Freeman, chairman in the early 1950s of Commonwealth Edison, described the utility's dominant challenge: "With the . . . reconversion to a peace-time economy, we thought that at last we would be able to restore the comfortable reserve capacity which had been dissipated by war conditions. But quite to the contrary, the principal problem facing us now in 1951 is the same which has plagued us from the end of the war, namely, that of constructing more and more generating, transmission, and distribution facilities to meet our customers' increasing demands for electric power."[2]

Electricity's potential caught the popular imagination. Futurists envisioned giant glass bubbles enclosing air-conditioned metropolises. They foresaw electric cars and an array of appliances that would provide "universal comfort, practically free transportation, and unlimited supplies of materials." The president of the Edison Electric Institute in 1961 gushed, "What we have seen in the first phases of electrical progress is marvelous enough. What may come in succeeding phases may well be beyond our present ability to comprehend, but it is not beyond man's ability to create."[3]

Utility marketers fanned these visions of an electrified future. Since electric lamps had saturated the market and radios and other small appliances consumed little power, they knew the industry's growth and prosperity demanded the adoption of air conditioners and other power-guzzling devices. The Edison Electric Institute advised its member utilities that "electric cooking and water heating must be vigorously pushed." And pushed they were. Power companies spent millions of dollars convincing consumers they would "live better electrically."

In addition to advertisements, utilities offered subsidies. They paid some builders $1,000 to construct all-electric "Gold Medallion" homes. Chicago's Commonwealth Edison provided $1.5 million to the Hancock Center's developer, double the gas company's proposal, to power the skyscraper with only electricity. Utilities also underwrote farmers adopting electric-powered irrigation.

Although advertising and payoffs helped, utilities were marketing a fairly reliable and reasonably priced commodity that consumers increasingly viewed as a necessity. As evidence of the nation's postwar dependence on electricity, in *The Day the Earth Stood Still*, a hit movie in the 1950s, an alien from another planet demonstrates his power by shutting off all electricity for half an hour. The action's effect is clear—the world very nearly stands still. Prosperity became defined, at least in part, by the refrigerators, air conditioners, and other electrical appliances that lightened daily burdens.

Even the system of utility regulation encouraged expansion. Because a power company's profits rose with the size of its investments, more power plants and transmission lines translated into larger returns. In more technical terms, regulators approved rates sufficient to pay for all fuel and operating costs, all construction costs associated with generators and other equipment, as well as a percentage profit on these fixed investments comparable to the profits earned by competitive businesses with similar risks. Protected by regulators from failure and competition, utilities had a built-in motive to expand and adopt expensive technologies.

CONTROLLING THE ATOM

The heady times inspired electrical engineers to think bigger and bolder. Perhaps their grandest scheme was to capture the tremendous energy released by splitting apart the large atoms of uranium. Such power, claimed the visionaries, would desalinate seawater, irrigate deserts, and run new factories. Since only a pound of enriched uranium fuel could produce as much electricity as 1,500 tons of coal, the new resource seemed limitless. And unlike dirty coal-fired plants, atomic power released little air pollution. The nuclear reactor was to be the crowning symbol of electricity's golden era.

Albert Einstein predicted the phenomenon, and Enrico Fermi demonstrated its possibility on December 3, 1942, at a squash court under the University of Chicago's football stadium. President Franklin Roosevelt subsequently sponsored the $2-billion Manhattan Project to build an atomic bomb that was to end World War II. Shortly after the bombing of Japan in 1945, *Newsweek* reported that "even the most conservative scientists and industrialists were willing to outline a civilization which would make the comic-strip prophecies of Buck Rogers look obsolete."[4]

Yet who should control this phenomenal source of power? Generals and diplomats, fearing Russia and other countries could obtain nuclear secrets, argued for military management, while industrialists, dreaming of huge profits in a new industry, pressed for the atom's commercial development. Lawmakers in 1946 sided with the diplomats and created an Atomic Energy Commission (AEC) to "conserve and restrict the use of atomic energy for the national defense, to prohibit its private exploitation, and to preserve the secret and confidential character of information concerning the use and application of atomic energy."[5]

The AEC initially tested bigger and bigger bombs at the Bikini atoll in the South Pacific's Marshall Islands. That strategy changed when President Harry Truman announced on September 22, 1949, "We have evidence that within recent weeks an atomic explosion occurred in the U.S.S.R." Truman quickly ordered the construction of a hydrogen bomb, far more powerful than "Little Boy" or "Fat Man," and he convinced Congress to allow the sharing of certain nuclear information with U.S. allies in the newly formed North Atlantic Treaty Organization (NATO). Although Truman's move strengthened opposition to the Soviet Union, industrialists questioned why foreign governments, but not U.S. companies, should receive atomic secrets.

The business sector's wish was granted with the 1952 election. While Truman had considered nuclear energy "too important a development to be made the subject of profit-seeking," business-oriented President Eisenhower wanted nuclear power commercialized. In his "Atoms for Peace" speech before the United Nations on December 8, 1953, Eisenhower declared, "It is not enough to take this weapon out of the hands of the soldiers. It must be put into the hands of those who will know how to strip its military casing and adapt it to the art of peace."[6] While some Democrats labeled Eisenhower's proposal a "giveaway" to utility monopolies, Congress approved an Atomic Energy Act in 1954 that encouraged private corporations to build and own reactors.

Cautious utility executives initially expressed skepticism of the unproven technology. Reactor construction costs, after all, were higher than those of coal-fired power plants. Nuclear plant reliability was unknown, and supplies of uranium fuel were not assured. Noting these practical problems, *Business Week* lamented, "You can find a great many more buyers for the Brooklyn Bridge than businessmen interested in doing something about atomic power."[7]

Fears of liability were particularly troubling. Charles Weaver, a Westinghouse vice president, described the industry's nervousness: "We cannot exclude the possibility that a great enough fool aided by a great enough conspiracy of circumstances could bring about an accident exceeding available insurance."[8] According to the Brookhaven National Laboratory, such a nuclear disaster could cause 4,300 deaths, 43,000 injuries, and $7 billion of property damage. Insurance companies and utilities, quite logically, refused to accept the gamble.[9]

Enter again the federal government. Representative Melvin Price and Senator Clinton Anderson in 1957 successfully pushed legislation that absolved utilities of most liability, regardless of any carelessness or recklessness on their part, and provided a $560-million fund to cover any damages. Senator Anderson later admitted $560 million was an arbitrary figure, high enough to provide confidence to potential victims but not so large as to "frighten the country and the Congress to death."

To further advance commercial reactors, the Atomic Energy Commission agreed to eliminate regulatory burdens that might slow a power plant's licensing. Eisenhower's Atoms for Peace program also granted $475 million for Euratom to build a 1,000-megawatt reactor if this consortium of European countries used American parts and U.S. fuel and enrichment facilities. The AEC by 1962 estimated the federal government had spent nearly $1.3 billion on research and development for nuclear power plants, more than twice the investment made by private companies.

The public generally supported such government subsidies as visionaries continued to speak of abundant energy that would be "too cheap to meter." Walt Disney produced a 1956 television show entitled "Our Friend, the Atom." Even the Sierra Club as late as 1972 consulted with a few utilities on the siting of atomic plants and refused to oppose nuclear power outright.

Despite such government and popular support, most utilities remained unwilling to take the nuclear gamble unless reactor manufacturers sweetened the pot. Westinghouse and General Electric were willing to negotiate, since both thought commercial reactors would allow them to break into the market for high-pressure steam generators that had been controlled by Combustion Engineering and Babcock & Wilcox. Both also needed a new line of business to boost morale after executives from the firms had been jailed for conspiring to fix prices on electrical equipment.

The equipment manufacturers devised an offer that utilities couldn't refuse—promising to assume all the risks associated with building this unproven technology and to charge a fixed construction fee that was competitive with coal-fired plants. General Electric in 1963 delivered a complete nuclear power station at a set price to Jersey Central Power & Light Company. Because Jersey Central simply had to start the generating equipment, the arrangement was called a "turnkey" contract. According to General Electric's John McKitterick, "Our people understood this was a game of massive stakes, and that if we didn't force the utility industry to put those stations on-line, we'd end up with nothing."[10]

The turnkey gamble produced mixed results. It certainly provided business for General Electric and Westinghouse. Since Babcock & Wilcox and Combustion Engineering refused to take the construction risks, GE and Westinghouse by the end of 1966 controlled 80 percent of the nuclear market. Yet the strategy hurt the reactor manufacturers dearly. Construction of the Jersey Central reactor, described as "the greatest loss leader in American industry," cost twice General Electric's initial estimates. A RAND study found Westinghouse and General Electric lost an average of $75 million on each turnkey contract, for a total of almost $1 billion. Still, GE's Bertram Wolfe concluded the gamble was worth it: "The turnkeys made the light water reactor a viable product. They got enough volume in the business that we could build an engineering staff, standardize our product, and put up facilities to mass-produce things so that the cost went down. That way we got over this tailor-made, one-of-a-kind, high-cost plant."[11]

The union of government subsidies and corporate loss-leaders finally persuaded utility executives. Orders for reactors jumped from seven in 1965 to 20 in 1966 and 30 in 1967. The "great nuclear bandwagon" had begun.

The combination of energy-guzzling appliances, utility advertising and subsidies, falling electricity prices, and favorable regulation increased electric power usage rapidly and predictably. At a compound annual rate of 7.8 percent, electricity demand after World War II doubled every ten years. Utility executives, at least for a couple of decades, expanded their operations with the benefit of engineering progress and without the fear of competition.

Power company managers, however, also became increasingly conservative and cautious. Trade journals acknowledged the management malaise as top engineering and business students turned to the more glamorous electronic, aerospace, and computer industries.[12] The shortage of talent, according to one publication, would have "a profoundly negative impact on the quality of [the industry's] leadership—its top executives, its middle managers, and its supervisors."[13] *Fortune* in 1969 described the utility industry as "sluggish" and "clumsy." The magazine suggested power company executive were "generally unimaginative men, grown complacent on private monopoly and regulated profits," and ill prepared for change.

Growth and stability could not last forever. By the mid-1960s, the deliverers of electricity began suffering a series of setbacks. Utilities no longer could assume that reliable service was assured, that larger power plants would be more efficient than older models, that power company stocks offered safe investments, and that nuclear energy was "too cheap to meter." The industry's fundamental concepts were challenged, and staid executives exacerbated their problems by refusing to accept the new realities.

The industry's setbacks did not translate into a lesser role for electricity. In fact, a growing array of appliances, computers, and robots demonstrated electric power's flexibility and usefulness. Electricity demand continued to rise, even if at a less rapid rate, yet the generators and deliverers of electricity were shocked from their predictable worlds by blackouts, protests, embargoes, accidents, and defaults.

THE BLACKOUT—NOVEMBER 9, 1965

On the evening of November 9, 1965, electricity demand began its normal rise as commuters returned home from work. High-voltage power lines passing through the Sir Adam Beck electric station near Niagara Falls wheeled, as usual, this increasing power between Ontario, Canada, and New England. Yet at 5:16 P.M., a transmission line suddenly "tripped out" to avoid being overloaded. As that line's power moved to other wires, four additional lines—with a total capacity of 1,500 megawatts—quickly shut down. Now a massive electric current, looking for another path, surged into upstate New York, where faulty switches failed to curb the cascade of power. Within less than twelve minutes, the overloaded system crashed and sent eight states and Ontario into darkness for almost thirteen hours.

Dale Chapman was piloting his United Airlines jet 33,000 feet above southern New England on that clear November twilight when he looked out the window and suddenly "the whole city of New York was missing." Declared a startled Chapman, "It looked like the end of the world."[14]

Some 30 million northeasterners on the ground watched lights flicker, surge for a brief instant, and then fall into darkness. Approximately 800,000 commuters in subways cars slowed to a stop, while millions of motorists confronted traffic snarls at dark intersections.

The power outage spread over 80,000 square miles—an area slightly smaller than Great Britain. "Black Tuesday" was not the nation's first blackout, but it was the most extensive, the longest, and the most publicized.

Most of those who spent the night without power "reacted sportively," said one participant, "as if it were all a gigantic game of blindman's buff." Hundreds of volunteers substituted for traffic signals. Occupants of several stalled subway cars passed their time singing and dancing. Numerous restaurants offered free food and drinks to the stranded.[15]

Northeasterners learned the full extent of their dependence on electricity, and many devised creative means to accomplish their tasks. At Fordham University, for example, students studied by car lights. Farmers deployed tractor motors to power their dairy pumps. Guests at New York's Hilton Hotel burned 30,000 candles, and Manhattan doctors devised makeshift operating rooms to deliver five-dozen babies.

The news media, headquartered in New York City, shared the experience with the entire nation. Hollywood later added to Black Tuesday's legend with Doris Day's comedy, *Where Were You When the Lights Went Out?*, perpetuating the image of thousands of couples spending the dark and quiet evening preparing families.

Utility executives, however, did not laugh about the bewildering accident. They had claimed interconnected power pools were reliable deliverers of electricity. Although subsequent investigations showed the power cascade was caused simply by an uninspected relay, a device about the size of a shoe box, executives and politicians feared more accidents would occur throughout the increasingly complex transmission system. A Federal Power Commission report could give "no absolute assurance" against a similar massive failure in the future.

New York's Consolidated Edison (Con Ed) conducted its own extensive investigation. Yet only three days after the utility's chairman "guaranteed" that a power cascade would not recur, another small malfunction spiraled into a widespread blackout, this time affecting 9 million people for as much as twenty-five hours. The Big Apple's July 13, 1977, blackout, unlike the first experience, was no carnival. In fact, chaos reigned that hot night as rioters and looters destroyed more than $50 million of property.

The power outages forced utility executives to redirect expenditures from building new power plants to improving the operations of existing facilities. Specifically, they had to upgrade the fragile distribution system in order to efficiently service larger power pools and more frequent sales among utilities. The new costs led to higher rates, and despite the industry's expensive image advertisements, the public grew increasingly critical of utility monopolies.

THE EFFICIENCY LIMIT—1967

No one missed the highly publicized blackouts, but few noticed that 1967 marked a profound turning point for the electricity industry. That year represented the peak in power plant efficiency. No longer would new generating equipment be more efficient than the machinery it replaced. The properties of construction materials had reached their practical limits. Rather than lower the average cost of electricity, a new station henceforth would increase it. Economies of scale didn't apply any longer for the utility industry. Continued expansion would no longer benefit the consumer.

Electrical engineers for the previous few decades had developed boilers that could withstand enormous and increasing amounts of heat and pressure. Supercritical steam reached temperatures exceeding 1,050 degrees Fahrenheit and pressures above 3,206 pounds per square inch, turning water into dry, unsaturated steam. The power companies had employed an array of new alloys to protect a power plant's metal from corrosion and fatigue. They also met rising power demands with larger turbines, and they demanded that equipment manufacturers build bigger and bigger units, often without taking the time to test and learn from each incremental increase.

Scientists long had predicted a steam generator's maximum efficiency to be approximately 48 percent. Thus, for every 100 units of fuel burned, thermodynamic theory holds that a power plant could generate at most 48 units of electricity. The remaining 52 units would become heat, usually disposed as waste into adjacent rivers or the air.

Yet even before efficiencies reached 40 percent, utility managers slowly began to realize that their larger systems were not performing well. Turbine blades twisted frequently, furnaces couldn't maintain high temperatures, metallurgical problems became apparent in boilers and turbines, and a slew of other defects retarded reliability and performance. Large plants also required expensive construction techniques since many components had to be custom built on site rather than prefabricated in a factory. A General Electric manager later admitted that the rapid growth in the size of generators and boilers caused "major failures leading to the need for costly redesigns, costly rebuilds in the fields, and the additional costs involved for purchased power."[16]

Outages became directly proportionate to size. The larger the power plant, the more likely it would fail unexpectedly or be shut down for repairs.[17] The probable failure of big units, moreover, required utilities to build more expensive backup systems.

Power executives slowly became skeptical of giant generators, and the era of centralization waned. "Central thermal power plants stopped getting more efficient in the 1960s, bigger in the 1970s, cheaper in the '80s, and bought in the '90s," stated the Rocky Mountain Institute. Reflecting centralization's efficiency limit, "smaller units offered greater economies from mass production than big ones could gain through unit size."[18]

THE PROTESTS—APRIL 22, 1970

With the 1962 publication of *Silent Spring*, Rachel Carson stimulated Americans to consider the health and environmental hazards of industrial practices. The damaging impacts of those actions became shockingly apparent with the bursting of an oil well off Santa Barbara, California, in January 1969 and the burning of Cleveland's polluted Cuyahoga River that June. A new breed of citizen activist began to target utilities for the air pollution that irritated eyes, limited visibility, and led to increased emphysema, lung cancer, and heart disease. These environmentalists complained that power generators discharged half the nation's sulfur dioxide and a quarter of its particulates and nitrogen oxides, and the National Academy of Sciences predicted sulfur-dioxide emissions would triple by the century's end unless utilities installed pollution-control equipment. The chairman of the Senate Air and Water Pollution Subcommittee also lamented that heated water from generators killed thousands of fish and organisms and that strip mines to feed coal-fired power plants destroyed an area larger than the state of Connecticut.

Utility executives either dismissed these problems or complained that adding "scrubbers" would double the price of electricity. Yet the popular mood turned against polluters on Earth Day—April 22, 1970. With a small staff and hundreds of volunteers, Denis Hayes, a Harvard Law School student, and Senator Gaylord Nelson mobilized thousands of schools, churches, and civic groups to sponsor debates, sit-ins, and demonstrations that attracted millions across the country. Events ranged from mock burials of automobiles to lectures by leading scientists. New York's mayor closed Fifth Avenue to automobiles most of the day in order to demonstrate the city's concerns about air pollution. A Gallup Opinion Index conducted shortly after Earth Day found that, of major domestic concerns, pollution had moved from ninth to second place.

Earth Day launched environmental activism and focused fresh attention on electric utilities. The Environmental Action Foundation in 1974 published *How To Challenge Your Local Electric Utility*, a popular step-by-step handbook on opposing rate increases and power plant constructions. Public-interest lawyers blocked Consolidated Edison from building a dam in upstate New York, arguing it would "deface Storm King Mountain and the Hudson Valley." Other lawyers used environmental impact statements to delay scores of reactors and coal-fired generators, causing much dismay and confusion among utility executives.[19]

Protests at power facilities accelerated throughout the 1970s. Clamshell Alliance organizers in 1976 marched to the reactor site in Seabrook, New Hampshire, camped out for several weeks, and obtained widespread media coverage. One march led to the arrests of 1,414 protesters, which sparked the creation of other alliances across the country. In addition to such young activists, farmers in Minnesota's Stearnes and Pope counties marched against the construction by two rural electric cooperatives of high-voltage transmission wires. They feared the lines would destroy 8,500 acres of prime farmland and reduce the milk output of cows. Complained one farmer, "Those damn lines, on a wet day, can throw shocks all over the place."[20] These protests got testy as normally conservative farmers set bonfires, blasted patrol cars of arresting officers with makeshift slingshots (which the farmers dubbed "wrist-rockets"), and toppled an $80,000 transmission tower.

Earth Day's popularity also mobilized politicians. Even Republican Richard Nixon, in his 1970 State of the Union message, declared, "The great question of the '70s is, shall we surrender to our surroundings or shall we make our peace with nature and begin to make reparations for the damage we have done to our air, to our land, and to our water." The president supported the creation of the Environmental Protection Agency, and Congress quickly approved the Clean Air Act, Clean Water Act, and more than thirty other environmental laws. States established their own environmental agencies and passed their own regulatory statutes.

Utility executives vehemently opposed environmental legislation and regulations, and they often responded to growing public concerns with modest actions, such as adding shrubbery around relay stations or painting transmission towers a sky-blue color. Con Ed launched its campaign against air pollution not by installing scrubbers, but by placing a staff assistant with binoculars atop the Empire State Building in order to monitor visibility. Most industry lobbyists argued for a "balanced approach" that would allow continued construction and modest clean-up efforts. Without such expansion, they predicted more blackouts and brownouts. In fact, the Potomac Electric Power Company in 1969 had to ask District of Columbia residents to turn off their air conditioners in order to not overwhelm the stressed power system on hot summer days.

Such efforts and claims could not hide the fact that utility executives faced an array of new regulations and costs that would change their business practices dramatically. The days of laissez-faire government oversight were over. According to the director of the White House Office of Science and Technology, "Environmental concerns now must be considered as an integral part of the [utility] planning process."[21]

THE GRID'S OPENING—1973

A utility's key monopoly investment had been its transmission lines. Other corporations might build a generating plant, but it was assumed that only one firm would (and should) be able to build and control the grid that distributed power. Transmission construction costs are high, and available corridors often are restricted by urban developments, wilderness areas, and military reservations. Installing high-voltage lines also tends to spark hostile reactions from residents worried about unsightly towers and electromagnetic radiation.

Senator George Norris had challenged the notion of a grid monopoly, but he made far more progress establishing government utilities than in opening high-voltage lines. Norris wanted the large investor-owned utilities to provide a more flexible distribution system, and he argued that their wires should be common carriers, available for a reasonable fee to municipalities, rural coops, and others. When lobbyists for the investor-owned utilities blocked the senator's effort—inserting giant loopholes into the Federal Power Act that prevented wheeling of electricity if it hampered power reliability or injured relations among utilities—Norris responded by proposing that the federal government construct a separate electricity grid that would circumvent the investor-owned utilities' transmission lines. His goal was to allow municipally owned firms to obtain electricity directly from federal hydroelectric projects. Private utilities squashed that effort, too.

President John F. Kennedy in the early 1960s revitalized Norris's efforts and called, on several occasions, for a cross-county, high-voltage transmission system available to all generators and consumers. Despite utility protests, the administration advanced a piecemeal federal grid by constructing government power lines in Idaho and along the West Coast. Federal officials also blocked several private utilities from building transmission wires across national forests, and they ordered utilities with existing lines over public lands to sell access to that grid.

The struggle shifted to the courts in the late 1960s. Four small communities in Minnesota, North Dakota, and South Dakota sued the investor-owned Otter Tail Power Company for refusing to wheel low-cost electricity from a federal hydroelectric project. Siding with Otter Tail, the Federal Power Commission ruled that the private company was not required to provide its equipment to its competitors. Yet in 1973, the Supreme Court disagreed, arguing that Otter Tail's distribution monopoly gave it "effective control over potential competition from municipal ownership. By its refusal to sell or wheel power [Otter Tail] prevents that competition from surfacing."[22]

The court's Otter Tail decision, while it reflected a close vote and prompted additional legal battles, marked the onset of competition. It challenged the utilities' wires monopoly and opened the door slightly to a competitive transmission market.

THE EMBARGO—OCTOBER 1973

Utilities turned increasingly to petroleum during the 1960s and early 1970s, in part because the fuel contains less impurities and burns cleaner than coal, which were real advantages in urban areas during an era of stricter environmental regulations. Oil also had become cheaper, having fallen some 30 percent in price throughout the 1960s. Petroleum, as a result, had risen from 6.9 percent of a utility's fuel mix in 1962 to 14.2 percent in 1970.

Oil's price advantage ended abruptly in 1973 for reasons outside of the power industry's control. Political tensions long had simmered in the Middle East, but in the fall of that year, Saudi Arabia's King Faisal expressed fiery frustration with Israel and warned the United States that if it wanted more Saudi oil at reasonable prices it must "disavow . . . Israeli policies and actions."[23]

President Nixon, distracted by Watergate scandals, believed the king was "calling wolf where no wolf exists except in his imagination." But the wolf pounced on October 6, 1973, in the form of Egyptian troops crossing into Israeli-occupied Suez and closing the canal. Nixon's initial reaction was to provide military assistance to Israel. Arab foreign ministers lobbied against the move, as did U.S. oil executives who feared the aid would "have a critical and adverse effect on our relations with the moderate Arab producing countries." Yet Nixon proceeded with a $2.5-billion arms shipment.[24]

Arab ministers reacted angrily. Meeting in Kuwait on October 17, the Organization of Petroleum Exporting Countries (OPEC) agreed to boost oil prices 70 percent and to cut production 5 percent each month "until the Israel withdrawal is completed . . . and the legal rights of the Palestinian people restored." Saudi Arabia quickly cut its production by 20 percent and announced a total embargo on oil sales to the United States and the Netherlands, Israel's chief allies.[25]

Arab cutbacks amounted to less than 10 percent of the world's supply, but panic ensued. Within a month, the price of oil on the spot market soared from approximately $3.00 to $17.00 a barrel. By December, OPEC ministers settled to a floor price of $11.65 a barrel, a 400 percent rise in just two months—an increase that would cost the United States more than the entire war in Vietnam.

Since utility reliance on petroleum had increased, OPEC's action had a direct effect on electricity rates. Yet the Arab action also caused a rise in the cost of other fuels, including coal, upon which the power industry depended enormously. Other economic factors were at work, too, including accelerated inflation and high interest rates resulting from an overheated Vietnam War economy. Higher borrowing costs proved to be a particular burden to capital-intensive utilities.

Most utility executives viewed the high costs as an aberration, and they maintained their estimates of rising consumer demand and their commitments to costly construction projects. They and many politicians argued that the embargo proved America needed vastly more electricity capacity. Presidents Richard Nixon and Gerald Ford, for instance, advanced "Project Independence" that would build 200 nuclear reactors, 150 coal-fired power plants, 30 oil refineries, 20 synthetic fuel plants, and 250 major coal mines. The utility industry and its political supporters simply failed to acknowledge that higher costs would encourage consumers to conserve and to reduce the growth of electricity sales for the first time since World War II.

THE MISSED DIVIDEND—APRIL 23, 1974

Consolidated Edison's construction expenses more than doubled between 1968 and 1974, evidence in part of the utility's efforts to continue its construction projects and to make its transmission and distribution system more reliable after the blackout. Another factor was a New York City regulation that required underground cables, which cost twenty times more to install and maintain than unsightly overhead wires. The utility's labor costs also increased 65 percent, an industry high, and the firm paid almost three times more than other power companies in state and local taxes.

Con Ed's prospects were not bright. The utility was penned in and could not expand into prosperous suburban industrial parks. Serving a densely populated urban area, it also faced citizen opposition when it tried to build nuclear or coal-fired power plants. Highly dependent upon low-sulfur coal and imported oil, Con Ed sat defenseless against OPEC's price hikes, which raised the utility's daily fuel costs from $720,000 to $2,480,000.

To help the utility overcome these financial burdens, New York's Public Service Commission in March 1974 granted an 85-percent rate increase, raising a New Yorker's average monthly bill to $250. Many angry customers delayed payment or simply refused to pay, further complicating Con Ed's cash crunch.

In February 1974, Moody's Investors Service downgraded the utility's bond rating, making it more difficult and expensive for Con Ed to borrow money. In early April, New York City Civil Court judge Bernard Weiss encouraged the utility to reduce its quarterly dividend in order to help relieve its cash plight. Several weeks later, on April 23, Con Ed chairman Charles Luce went beyond the judge's suggestion and canceled the dividend for the first time in the company's eighty-nine-year history.

That move, according to Florida Power & Light's president, Marshall McDonald, "really clobbered all the utilities. They have long been considered the best stocks for widows and orphans, and now we have the largest of them in trouble and passing a dividend. This throws the viability of the entire industry in doubt."[26] Luce's dividend cancellation sparked a selling frenzy on Wall Street that quickly drove the average utility stock price down 18 percent. By September, power company values fell 36 percent, the greatest decline since the Great Depression.

Con Ed's bond rating dropped so low that several institutions, included savings and loan associations, were legally forbidden to invest in its bonds. Luce, desperate for a short-term solution, asked New York State for additional help. Swayed by Con Ed's political connections and fearful that bankruptcy would turn out the lights of their constituents, politicians approved an $800-million bond and the state purchased two of the utility's partially completed power stations, a nuclear reactor at Buchanan and an oil-fired generator in Queens. The utility's delighted financial manager, reflecting Con Ed's financial straits, declared, "When we sell those plants, we will get more money than we normally raise in a year."[27]

Despite such short-term fixes, electric companies continued to flood the financial markets with securities in order to pay for rising construction costs. In 1973 alone, utilities issued $4.7 billion in new common and preferred stock, almost seven times more than was sold by all manufacturing companies combined. The cash crunch forced several firms, including Carolina Power and Public Service Electric & Gas Company of New Jersey, to sell new common stock below the book value of the company's assets, decreasing shareholder equity.

Most power industry officials ignored such troubling prospects and refused to abandon their commitment to growth. American Electric Power's Donald Cook, considered by *Business Week* to be "one of the most thoughtful of utility executives," continued to project widespread blackouts if utilities did not build more power plants.[28]

Con Ed's problems, however, convinced a few utility executives and Wall Street analysts to avoid expansion. Detroit Edison, for instance, adjusted downward its power-demand projections and announced a $650-million cut in its five-year building program. Charles Benore, then with the Mitchell Hutchins investment company, advised his clients against buying stocks and bonds in utilities with large construction programs. These few recognized that the vision of more and larger power plants was becoming a financial nightmare.[29]

THE ACCIDENT—MARCH 28, 1979

Americans in early March 1979 flocked to movie theaters to watch Jane Fonda and Jack Lemmon confront a nuclear accident and a utility's efforts to cover it up. *The China Syndrome* became a box office hit and "meltdown" a household word.

Fiction became reality on March 28. About three miles from Harrisburg, Pennsylvania, on a thin island in the Susquehanna River, a pressurized-water reactor lost its coolant, causing its radioactive fuel to overheat. For the next five days, televisions and newspapers featured fearful news about "the worst nuclear power plant accident in history."[30]

Shortly after 4:00 A.M., pumps feeding water into the steam generators for Three Mile Island's Unit 2 stopped working. As called for in the plant's safety plan, both the steam turbine and the electric generator it powered shut down, excess steam heated the reactor's coolant, enormous pressure developed within the reactor vessel, and operators opened a valve to release the pressure. Then serious mistakes were made. Believing incorrectly that cooling water covered the radioactive core, plant engineers shut off the emergency pumps, causing the core to overheat. For two hours and twenty-two minutes, about 32,000 gallons of vital coolant became radioactive and leaked out of the chamber. Without sufficient liquid, part of the intensely hot uranium core melted and produced a hydrogen gas bubble within the reactor.

No one knew the full extent of the accident's seriousness, yet officials with Metropolitan Edison, Three Mile Island's operator, arranged hasty press conferences to assure the public that everything was under control. It was not. Three days after the first pump stopped working, a helicopter with monitoring equipment detected a sudden release of radioactivity from the reactor. Volunteers quickly evacuated pregnant women and young children from nearby Middletown, and residents as far as 200 miles away began to worry about the wind bringing deadly radioactivity into their backyards.

Government regulators provided little assurance. For long hours during the crisis, they ineptly debated the wisdom of evacuating entire communities. Joseph Hendrie, chairman of the Nuclear Regulatory Commission (NRC), later admitted, "We were operating almost totally in the blind."[31]

Reporters from around the world descended upon Harrisburg, Middletown, and Three Mile Island as they tracked technical developments and interviewed frightened residents. Some reporting was clearly sensational or politically motivated. The tabloid New York *Post*, for example, blazoned the headline: "Race with Nuclear Disaster," while the conservative Manchester (New Hampshire) *Union Leader* announced: "No Injuries Reported in Nuke Mishap." Many of the stories, however, accurately investigated the power company's lack of control and the uncertainties associated with reactors. The constant news coverage convinced most Americans that utilities and nuclear power were in trouble. A CBS/*New York Times* poll found "only 46 percent of Americans now favor further development of nuclear power, compared with 69 percent who were asked the same question in a July 1977 CBS/*New York Times* poll."[32]

Utility executives, however, continued to applaud nuclear power's safety record. John Herbein of Metropolitan Edison maintained enough confidence to declare, "We didn't injure anybody with this accident. We didn't seriously contaminate anybody, and we certainly didn't kill anybody."[33]

The Nuclear Regulatory Commission's investigation, headed by lawyer Mitchell Rogovin, revealed a far more frightening picture. The Rogovin account explained that Three Mile Island had been within one hour of a catastrophic meltdown. It declared that the release of substantial radioactivity into the air and water was avoided mainly by dumb luck.[34]

Three Mile Island certainly was the best known reactor accident, yet it was not a singular event. In 1952, engineers mistakenly lifted four of the twelve control rods from the fuel core at Canada's Chalk River experimental reactor, causing a chain reaction that melted almost all of the uranium. In 1957, operators at a British plutonium-production reactor failed to realize for forty-two hours that radioactivity was leaking from the plant; while officials subsequently refused to admit a problem, they quietly destroyed half-a-million gallons of milk from dairy farms surrounding the facility.

The first major U.S. reactor accident occurred at a small military power plant in Idaho. On January 3, 1961, three servicemen—John Byrnes, Richard McKinley, and Richard Legg—were finishing routine chores when, suddenly, the control rods fell from the core. The now "supercritical" fuel created a steam explosion that projected debris throughout the reactor, including a control-rod plug that speared McKinley's body and hurled it into the ceiling. Byrnes and Legg died of radiation burns, and their bodies were so radioactive that the military would not handle them for three weeks and then buried them in lead-lined caskets within lead-lined vaults.

One of the more bizarre accidents occurred on October 22, 1975, at the Tennessee Valley Authority's Browns Ferry reactor near Decatur, Alabama. A worker, for some reason, was using a candle to check for air leaks around electrical cables, when the flame set fire to the polyurethane insulation. Other workmen tried to douse the fire, but automatic sprinklers had not yet been installed. The fire quickly destroyed 1,600 cables, including those controlling key safety equipment. Hours went by while the fire department and reactor personnel debated whether to spray the fire. Engineers later admitted privately that a meltdown was avoided "by sheer luck."[35]

Underlying these specific problems were the government's premature licensing of a complex technology, as well as the aggressive competition among reactor vendors. Struggling to gain business, General Electric, Westinghouse, and other equipment manufacturers had promoted larger reactors aggressively without waiting for operating experience associated with current designs. James Deddens of Babcock and Wilcox later admitted, "When you get into that kind of competitive situation, you may sell something that hasn't been tested as thoroughly as it would be today."[36]

After the Three Mile Island accident, the public and politicians demanded stricter (and more costly) safety regulations and enforcement. Utility executives tried to restore public confidence, yet they faced another problem: Reactor cost overruns were sending power companies to the brink of bankruptcy.

THE DEFAULT—JULY 25, 1983

Perhaps the poster child of troubled utilities was the Washington Public Power Supply System (WPPSS, commonly known as "Whoops" for its mangled acronym and problems). The utility's cost estimate for building five reactors in the Pacific Northwest had almost tripled between 1975 and 1980, soaring to $15.9 billion. It had been fined $61,000 by the Nuclear Regulatory Commission for inadequate welds in a shield surrounding a reactor vessel. Workers at three of the plants had been on strike for five months, and more than forty-five general contractors at each reactor jockeyed to get their equipment into crowded, poorly managed construction sites.

In August 1980, WPPSS officials asked Robert Ferguson to clean up their mess. The engineer and administrator enjoyed a reputation for getting jobs done, having spent more than twenty years completing government nuclear projects on time and within budget. Ferguson quickly decentralized the cumbersome administrative system and centralized the hiring of contractors, prompting many in the Northwest to declare that he had performed a management miracle.

The hard-nosed manager also began a "bottoms-up" review of the WPPSS budget, systematically calculating the amounts of concrete, pipe, cable, and labor needed to finish the job. Each time he checked the numbers, to his great disappointment, the cost estimates rose. In May 1981 Ferguson concluded that the true figure was $23.8 billion, a 50-percent increase over the $15.9 billion he was told when he became managing director.[37]

Ferguson realized that WPPSS could not raise the extra funds needed to continue its construction projects. The utility already had saturated the U.S. bond market with $6 billion of tax-exempt offerings, including $1.6 billion in 1981. The manager reluctantly recommended a moratorium on Units 4 and 5, shocking the WPPSS board, which included farmers and ranchers committed to bringing more electricity to the Pacific Northwest.

Investors in those reactors assumed their bonds were secured by "take or pay" contracts that obligated the eighty-eight participating utilities to take the electricity as soon as it was produced or to pay WPPSS for the power even if it was not delivered. Bondholders, however, failed to anticipate the unwillingness of Northwest consumers to pay higher rates, even though their electricity costs were among the nation's lowest. Eighty-six of the eighty-eight utilities decided to break their contracts, calling them invalid and arguing they never had the authority to sign such agreements. The Chemical Bank, representing bondholders, filed suit against the power companies, but the Washington State Superior Court unexpectedly ruled in June 1983 that the utilities could avoid paying WPPSS for the over-budget and unfinished reactors.

WPPSS, unable to repay its bondholders, filed on July 25 a $2.25-billion default, the largest to date in U.S. history. Investors suddenly held bonds worth only 12 cents on the dollar, and WPPSS terminated some 15,000 construction workers.[38]

More than sixty lawsuits were filed as participants tried to blame someone else for the economic mess. The WPPSS utilities complained that the Bonneville Power Administration, a federal agency, bullied them into signing contracts for the unneeded power. Bonneville, in contrast, charged that "the project simply ran away from the Supply System" and its inexperienced managers. Bondholders blamed investment houses for providing misleading information about WPPSS's financial condition, while the brokerage firms and rating companies said they couldn't foresee a judge allowing utilities to "walk away from contracts."[39]

The WPPSS fiasco was not an isolated incident. The Department of Energy in 1984 calculated that more than three-quarters of the operating reactors cost at least twice their originally estimated prices. The default, however, shattered many of the power industry's basic assumptions about the safety and security of utility investments, and it marked a turning point in electricity economics.

The nuclear reactor, once a symbol of so much promise, had become a financial lemon. Utility executives only two decades before had predicted 1,000 reactors would be operating in 2000 and providing electricity "too cheap to meter." The reality was that only eighty-two atomic plants operated in 2000, and no new orders had been placed in more than two decades. Reactor cost overruns produced rate shocks, with average power prices soaring 60 percent between 1969 and 1984.

"The business of generating electricity has ceased to be a commercially viable enterprise," declared I. C. Bupp of the Harvard Business School in the early 1980s. Although some nuclear advocates today speak of a pending renaissance, the history of soaring construction costs does give pause. One industry spokesman rued that "estimating capital costs for power plants is like shooting at a moving target."[40]

Utility executives blamed their woes on government regulators and environmentalists, saying new rules and associated delays escalated costs. Safety requirements to contain radioactivity, for example, demanded thick and expensive concrete walls. After accidents or "incidents" at one reactor, regulators frequently forced other utilities to rebuild many of their systems, as when Northeast Utilities of Connecticut spent $85 million to add new pipes at its Millstone 2 unit, then 50 percent complete.

Yet the rush of regulatory changes began only after large reactors ordered in the mid-1960s began to break down. Pipes and valves cracked under intense radiation and high temperatures. Tubes corroded, fuel rods bent, and cooling systems malfunctioned. After hearing of an increasing number of safety problems, the public and politicians demanded that the Atomic Energy Commission and its successor, the Nuclear Regulatory Commission, alter their habit of routinely granting nuclear licenses. The more regulators investigated, the more problems they discovered. At Wisconsin's Lacrosse reactor, for instance, investigators found that a 3,000-gallon tank of radioactive wastewater had been inadvertently connected to the plant's drinking water system. At the Diablo Canyon reactor atop a California fault line, the Nuclear Regulatory Commission provided a preliminary start-up license to Pacific Gas & Electric in September 1981, only to discover two months later that the plant's anti-earthquake structures were installed backward due to a blueprint error. In 1983 alone, utilities reported more than 5,000 mishaps at nuclear power plants, 247 of which were considered "particularly significant" by the Nuclear Regulatory Commission. The *Wall Street Journal* concluded that reactor troubles "tell the story of projects crippled by too little regulation, rather than too much."[41]

Utility engineers had misjudged nuclear technology by initially considering it to be "just another way to boil water." A reactor, in fact, is anything but simple. Some 40,000 valves weave through a large plant, ten times more than for a coal- or oil-fired unit of comparable size. Fuel rod temperatures soar to 4,800 degrees Fahrenheit, and highly refined zirconium alloys are required to contain the fission products. One industry executive admitted his colleagues were "darn good at building big coal plants" but didn't appreciate that nuclear technology demanded "ten times the management intensity."[42]

Some utility analysts issued even harsher conclusions. "Many of the worst problems to befall the nuclear industry have occurred as a result of its own management failures," concluded the engineering department of the Massachusetts Institute of Technology.[43] A 1984 report by the congressional Office of Technology Assessment attributed reactor cost overruns to the lack of competence and experience of utility managers.[44] In February 1985, *Forbes* ranked the U.S. nuclear program "as the largest managerial disaster in business history, a disaster on a monumental scale."[45]

Not all utilities, of course, suffered rate hikes and plant cancellations. Those that avoided the nuclear bandwagon of the 1970s fared fairly well throughout the 1980s, largely because regulators continued to protect them from competitors and to guarantee them healthy rates of return on their investments. Power monopolies, moreover, obtained substantial help from Washington.

TURNING TO GOVERNMENT

The electricity market was anything but free. Power companies long had enjoyed government-sponsored monopolies and guaranteed profits. More obvious direct subsidies went to government-owned utilities, including the Tennessee Valley Authority, Bonneville Power Administration, municipal power companies, and rural electric cooperatives. Munis and co-ops paid no taxes and obtained taxpayer-supported financing through tax-exempt bonds or low-interest Rural Electrification Act loans. They also received preference to the low-cost power generated at huge government dams like Hoover and Grand Coulee.

Investor-owned utilities also benefited from numerous government incentives, including investment tax credits and accelerated depreciation benefits. The nuclear industry stood out as a particular beneficiary. U.S. reactors probably would not exist were it not for government-supported insurance, liability limits, research, and fuels processing.

Utility executives, however, tended to argue that the government imposed more burdens than benefits. Some complained that state regulators limited their profits and that a mountain of requirements increased their costs.

Politicians no doubt had whipsawed utilities. The Clean Air Act of 1970 and other environmental legislation virtually forced many utilities to convert from dirty coal to relatively clean oil, which was abundant and cheap before the embargo. But after OPEC's price hikes in 1973, politicians, wanting to conserve oil and get their angry constituents out of gasoline lines, directed utilities back to coal, despite the substantial expense of pollution-control equipment. Some power-industry executives also complained that Washington urged them to adopt reactors and then, after the Three Mile Island accident, burdened the technology with expensive safety requirements.

Reactor-troubled utilities in the 1980s turned to Washington for more help, but conservative President Ronald Reagan would not countenance a high-profile bailout. Still, the administration quietly provided a diverse package of very expensive benefits for the struggling electricity industry. A dividend reinvestment plan, for instance, deferred the collection of taxes payable by investors, thereby adding $3.4 billion to utilities' cash flow (more than twice what the government provided to Chrysler after its collapse). *Business Week* labeled the effort an "unabashed—and unneeded—subsidy."[46]

President Reagan also offered a 36-percent increase to the nuclear research budget, authorized the government to collect utilities' radioactive wastes, and approved reactor sales to China. He also endorsed an obscure Internal Revenue Service ruling that allowed utilities to use tax-exempt pollution-control bonds to finance as much as a quarter of their nuclear construction projects. Even more important to a utility's balance sheet, Reagan's Federal Energy Regulatory Commission loosened accounting rules in ways that allowed wholesale power producers to earn a return on their costs of so-called construction work in progress (CWIP) before their plants were completed. Utilities said CWIP, which allowed an immediate return on their expenditures, lowered borrowing costs, eased financing burdens, and cushioned rate shocks. Critics argued the provision only encouraged utilities to make poor investments in unneeded power plants.

Substantially more government benefits came from the Rural Electrification Administration (REA), a unit within the Department of Agriculture. REA's most obvious subsidies were for the investments by cooperatives in seventeen reactors. Yet in May 1984, the government agency quietly committed $57 million to purchase the Public Service Company of New Hampshire's share of an operating Maine reactor so the private utility could continue financing its troubled Seabrook nuclear plant in New Hampshire.

These complex, indirect, and expensive subsidies demonstrated the political clout of both private and public utilities. Yet they came at a price not initially noticed by power industry lobbyists. First, the problems of the 1960s and 1970s prompted engineers to consider more innovative and efficient technologies, and, second, the rising costs of defaults and subsidies during the 1980s led politicians to consider alternative regulatory approaches.

Most utility executives argued that blackouts, accidents, and defaults were simply isolated instances that demanded isolated responses. If transmission wires were stretched, the industry answer was to build more lines. If pollution posed a problem, utilities would add a few scrubbers, even if rates would subsequently rise and efficiencies fall.

Yet more profound trends were confronting the power industry, and challenged the very ways electricity was generated and priced. No longer could utility planners accurately plot a steady rise in electricity demand. No longer could they count on low-cost fuels or the promise of the atom. Despite their best efforts, they could no longer construct larger and more efficient generators, nor could they avoid the costs associated with their pollution. Despite their desire to maintain monopoly control, executives also could no longer block innovative technologies, hustling entrepreneurs, or the growing chorus suggesting competition would be an effective cure for the electricity industry's woes.

5

Partial Competition

The opening of utility monopolies to limited competition—perhaps the most significant change in electricity law during the last half of the twentieth century—occurred with no fanfare, and almost no notice. It resulted largely from a single company in 1978 wanting a provision to resolve a specific problem and utility lobbyists being distracted by other measures within a huge legislative proposal.

Wheelabrator-Frye Corporation, a New Hampshire-based firm, had built a waste-to-energy plant near Boston that burned garbage and sold heat to an adjacent General Electric factory, but the company also wanted to use some heat to generate electricity that it would sell to the local utility. Since the region's power monopoly had no interest in buying electricity from an independent generator, Wheelabrator-Frye executives hired a Washington lobbyist and contacted their senator, Democrat John Durkin.

The New Hampshire lawmaker did push the momentous—if little understood—provision, yet several other individuals played key roles. The story actually began when the Organization of Petroleum Exporting Countries (OPEC), angry at U.S. support for Israel, imposed oil embargoes. A sweater-clad Jimmy Carter in 1977 responded by announcing the "moral equivalent of war" and asking Congress to approve his National Energy Plan that stressed energy efficiency, which the president described as "the quickest, cheapest, most practical source of energy."[1]

The Carter plan frightened utility lobbyists, who felt it placed too much emphasis on conservation (which they equated with lost sales), usurped state jurisdiction by imposing federal rate regulations, and forced power companies to convert their generating plants from oil and natural gas to coal. One industry newsletter reported that the energy plan represented "perhaps the deepest federal push into utility affairs since the 1935 breakup of holding companies," and another noted that the Carter proposal frightened utilities into "an evangelic fervor they haven't displayed in years." A Mississippi Power and Light Company executive went so far as to argue that the president's provisions threatened "the very survival of the United States as a free nation."[2]

Industry lobbyists became even more outraged after House Democrats, led by energy committee chairman John Dingell, held eight days of hearings and crafted provisions that were, according to *Electrical World*, "broader and tougher than the administration version."[3] The utility trade associations responded with a steady bombardment of lobbying visits, meetings with editorial writers, appeals to mayors and other opinion leaders, and campaign contributions. As a result, the Senate bill, according to the industry newsletter, appeared "tame" as it had "scuttled or weakened" every Carter rate-reform provision.[4] Negotiations over the differing House and Senate provisions were lengthy and testy.

Distracted by the proposed rate-making standards and coal-conversion requirements, utility lobbyists paid little attention to a small section of the president's proposal on incentives for nontraditional technologies. President Carter was particularly interested in cogeneration units, which provide electricity as well as capture the resulting heat for industrial processes. Utilities had shunned cogenerators throughout the twentieth century as they built larger and more distant generators that simply released waste heat into the atmosphere. In 1912, independent companies using cogenerators—such as lumber yards, refineries, and office buildings—produced more kilowatt-hours than did utilities, but cogeneration's share dropped to only 3.5 percent of U.S. electricity by 1978. Utility monopolies over the years not only enticed industrialists to abandon their power plants, but they also blocked new independents by refusing interconnections with the transmission and distribution grid.

The Carter and House proposals, designed to spur energy efficiency, required utilities to interconnect as well as to purchase an independent producer's power at rates equal to the utility's own generation costs, what became known as the utility's "avoided cost." Senators on the energy committee watered down these provisions, stripping benefits from solar and wind entrepreneurs and changing the language so that utilities were "recommended" (rather than "required") to buy power from cogenerators at "nondiscriminatory" (rather than "avoided cost") prices.

That's when Senator Durkin became involved. While not initially addressing interconnection and resale rates, the New Hampshire Democrat, in close contact with Wheelabrator-Frye's lobbyists, introduced an amendment that would exempt small power producers, those generating less than 80 megawatts of electricity, from being regulated as utilities under the Great Depression-era Public Utility Holding Company Act (PUHCA). Most senators assumed the amendment affected only Durkin's constituent. In fact, the chairman of the energy committee sought on the Senate floor to clarify that the measure's "real purpose . . . is to protect an existing facility in New Hampshire from dismemberment." Durkin agreed, while noting the facility actually was in Massachusetts.[5]

Even with the Durkin amendment, the Senate's provisions associated with independent generators called mostly for voluntary actions by utilities. Almost nothing would be mandatory. Yet during the Senate-House conference, when members from both chambers tried to compromise their distinct bills, Durkin argued for an exchange. The House, he said, should accept his Senate language on exempting small producers from PUHCA if the Senate approved the House language mandating interconnections and avoided-cost rates for independent generators. "I don't think we can afford the guideline approach," the senator argued in favor of the House language. "It will take too long and may never create the kind of atmosphere we need to encourage as much cogeneration and small power production as possible." He stressed that mandatory provisions for independent producers would make a substantial contribution to solving the nation's energy challenges.[6]

Durkin wisely made his case late in the conference process, when lawmakers and utility lobbyists were exhausted by months of haggling about the legislation's higher-profile aspects. When the conference report was released in September 1978, it included Durkin's "compromise," a three-page provision—identified as Section 210—buried within the sixty-one pages and seventy-eight sections of the Public Utility Regulatory Policies Act (PURPA), one of five energy bills approved in 1978. Yet that tiny section provided special privileges to "qualified facilities," or QFs, allowing them to avoid Securities and Exchange Commission registration and to take advantage of more-favorable financing. It also enabled these small generators to receive for their power a price equal to a utility's incremental cost of building a new generator. Most fundamentally, by preventing utility monopolies from using their market control and financial resources to block independents, the law opened the electricity market to limited competition.

Most utility lobbyists did not notice the provision's significance, at least initially. The editor of *Electrical World*, in fact, commented that the energy bills contained several setbacks but concluded that "utilities escaped relatively easily. . . . The Public Utility Regulatory Policies Act appears to contain no nasty surprises."[7]

Yet when the Federal Energy Regulatory Commission (FERC) crafted rules to implement the law, utilities became alarmed. This fear resulted in part from Ross Ain, the congressional staffer who had helped write the House's aggressive legislation and who subsequently moved to FERC in order to promote a new class of generators. On the issue of rates, for instance, FERC could have established a lengthy and costly process by which independent generators would have to prove their costs. Instead, Ain and the commissioners declared that QFs should receive the utility's "avoided costs," or the construction and fuel expenses that monopolies would assume if they built their own generators. FERC also ruled that independent generators could purchase supplemental and backup power, needed during their normal maintenance or outages, at normal retail rates. From the utility perspective, that decision allowed QFs to buy electricity at discount rates but to sell it at premium prices. FERC, moreover, limited utilities from owning more than 50 percent of a QF's assets, arguing that they should not use their monopoly positions to dominate the market of independent producers.

Utilities quickly challenged the law and FERC's rules. Mississippi Power & Light Company, for example, convinced a Mississippi-based judge that PURPA was a "direct intrusion" of the federal government into the affairs of the "sovereign state of Mississippi," and that only states could regulate utilities. In June 1982, however, the U.S. Supreme Court unanimously overturned the judge's ruling, arguing that Congress and federal agencies could set guidelines for utilities because the sale of electricity often represented interstate commerce.[8]

Utilities continued fighting. Electricity companies in Georgia, Louisiana, Mississippi, the District of Columbia, and several New England states canceled their contracts with independent producers. One utility executive described power entrepreneurs as unreliable hustlers wanting "only tax breaks and fast bucks." He complained that PURPA caused uncertainty: "How can I supply electricity . . . when I don't know how many entrepreneurs will be operating next year?" Disliking a federal mandate, he argued that "when I'm required to buy power from someone else, I can no longer plan for the future."[9]

The newly formed independent generators, of course, responded, but stronger efforts came from large industrialists wanting energy options and lower costs. The Electricity Consumers Resource Council (ELCON) began an aggressive lobbying and legal campaign arguing that manufacturers should enjoy the inexpensive power of combined-cycle gas turbines deployed by independent generators and avoid the high costs of utilities' over-budget reactors. Such efforts were fairly effective, as industrial electricity costs fell 35 percent by 1994 from their 1982 peak.

Several utilities launched further legal challenges. American Electric Power, Consolidated Edison, and Colorado-Ute Electric Association attacked PURPA before the U.S. Court of Appeals, arguing that utilities should not be required to interconnect with or pay full avoided costs to independent power producers. The Appeals Court agreed in 1982, arguing that FERC should not have allowed QFs to buy power from utilities at a lower rate than they could sell power to the same utilities.

The Supreme Court put the matter on hold while it conducted another review of the law. Finally in May 1983, the High Court again unanimously upheld PURPA's provisions, ruling it important to "provide a significant incentive to the development of cogeneration and small power production, and that ratepayers and the nation as a whole would benefit from the decreased reliance on scarce fossil fuels and the more efficient use of energy."[10] Independent power producers sighed with relief, although they knew many utilities would still oppose signing the long-term contracts entrepreneurs needed to obtain financing.

After this Supreme Court ruling, states issued a variety of different rules, making the progress of independent power producers dependent, to a large degree, upon the strength of those regulations and the willingness of local officials to prod unenthusiastic utilities. Regulators in most southern states, who long had been under the influence of large utility monopolies, did relatively little to advance competition. California, in contrast, proved to be particularly aggressive, in part because analysts were projecting a huge increase in the state's electricity demand, enough to require the construction of 130 new generators, or 150,000 megawatts, by the year 2000. The advance of electric entrepreneurs in California also resulted from Governor Jerry Brown's support for solar, wind, and biomass projects, which he saw as environmentally sound alternatives to oil and natural gas, upon which the state depended for much of its power. Brown's appointees blocked the construction of several large utility power plants, and they established a series of standard contracts between independent generators and utilities that allowed QFs to save time and money by not negotiating multiple agreements.

While taking a slightly different approach, George Deukmejian, the next California governor, continued to endorse competition within the electricity market. Many of the state's largest businesses, which used cogeneration equipment and contributed generously to the Republican Party, convinced Deukmejian to support the emerging industry.

California's "standard offers" were generous to independents—providing energy payments from utilities that rose from 5.6 cents per kilowatthour in 1984 to 10.1 cents in 1983 and even to 15 cents in 1998—and they prompted a multitude of new power offerings—15,000 megawatts of independently generated electricity by the end of 1985. The contracts also required no financial commitment from the independent generator, who had five years to complete a project or walk away without penalty.

The state based its rising avoided-cost contracts on the expectation that prices for natural gas would continue to increase. When they began to fall in 1983, the standard offers appeared to be an even greater deal for QFs, and utilities again balked. Pacific Gas & Electric asserted that it was forced to pay 2 cents more per kilowatt-hour under the standard contracts than its actual avoided cost. Since electricity demand did not rise as quickly as projected, utilities also complained they were paying for independently produced power that was not needed. Regulators in several states eventually responded by shifting to a bidding system for the purchase of a finite amount of independently produced electricity, forcing QFs to compete against each other. Virginia Power, as an example, offered to buy 1,000 megawatts of capacity, for which it received offers from fifty-three companies for more than 5,000 megawatts. The move toward market-based bidding lowered the avoided cost available to QFs, but it maintained competition opportunities for independent producers.

PURPA's Section 210, despite its pricing controversies, helped spur the deployment of new and more efficient technologies. Combined heat and power units, for instance, achieved efficiencies of 70 to 90 percent, well above the utility average of only 33 percent. U.S. cogeneration capacity rose from 10,500 megawatts in 1979 to 40,700 megawatts in 1992. Although the competition allowed by Section 210 is quite limited and utility monopolies still control virtually all transmission and distribution lines, the law's impacts have been noteworthy as the nation's average electricity rates dropped by approximately 30 percent, saving the country $150 billion annually. Entrepreneurs argue that full-scale competition in the power business would reduce rates further and dramatically enhance environmental quality, consumer options, and economic productivity.

RESPONDING WITH MORE REGULATION

Many state regulators—and the lobbyists who were used to dealing with them—disliked competition, even if it was limited, and preferred responding to the utility industry's woes with new forms of regulation. Most environmentalists, for instance, advanced several initiatives—including demand-side management (DSM), least-cost planning (LCP), and integrated resource planning (IRP)—that required utilities to adopt conservation and environmental protection. They convinced numerous regulators to treat conserving power as the functional equivalent of generating electricity, to link a utility's profitability to its efficiency, and to provide incentives for power companies to consider conservation. No doubt traditional rate-setting formulas—which provided a percentage return on all utility expenses, including power plants, transmission lines, and office buildings—encouraged expansion and gold-plating. One utility executive, as noted earlier, humorously observed, "This is the only industry I've ever seen where you can increase your profits by redecorating your office."[11]

The environmentalists' theory was that if utilities invested in conservation they would spend less on new construction projects, which would reduce their borrowing costs and the rates they needed to charge consumers. Fewer power plants also promised fewer pollutants. Yet perspectives on the array of new regulations depended as much on theory as how those measures would allocate clout and control within the electricity industry.

Environmentalists had a clear, if unacknowledged, self-interest in the regulatory provisions since they won a seat at the table when millions of dollars were distributed for utility planning and the purchase of florescent light bulbs, solar collectors, and efficient appliances.

Regulators also obtained more political and economic control through these acronym-laden initiatives. A Nevada commissioner admitted, "There are two reasons why we have regulation. One is we need to protect customers from abuses by regulated monopolies, and the other is because it's fun."[12]

A few utility managers saw DSM/ICP/IRP measures as a new source of revenue, and several realized that conservation measures could retard the opportunity for competitors to build new generators. Most power company executives, however, felt conservation meant decreased sales and that the regulatory measures simply created "a whole new bureaucracy at state commissions to keep the existing bureaucracy in place."[13] Some complained the programs "may transform regulators from civil servants into utility executives."[14] John Rowe, now president of Exelon, argued that regulators created a "welfare society when they subsidized activities that individuals should have pursued in their own best interests."[15] Alfred Kahn, a Cornell University economist who advanced the deregulation of airlines and other industries, joined the protests, declaring that such regulations gave state officials the opportunity "to play the role of a paternalistic central government planner."[16] Kahn argued that instead of promoting conservation for its own sake, regulators should impose higher, marginal-cost rates that would prompt consumers to use electricity efficiently and in ways that caused the least amount of environmental damage.

Independent power producers and industries wanting to generate their own electricity were even more harsh. Electricity Consumers Resource Council (ELCON), the trade association of industrialists, criticized the regulatory programs as wasting ratepayer funds and forcing large businesses to subsidize other consumers who were unwilling to use their own resources to conserve power.

ANOTHER STAB AT COMPETITION

Another Middle East crisis prompted another U.S. energy plan. In August 1990, Saddam Hussein's army invaded and annexed Kuwait, and the United Nations reacted with a trade embargo on Iraq. As a result, the

United States lost 10 percent of its oil imports, gasoline prices rose about 20 cents per gallon, and American consumers paid some $21 billion more for petroleum products.

Congress responded in 1992 with the Energy Policy Act, which aimed to reduce U.S. dependence on foreign oil. In the electricity title, the law opened the door to more competition by establishing a new class of "exempt wholesale generators" that could sell power in the wholesale market. Unlike the "qualifying facilities" regulated under PURPA, these merchant generators could charge market rates, sell their power to non-utilities, and avoid cogeneration and renewable-energy requirements. Utilities, however, were not required to buy this independently produced power. The legislation also authorized the Federal Energy Regulatory Commission (FERC) to order utilities to "wheel" or transmit a competitor's power across their lines.

Technological developments played a key role, along with the Kuwait war, in forcing the policy reexamination. Equipment manufacturers had profited greatly from airplane engine advancements and improved a gas turbine's efficiency, which rose above 50 percent in combined-cycle units that ran steam twice through the unit. These manufacturers also employed mass production techniques that lowered turbine costs significantly.

Another factor influencing the 1992 debates was the deregulation of natural gas prices in the 1980s, which prompted exploration companies to drill additional wells and discover expanded supplies, making gas a more available and affordable fuel for electricity generation. These drilling companies employed new three-dimensional seismic techniques in order to increase their odds of discovery, leading to a six-fold boost in the estimated amount of recoverable natural gas in the lower forty-eight states. As a result, most of the new electricity provided by exempt wholesale generators would come from natural-gas-fired units. The combination of better technology and lower prices had changed the economics of electricity generation, whereby gas turbines had become more attractive than new coal-fired units for generating electricity's base load.

The political debates featured unexpected alliances. Although it usually sided with utility positions, the first Bush administration, showing a strain of conservative free-market ideology, argued for allowing both non-utility and utility companies to participate within the wholesale electricity market. An enlarged market, however, meant that power producers would need access to customers, and such access required that transmission networks be available to all parties. According to Henson Moore, the administration's deputy energy secretary, "We believe increased access to electric transmission facilities for wholesale power buyers and sellers would increase economic efficiency, stimulate competition, and ensure that the nation's industries, shops, and residences benefit from their local utility having access to electricity at the lowest reasonable cost."[17]

Competition advocates formed a diverse and unusual coalition. Large industrialists, under the umbrella of the Electricity Consumers Resource Council (ELCON), obviously wanted increased electricity-supply options, hoping that their energy costs would fall. Independent power producers, moreover, envisioned open transmission as their means to sell more electricity to more customers. More surprisingly, several environmental and consumer groups argued that new non-utility companies would likely employ renewable resources and relatively clean-burning natural gas. In the House of Representatives, this coalition negotiated a "delicate compromise" to reform the Public Utility Holding Company Act (PUHCA), increase transmission access to third parties, and "reduce the price of electricity for all consumers and reduce emissions by making more efficient use of electricity generating facilities."[18]

Electric utilities, in contrast, splintered. Most opposed competition, as evidenced by the blunt comments of Philadelphia Electric Company's CEO: "The only ones who will benefit are the independent power producers and their select customers. Outside of this small group, everyone else stands to lose through higher costs and less reliable service."[19] That utility and about forty others formed the Electric Reliability Coalition that published newspaper advertisements in the states of swing senators declaring that "powerful special interests are urging the U.S. Congress to dismantle a law that for more than 50 years has protected you and your family and millions of other electricity consumers."[20] (There is some irony in that argument, of course, because it was these very utilities that wanted to repeal PUHCA.) Yet seven utilities argued for increased competition. While these insurgents did not favor totally open access to transmission lines, they predicted their profits would increase if they purchased and wheeled power from new sources.

Congress sided mostly with the competition advocates, and the Energy Policy Act of 1992 opened the electricity grid to many more players. Utility monopolies, however, did not suffer anything approaching a total defeat. The law allowed them to own "exempt wholesale generators" outside of their own service territories or to establish subsidiaries that would produce and sell power across the country. It enabled them to purchase interests in foreign power companies. Perhaps most important from the utilities' perspective, the final bill did not include the House provisions associated with "retail wheeling," whereby utilities would have had to transmit electricity from an independent generator directly to a residential, commercial, or industrial customer. Federal lawmakers punted that issue to the states, where monopolies held substantial political clout and could ensure that they remained the sole buyers of independently produced power. Yet while the compromise legislation may have been limited to wholesale transmission, it permitted independent generators, for the first time, to transmit electricity over a utility's wires.

The bill's passage did not result in immediate restructuring. Noting the continuing controversy, the Federal Energy Regulatory Commission (FERC) took another four years to develop a set of specific rules, bureaucratically titled Order 888, that outline the conditions by which utilities must provide open, nondiscriminatory access to the nation's transmission system. Suddenly, anyone selling electricity wholesale—including independent generators, government-owned utilities, and industrial producers—could obtain transmission service at "just and reasonable" rates. By mandating a universal transmission tariff, FERC saved independents from the agency's usual time-consuming review of individual wheeling requests. The April 1996 order also declared that a transmission owner must charge the same rate for moving an independent's electricity as it would impose on its own power. It even said that a transmission company must expand its capacity if an independent generator is willing to pay its share of the expansion costs. To further streamline the flow of wholesale electricity, FERC in December 1999 issued Order 2000 and asked all transmission-owning utilities to join an independent regional transmission organization. Together, these orders reflected FERC's efforts to eliminate discrimination in the management of the nation's transmission system.

Traditional utilities, while lamenting FERC's move toward open-access transmission, did win a few plums in Order 888. Most notable was the regulatory embrace of "stranded costs," or the requirement that consumers pay for the power plants and other utility assets that would become less valuable (or even worthless) in a restructured and competitive market. The most obvious stranded assets were expensive generators, built years before with state regulatory approvals, that could not compete against lower-cost merchant power. FERC left it to the states, where power monopolies enjoyed substantial sway, to determine how consumers should pay for those stranded assets; utilities, of course, argued for huge reimbursements, while competitors asserted that high charges would kill competition and eliminate its benefits.

Still, FERC's orders, particularly its encouragement of independent system operators (ISOs), took significant steps toward ensuring fair and nondiscriminatory access to the nation's transmission grid. Having no financial interests in any market participants, regional ISOs, whose operating procedures must be approved by FERC, are to set a single, open-access tariff and be responsible for system security and power dispatch. The ISOs (and similar "RTOs," or regional transmission operators) are key components of competition since they offer the means for ensuring fair transmission of power. As of 2005, six regional ISOs had obtained control of power allocations, although utility monopolies in the Pacific Northwest and Southeast continue to oppose such independent market enablers.

FERC's rulings highlight two obvious, but still-debated, realities. First, a competitive electricity market will evolve only if competitors have unfettered access to the power delivery system. Second, since electricity now is largely traded wholesale across state lines and is part of interstate commerce, the federal government, rather than the states, holds the key regulatory responsibilities.

The Energy Policy Act and FERC's subsequent regulations also prompted a dramatic change in the ownership of electric generation. For most of the twentieth century, private utilities—regulated monopolies controlling power plants and distribution lines—dominated the industry. Within the past decade, however, non–utility generators captured 30 percent of the generation market. That amount exceeds the combined ownership of rural co-ops (4 percent), the federal government (8 percent), and municipal utilities (11 percent), and the share controlled by investor-owned utilities fell to 47 percent. Wholesale electricity trading also soared, from approximately 100 million kilowatt-hours in 1996 to almost 4,500 million kilowatt-hours in 2000. Change quite suddenly had replaced stability within the electricity industry.

6

Stresses

The twenty-first century did not begin well for power generators and distributors. The biggest electricity marketer, Enron, collapsed and faced a slew of lawsuits for shady accounting and sham trades. One of the nation's largest investor-owned utility, Pacific Gas & Electric, filed for bankruptcy amid chaotic power markets in California. Fifty million people in the Northeast and Midwest lost electricity because of a cascading power failure that could have been prevented by better coordination among utility operators. High natural-gas prices and the economy's overall slowdown caused electricity demand to falter, wholesale prices to fall, and several independent power producers to collapse.

These stresses prompted a financial tailspin as investors, regulators, and even consumers lost trust in power companies. By early 2003, the electricity industry had suffered a staggering $238-billion setback in market valuation, faced scores of downgrades from bond rating agencies, and confronted its worst credit environment in more than seventy years. Energy trades, moreover, plummeted 70 percent in the early years of the twenty-first century, and construction on more than 60 percent of proposed power plants was halted. In stating the obvious, David Owens, executive vice president of the Edison Electric Institute, declared, "The industry's top priority must be to restore investor confidence."[1]

The industry's prospects remain uncertain. In late 2004, despite several months of economic expansion, Standard and Poor's Rating Services declared that more than 40 percent of the electricity industry had negative outlooks or were on CreditWatch with negative implications.[2] Fitch Ratings offered a bit more optimism, projecting the near-term outlook for utilities as "stable" and declaring that prospects for energy merchants have "shifted to positive from stable."[3] Yet the stock prices of several utilities increased handsomely, with shares of Duke Energy rising 48 percent from 2004 to 2005.

Financial setbacks for some power makers certainly presented opportunities for the well-heeled. Those utilities maintaining good credit ratings and stable stock prices bought scores of power plants and transmission lines from weaker firms. In early 2003, an estimated $100 billion of utility assets were for sale.[4] Entergy, a Louisiana-based utility giant that benefited from monopoly regulation in its home territory, allocated $3 billion to buy up generators throughout the country.

Such purchases may continue a consolidation trend from the 1990s, when investor-owned utilities completed almost forty mergers. The biggest combination occurred in December 2004 when Chicago-based Exelon Corporation agreed to pay $12.8 billion for New Jersey-based Public Service Enterprise Group, creating the nation's largest power company. In May 2005, Duke Energy offered $9 billion for Cinergy, creating a company with 5.4 million customers. Many executives believe that to prosper in today's more competitive environment a utility needs to be larger, in part because it could negotiate lower prices when purchasing higher volumes of fuel or equipment. One result of this trend is that fewer investor-owned utilities control a larger proportion of utility generation. The share of the largest ten firms rose from 36 percent in 1992 to 51 percent in 2000.

Looking for growth opportunities, many utilities also have merged with or acquired natural gas companies, creating a convergence of the electric and gas industries. Since natural gas fuels most new generators, these combinations allow a power company to better control its costs as well as to offer both electric and gas services for its customers.

The merger trend, however, has been offset by widespread divestitures of utility power plants. In the final years of the 1990s, about one-third of the investor-owned utilities sold generators, and independent producers expanded their capacity by almost three-quarters. Put another way, the share of electricity generated by non-utilities soared from only 1.7 percent in 1993 to over 30 percent in 2003.

Also stressing the electricity industry are struggles between residential and business consumers. As utilities ask regulators for rate increases to cover higher natural gas prices and increased reliability costs, businesses are complaining they bear a disproportionate share of utility charges and are demanding rate relief. They seem to be winning their battles, as evidenced by Pacific Gas & Electric in 2004 proposing a 17.4-percent boost for residential rates and a 7.9-percent drop for corporate consumers. Detroit Edison, moreover, will raise home rates by 22 percent over the next decade while reducing commercial charges by 15 percent.[5]

This combination of mergers, divestitures, and pricing battles is complicating the electricity business. Consensus among even utility executives has become a relic of the past. One industry leader observed that utility managers from different companies "can't sit around in a room anymore and agree on which direction the industry is headed, then charge off and bring it about. There are vast differences of opinion now among utilities as to where the industry is going and how it ought to get there."[6] The Enron and California debacles, as well as the 2003 blackout, only added to the power industry's stresses and uncertainties.

STAR WARS ACCOUNTING

Kenneth Lay for more than a decade appeared to be a financial genius. The courtly executive had converted a low-profile gas-pipeline company, Enron, into the nation's largest energy trader. As Enron's chairman Lay had also become the chief spokesman for deregulating electricity markets and for the promise that competition would lower power costs and enhance innovation and productivity. Because of his large contributions to political campaigns, including those of President George W. Bush and Vice President Cheney, Lay's arguments carried substantial political weight.

Enron's leader, however, now appears to be little more than a brilliant deceiver. On the very day in August 2001 that Jeffrey Skilling, Enron's CEO, unexpectedly resigned and the company filed a financial report with the Securities and Exchange Commission (SEC) vaguely mentioning problematic partnerships, Lay declared, "I can honestly say the company is in the strongest shape it's ever been in."[7] The Houston-based firm filed for bankruptcy four months later.

In October 2001, Enron released its third-quarter earnings, which included another cryptic reference to those investment partnerships. When

Kenneth Lay. Courtesy of AP/Wide World.

asked about the matter, Lay snapped, "I don't think we need to say anything more about that."[8] Only after investigative reporters discovered embarrassing documents did company officials admit the partnerships caused a "$35-million setback," which they subsequently revealed was actually a staggering $462-million loss.

These problematic partnerships, which were managed by Enron's chief financial officer, were the source of much consternation among some Enron executives, who internally argued that the CFO exposed the company to conflicts of interest. Indeed, private documents associated with one investment partnership boast of "preferred access" to Enron assets and of the full involvement of Enron's top financial manager. The company later admitted that the CFO personally made more than $30 million from the partnerships, even as they ended up costing Enron many times that amount.[9]

When Enron in late 1997 was having trouble meeting Wall Street's earnings expectations, it created partnerships known as JEDI and Chewco, named for Star War character Chewbacca, which now appear to be nothing more than sham enterprises designed to boost the appearance of Enron profits. For several years, Chewco and JEDI assumed hundreds of millions of dollars of debt, kept it off Enron's books, and allowed the company to declare $390 million in net income.

Although Enron treated Chewco and JEDI as totally independent enterprises, the partnerships were managed by an Enron officer, and Enron supplied almost all of the initial funding. When the Securities and Exchange Commission began to investigate Enron's accounting, the company finally admitted that Chewco and JEDI should have been considered part of Enron's regular operations. That admission forced the company to restate its earnings for the previous four years, revealing a loss of $586 million, or 20 percent.

The restatement shocked an already nervous Wall Street. No longer confident of Enron's audited statements, investors sent the sagging stock price into a deep plunge. After a potential merger/rescue effort collapsed, Enron lacked the cash needed to pay off creditors or to finance continuing operations. Rating agencies in late November 2001 declared the company's credit to be "junk," or below investment grade. With no options, Enron—which, with its 3,500 subsidiaries and affiliates around the globe, was once valued at $60 billion—declared bankruptcy on December 2, 1997, marking the largest such filing in U.S. history.

Tape recordings of Enron traders subsequently revealed numerous market-manipulating scams, including delivering false data to California's independent system operator; creating unnecessary congestion on power lines and shutting down generation plants in order to drive up the price of electricity; and sidestepping the state's price cap by selling power across the state's borders before wheeling it back in. On one tape an Enron trader boasts of stealing money "from those poor grandmothers in California" and of "over-scheduling load and making buckets of money on that." Another trader, who confessed to one count of wire fraud, claims that the company's California revenues soared from $50 million in 1999 to $800 million in 2001 in part because of manipulation and a corporate attitude to do whatever was necessary to "maximize profit for Enron."[10]

Enron faces scores of lawsuits and investigations. Former employees rail against company executives who sold millions of dollars in Enron stock while they were forbidden from trading their Enron-laden retirement accounts, which now sit virtually worthless. Stockholders, who watched their stock values drop from $90 to dimes, complain that Kenneth Lay should not have profited from selling his Enron shares while simultaneously issuing earnings statements that the company later admitted were bogus and misleading. Creditors, a list of which runs for fifty-four pages, want to be paid for everything from toilet paper to computers they sold to Enron.

The political fallout remains uncertain. Opponents of utility restructuring highlight Enron's woes as an excuse to block further competition. They tend to equate the company's abuses with its advancement of energy trading and other innovations. Deregulation advocates, in contrast, argue that Enron's fall proves free markets work since competitors kept energy flowing and prices stable despite the bankruptcy of a giant firm. Detailing the difference between outright fraud and successful policies, one industry executive declared, "The failure of Enron did not come from energy trading."[11]

The Enron debacle, of course, is not the first time an innovative entrepreneur rocked the electricity industry with questionable accounting practices. Enron's Kenneth Lay may have been born five years after Commonwealth Edison's Samuel Insull died, but similarities between the executives are informative. Raised in modest households, the two were lionized as business geniuses and then demonized as corporate scoundrels, but both launched significant transitions in power markets.

Insull, who had served as Thomas Edison's personal secretary, built a giant empire throughout the Midwest that in the late 1920s supplied almost one-eighth of the nation's electricity. While most people thought electric power was a luxury only for the rich, Insull took advantage of emerging technologies—especially coal-fired steam turbines—to build larger power plants that integrated the demands of electric streetcar companies, buildings, and factories. Based in Chicago, he slashed the price of power and delivered the wonders of electricity to millions of Americans.

Insull was the industry's visionary in the early twentieth century, leading the utility trade association for more than a decade. Along with progressive politicians, he advanced a new business model—state regulatory commissions overseeing utility monopolies—that survived for more than nine decades and supplied reliable power throughout the United States.

Lay in the late twentieth century challenged Insull's assumption that electricity must be monopolized, and he adopted innovative technologies—especially combined-cycle natural-gas-fueled turbines—that allowed competitive power producers to cut prices and pollution. He promoted marketing advancements, including Internet-based trading of electricity, and his business vision challenged the nation's power monopolies that had failed to innovate.

Widely admired in their eras, the two executives were generous and community oriented. Insull gave away most of his salary to an array of charities, including many for minorities. He built several Chicago institutions, including an opera house designed to bring music to average men and women. Lay supported many Houston-based causes.

Both Insull and Lay, however, overextended. Insull incorporated holding companies to manage utilities scattered across the Midwest. Investors flocked to these firms, sending stock prices skyward. Yet Insull's corporate pyramids relied increasingly on questionable accounting, and when the value of the underlying utilities began to fall during the Great Depression, his empire collapsed, and thousands of investors lost their life savings.

In an odd coincidence to the current Enron scandal, New York and Chicago bankers appointed Arthur Andersen, founder and director of the accounting firm Arthur Andersen and Company, to oversee all Insull expenditures during receivership because of the auditor's reputation for fairness and diligence. That same firm, ironically, was accused recently of endorsing Enron's accounting gimmicks.

When financiers finally ousted Insull and he set sail for Europe, the seventy-one-year-old executive became the symbol of corporate excess, the scapegoat for the depression, and the focus of numerous investigations. President Franklin Roosevelt lambasted Insull's network of holding companies as "challenging in their power the very government itself." In muckraking tones that would make even Ken Lay blanch, the Hearst newspapers, as noted before, characterized the utility titan as "the embodiment of avarice, the fat plutocrat of capitalism defiled."[12] Federal officials eventually indicted the former executive and extradited him dramatically from a boat in Turkey in order to stand trial in Chicago.

Although a jury acquitted Insull of all charges, he remained a pariah. The utility industry quietly expunged his name from its official history, while Franklin Roosevelt and the Congress quickly passed legislation to limit holding companies and to increase government control of utility assets. Virtually forgotten were Insull's enormous contributions to electrifying America and establishing a system of regulated utility monopolies.

Lay's legacy is not yet clear. The secret partnerships and the pain caused to Enron investors and employees have been well publicized. Even if Lay is not found guilty of any crime, his reputation is tarnished. It's also likely that today's lawmakers will react to the Enron scandals with new legislation and regulations that hold accounting firms accountable and limit the use of off-balance-sheet transactions.

Yet like Insull, Lay's horrendous deceits probably will not stop the revolution he advanced within the power industry. The Enron executive exploited technological innovations and made the Insull model of utility monopolies obsolete. He effectively highlighted the inefficiencies and pollution associated with the status quo. As a result, Lay's name may be vilified, but his business vision of competitive power markets may mold the electricity industry for several decades.

CALIFORNIA DEALING

California's 2001 electricity disaster, when prices skyrocketed and the state's largest utility declared bankruptcy, resulted largely from political deals made in the mid-1990s that tried to appease virtually every interest group. The compromises on utility deregulation may have produced a unanimous vote in the state legislature in 1996, but in hindsight, according to one researcher, "getting it done fast and in a way that pandered to the many interests involved become more important than getting it right. The end result was the most complicated set of wholesale electricity market institutions ever created on earth and with which there was no real-world experience."[13]

Californians for many years had complained that their system of regulated monopolies kept power rates artificially high (some 30–50 percent above the national average) and retarded the development of efficient and innovative technologies. The notion that competition would lower electricity costs and increase power options was advanced most aggressively by industrialists that consumed lots of energy, but competition advocates argued effectively that deregulation's benefits would be widespread. The California Public Utility Commission in 1994 issued a policy statement—known as the "Blue Book" because of its cover—that asserted the state should rely on "the discipline of markets to replace often burdensome, administrative regulatory approaches."[14] The publication argued for a radical shift in the electricity market, and *Business Week* observed that it "sent shock waves through the staid utility industry."[15]

Any change in the decades-old system, of course, meant some stakeholders would win and others would lose. Environmentalists feared competition would destroy the state's energy-efficiency programs, while utility executives worried that market forces would decrease the value of their shares. In such situations, lawmakers typically seek compromises. From 1994 to 1996, California legislators negotiated wildly.

Many of the deals were cut in marathon sessions orchestrated by Steve Peace, a California legislator perhaps best known for his production of the cult-classic movie *Attack of the Killer Tomatoes*. Some negotiators complained that Peace virtually locked them in a room, but he did produce legislation that offered some concessions to everyone.

Consider the advantages provided to utilities. Although the restructuring bill's purported purpose was to open electricity markets to competitors, state lawmakers gave to the state's three traditional monopolies a windfall subsidy as well as protection from new power producers. The state agreed to issue bonds in order to pay off the utilities' bad debts, and then it imposed a "competitive transition charge" on any new electricity generator trying to enter the California market. According to a consumer-activist group, "Consumers [were] forced to invest in and underwrite the utility companies."[16] Several well-heeled and savvy independent generators realized the cards were stacked against them and backed out of the California market, leaving Golden State consumers nowhere to go for a better deal. Reflecting the lack of real competitive options, less than 2 percent of Californians switched from traditional utilities to new providers.

Politicians also tried to appease consumers by providing an immediate 10-percent rate reduction and a cap on future increases. They might have appreciated intellectually the argument that higher prices would lead to more efficiency, which would benefit the state in the long run, but they were unwilling to face the near-term wrath of angry consumers. Responding to another concern of consumer advocates fearful of giant corporations, lawmakers required utilities to sell many of their power plants. The combination of these actions was that as prices for electricity and natural gas rose utilities had to buy power for more than they could charge their customers, leaving them with billions in debt.

Wanting to satisfy environmentalists, state officials set aside a bit more money for renewable energy development. They also kept restrictions on building power plants, without realizing a consequence could be electricity shortages.

Trying to protect against one company obtaining too much market control, California politicians also restricted long-term power contracts and forced all generators to deal in the volatile spot market. Electricity suppliers, therefore, had to hash out prices daily in a centralized power exchange, which mandated that utilities pay the highest price offered on any given day.

Legislators celebrated their compromises, approving the legislation in August 1996 by unanimous votes. Governor Pete Wilson signed the bill and declared: "We are shifting the balance of power in California. . . . We've pulled the plug on another outdated monopoly and replaced it with the promise of a new era of competition." The Republican governor went on to declare that the "landmark legislation" would "guarantee" lower rates.[17]

Yet this combination of compromises slowly produced chaos. Contrary to popular myth, problems did not result from soaring electricity demand since California's peak consumption actually fell 4.5 percent in 2000 and 5.4 percent in 2001. They also were not caused by a lack of power plant construction since independents in the 1990s added at least 4,500 megawatts, most of it distributed generation not noticed by analysts. The supply/demand balance tightened in part because other western states and provinces were experiencing brisk population and economic growth and did little to encourage energy efficiency. A drought in the Pacific Northwest also cut about 5,000 megawatts of hydropower exports usually sent to the Golden State. Another cause of the power shortage was the suspiciously large number of power plants that were shut down, ostensibly for maintenance. Outages soared from a typical 2,440 megawatts in 1999 to 10,000 megawatts in November 2000, and allegations were made that suppliers purposely withheld electricity in order to drive up its price.

The price increases were extraordinary . . . and perplexing. According to one study, "The price of wholesale electric energy dispatched from the new statewide pool soared by 13-fold, and that of spinning reserve (bought a day ahead) by 120-fold, even though the pool's load rose only 0.7 percent and its monthly peak load *fell* 1.9 percent."[18] In what has been described as the nation's greatest interstate wealth transfer, Californians' electricity bills went from $7.25 billion for all of 1999 to $7.5 billion for just the first six weeks of 2001.

Clever marketers certainly "gamed" the spot market. With secret schemes named "Get Shorty" or "Death Star," several traders pretended to overload the system at choke points only to obtain extra payments for relieving that very "congestion." They concocted "round trip" trades to inflate sales volumes and artificially drive up short-term prices.

Unable to pass on the higher costs, Pacific Gas & Electric filed for bankruptcy, and the state's two other utilities teetered. Rolling blackouts became common, forcing motorists to navigate intersections without traffic lights and consumers to use flashlights at grocery stores.

Politicians in 2001 responded to the chaos and confusion by blaming others—out-of-state power suppliers being the favorite targets—and switching course. Rejecting even the rhetoric of relying on private markets, Governor Gray Davis transformed the state government into the biggest buyer of power in the West.

California's electricity woes, unfortunately, continued. Although prices stabilized and supplies increased—largely because buyers and sellers were finally allowed to negotiate long-term contracts—the sudden surplus of electricity forced the state to sell back some of its purchased power at a loss. Those losses, as well as earlier government payments for high-priced electricity, helped transform a once-flush state budget into a huge deficit that will burden California's taxpayers for decades.

Peter Navarro, an economist at the University of California, Irvine, declared that the state's power deregulation fiasco "borders on the most expensive blunder in national history." He calculated the impact of rate increases and long-term bonds at $100 billion.[19]

Opponents of competition point to the California debacle as a reason not to change regulations or restructure electric utilities. According to one newspaper, "Deregulation has become synonymous with corporate greed, government incompetence, and the failure of free-market economics."[20] Yet the Congressional Budget Office concluded, "Deregulation itself [in California] did not fail; rather, it was never achieved."[21] Perhaps the Golden State's best lesson is that a transition to competitive power markets should not be fashioned as a combination of political deals offered to demanding stakeholders.

BLACKOUT 2003

August 14, 2003, began as a rather ordinary summer day. The Midwest and Northeast were hot but not that hot, and no significant storms threatened the region. Yet the electricity-delivery system was uncoordinated and stressed, and by late that afternoon a series of rather small problems cascaded into a massive blackout that left 50 million people without power and would cost an estimated $10 billion.[22]

The first minor sign of trouble occurred at 1:31 P.M., when a medium-sized power plant near Cleveland—FirstEnergy's Eastlake unit—shut down unexpectedly. The overall system can easily accommodate such a plant closure, yet how electricity managers handled the setback suggested future troubles. Unfortunately, the midwestern transmission coordinator, known as the Midwest Independent System Operator (ISO), did not have the sensors needed to detect the outage and only learned of the shutdown forty minutes later when FirstEnergy's engineers decided to telephone the Midwest ISO.[23]

A more serious problem appeared at 3:05 P.M., when one of FirstEnergy's large transmission lines—the 345,000-volt Chamberlin-Harding wire near Cleveland—went out after it sagged into a tree. Loaded power lines do sag, and the utility industry sets clear but voluntary standards to control vegetation, yet FirstEnergy had skimped for several years on tree trimming, as evidenced by forty-two-foot-tall trees growing in the transmission rights of way. Electricity systems are also designed to handle such a line loss by having other wires pick up the slack. Yet FirstEnergy's energy-management alarms failed to function, engineers did not realize they were losing lines and voltage, and the Midwest ISO was not told of the wire's failure until another delayed phone call from the utility.

A second 345-kilovolt line in the same area—which had heated up and expanded as it assumed some of the power from the Chamberlin-Harding wire—sagged into a tree at 3:32 P.M. and failed. With each line loss, larger power loads shifted abruptly.

"I wonder what is going on here," said Don Hunter of the Midwest ISO at 3:36 P.M. "Something strange is happening."[24]

The strangeness accelerated twenty-nine minutes later when two more lines failed, and a minute after that—at 4:06 P.M.—yet another FirstEnergy transmission wire tripped. Again, the transmission network should have isolated the problem and shut off power only to Akron and the surrounding area, yet transmission coordinators and utility engineers were neither communicating nor understanding the problem's growing depth.

According to Jerry Snickey in FirstEnergy's control room in Akron: "We have no clue. Our computer is giving us fits too. We don't even know the status of some of the stuff around us." Responded Don Hunter of Midwest ISO: "I can't get a big picture of what's going on. Strange things are happening all at the same time."[25]

The speed with which 50 million people can lose their electricity is staggering. Within less than three minutes—beginning at 4:08:58 to be exact—the last two lines carrying power from the South up into northern Ohio tripped their circuit breakers. Desperate for electricity, northern Ohio tried to pull from Michigan a massive 2,000 megawatts of power, the equivalent of three large generating plants. Michigan could not supply that load on short notice, and the unbalanced transmission system began to demonstrate huge swings in voltage and power surges. Since relays, the automatic devices that control the circuits, had not been coordinated throughout the region in ways to rebalance the grid and avoid a cascade, transmission lines and power plants across a vast area almost instantaneously went down as their safety equipment tried to protect against the dangerous power fluctuations. The power oscillations grew, the grid could not stabilize, and North America's largest cascading blackout occurred at 4:11 P.M.

Fifty million Americans and Canadians quickly experienced life without electricity. New York City subways stopped, many stuck between stations. Lacking power, security guards could not screen passengers, so airlines in New York, Newark, Detroit, Cleveland, Toronto, Buffalo, and dozens of other cities were grounded. Sewage treatment plants closed, forcing Detroit residents to boil their water and Clevelanders to avoid swimming in Lake Erie. Handcuffed prisoners were transferred to jails that still had lights and air conditioning. Hotels set up cots in conference rooms for their guests who could not open their rooms' electronic locks. Ice cream melted, and beer became warm. New York City businesses lost an estimated $1 billion, Ohio manufacturers suffered $1.08 billion in direct costs, and estimates of total U.S. damages reached at least $10 billion.

Many police officials initially feared terrorists caused the power failure, and heavily armored officers quickly surrounded dams, bridges, and other likely targets. The Pentagon even added air patrols over eastern U.S. cities. Yet most residents responded calmly. Some businesses offered free water to commuters forced to walk home. One community theater moved its performance outdoors and illuminated the actors with the headlights of several cars. Many families transferred their evening meal from the oven to an outside grill. Detroit police made only seventeen felony arrests, far fewer than typical for a summer evening.

Not all of the Northeast and Midwest went black. Mid-Atlantic utilities were able to disconnect from the grid before the power surges became dangerous. The same was true for suburban power companies around Albany and Rochester. Several businesses, particularly hospitals, continued basic operations with emergency generators. New York's Bellevue Hospital Center, for instance, had stocked a ten-day supply of fuel and a week's supply of medicine. Those offices or industries with their own power plants also operated normally. The Rochester headquarters of Eastman Kodak, for instance, generated its own electricity and steam with a 200-megawatt coal-fired cogenerator, natural-gas-powered microturbines kept the lights and air conditioning on at the Reuters skyscraper in Manhattan, and fuel cells and solar panels continued to supply limited power to the Condé Nast Building in Times Square.

The 2003 blackout demonstrated the grid's complexity . . . and vulnerability. The nation's 200,000 miles of high-voltage transmission lines are an engineering marvel that must balance second-by-second the volatile flow of electrons. Unlike the telephone system, the grid is not a programmable network, but rather a vast reservoir in which power production must instantaneously match electricity consumption.

The blackout prompted New Mexico governor Bill Richardson, a former secretary of energy, to declare, "We're a superpower with a Third World grid." That claim is exaggerated, but it does suggest that, despite the recent introduction of advanced computers, much of the electricity transmission system relies on mechanical circuit breakers and controls from the 1950s. The North American Electric Reliability Council, a voluntary association of utilities that encourages stable electricity deliveries, warned: "The nation is at a crisis stage with respect to reliability of transmission grids."[26]

August 2003 may have affected the most people, but it marked the grid's fourth catastrophic failure in the past ten years. In July 1996, some 2 million customers lost power when a line in Idaho sagged into a tree and a squirrel burned on a transformer. Two years later, an ice storm cut power in parts of the United States and Canada.

Threats to the grid are legion and complex. In addition to the problems of sagging power lines, tall trees, and poor coordination, Florida's hurricanes in fall 2004 demonstrated the system's vulnerability to extreme weather. Terrorists could also attack the far-flung grid, and not just with pipe bombs and rifles. One U.S. commission in August 2004 found that

70 percent of the U.S. power grid could be destroyed by a lone nuclear-weapon explosion at high altitude. The blast would produce an electromagnetic field that would cause "unprecedented cascading failures of U.S. major infrastructures."[27]

Electrons are disorderly and often move, at the speed of light, in unexpected ways. One writer described the grid to be "like a system of canals. Power plants pump energy into the canals, it sluices around, and then substations draw it off and siphon it to the consumer. A single power transaction sends eddies of electricity through the grid." The journalist further suggested that "trying to precisely manage activity on the grid with electromechanical relays has become the art of narrowly averting disaster."[28]

The August 2003 disaster could have been averted. FirstEnergy, for instance, should have trimmed trees in its rights of way, yet the existence of fourteen-year-old growths demonstrates the utility's negligence. Power operators also should have had far more training to manage the complex and dangerous machine under their control. One regulator complained that cosmetologists participate in more annual training than do grid operators.

An underlying problem, however, is the split nature of deregulation. Since the Public Utility Regulatory Policies Act in 1978 and the Energy Policy Act of 1992, wholesale electricity generators have been able to charge market rates, providing a clear incentive for entrepreneurs to construct more power plants. Yet the transmission and distribution sides of the electricity business have remained mostly regulated. Faced with a relatively low, government-set return on grid investments, companies have allocated far more funds to the generation than to the delivery of electricity. In fact, power demand over the past decade is up 30 percent, while transmission capacity has grown only 15 percent. The Energy Department predicts line investments during the next decade will expand only 6 percent compared to a 20-percent boost for electricity generation. The North American Electric Reliability Council calculates that $56 billion is needed to upgrade transmission wires, but it fears only $35 billion will be available.

The grid, moreover, was designed when utilities were independent fiefdoms and exchanged relatively little electricity. As more and more power is wheeled throughout the country, the grid's limitations are becoming obvious. The voluntary measures advanced by the utility-supported National Electricity Reliability Council worked reasonably well when power transmission was dominated by a small number of players, but today's electricity industry is splintered into many energy companies, and the council reports, "The adequacy of the bulk power transmission system has been challenged to support the movement of power in unprecedented amounts and in unexpected directions."[29] To its credit, the council has asked Congress for years to approve mandatory reliability standards and coordination rules, yet legislative debates on energy have been bogged down by regional conflicts.

Yet another problem is the patchwork of cooperation among utilities. The mid-Atlantic region long has had a formal institution to synchronize its power flows, while the midwestern system is relatively new and weak, and southern states have largely avoided any organized coordination among independent monopolies. In summer 2003, the Midwest ISO monitored, but did not manage, the flow of power; that responsibility remained divided among twenty-three utilities throughout Ohio, Michigan, and Indiana. According to Michigan's top utility regulator, "It would surprise a great number of Americans to know there is presently no government oversight of the reliability of this country's electric transmission system."[30]

Such patchwork approaches demonstrate the regionality of electricity politics. Rather than continue a balkanized system, the Federal Energy Regulatory Commission has argued for regional transmission organizations to coordinate the flow of electricity over state lines and to oversee improvements to the U.S. grid. Despite the clear need for such multistate organizing, southern and Pacific Northwest utilities bitterly oppose such a move. They argue that the feds should not challenge state regulations, but their real concern is that improved transmission lines may move to other sections of the country their relatively inexpensive power—made possible in part by taxpayer subsidies for federal utilities, and in part by the presence of already-paid-for, pollution-exempted, and cheap-to-operate hydroelectric and coal plants. That greed, of course, only forces the rest of the nation to live with an old and uncoordinated transmission system.

POLITICS

The U.S. electricity system's stresses go far beyond Enron, California, and blackouts, and the consequences, although largely unnoticed, are staggering. Inefficient power production is the principal cause of pollution. High energy prices are driving manufacturers and their U.S. jobs to locate in other countries. Unreliable supplies are shocking the nation's high-tech industry.

The system's waste is substantial. As mentioned earlier, Americans pay roughly $100 billion too much each year for heat and power. Two-thirds of the fuel burned to generate electricity is lost. Because of inefficiencies, U.S. power generators throw away more energy than Japan consumes.

The U.S. electricity system, moreover, employs decades-old technology. The average generating plant was built in 1964. Most of the switches that control electricity's flow are mechanical rather than solid state. Today's high-voltage transmission lines were designed before planners ever imagined that electricity would be sold across state lines, and, consequently, they are overloaded and subject to blackouts.

While California's disastrous restructuring received widespread attention, other states have realigned their power industries and obtained positive results. Pennsylvania officials calculate that the commonwealth's pro-competition efforts have saved residential and industrial customers some $8 billion. While admitting that century-old monopolistic practices are painstakingly slow to change, Texas, New York, and Massachusetts officials also profess a positive experience with electricity industry restructuring. In Texas, independent suppliers in 2004 offered 60 percent of the electricity used by commercial and industrial customers and 14 percent of the power demanded by residential consumers. Unlike California, Texas allows distribution utilities to purchase power on the spot market or through long-term contracts; that flexibility and the ongoing effort by state officials to resolve constraint points have produced a vibrant electricity market that embraces innovative technologies.

While restructuring efforts vary from state to state, they reveal three commonalities. First, utility sales of power plants, often demanded by reformers, have disclosed the true value of the industry's past investments. Nuclear generators in particular proved to be worth a lot less than anticipated. Some reactors, in fact, fetched about a tenth of their book value, whereas non-nuclear facilities sold at about twice their book value. Second, most of the new construction by non-utilities represent relatively small power plants, less than 100 megawatts, and confirm a shift away from centralization and towards distributed generation. Third, restructuring might have threatened utilities, but many monopolies benefited handsomely by arguing they needed to be compensated for their "stranded assets," those power plants and other equipment that would not be viable in a competitive market. Some utility lobbyists estimated such shaky investments nationwide totaled $300 billion. The exact utility benefit is impossible to calculate, but most states bowed to aggressive industry pressure and they shielded the monopolists from the consequences of their questionable outlays.

The shift to competition will take time, and establishing market rules will require a good bit of trial and error. As one researcher put it, "Electricity markets are made, they don't just happen."[31] With natural gas deregulation, the Federal Energy Regulatory Commission went through numerous revisions over a seven-year period before effectively opening access to alternative natural gas suppliers. Part of the ongoing experimentation with electricity competition is setting "standard prices" for customers not wanting to shop for power. Set that price too high and regulators will face angry consumers, but too low a price will discourage alternative suppliers from entering competitive markets.

Just as restructuring's opponents must develop patience for pricing adjustments, its advocates must acknowledge that deregulation does not mean no regulation. Competition demands that markets work fairly and effectively. Regulators remain necessary, at a minimum to police against the fraud and abuse that Enron and others advanced in a poorly structured California market.

With assets exceeding $600 billion and annual sales above $260 billion, electric utilities are this nation's largest industry. No doubt restructuring such a behemoth is difficult, the obstacles to change are formidable, and most utility monopolies are working aggressively to remain protected from competitors. Utilities, for instance, lobby for current clean air regulations that allow their old and dirty plants to keep polluting, while emission reductions must be borne by the small subset of new generators. The monopolists even argue that anyone stringing their own electric wires across a street, rather than relying on the utility's lines, should be sent directly to jail. To achieve the benefits of innovation, therefore, regulators and lawmakers must challenge vested interests and eliminate the outmoded regulatory, financial, and environmental barriers to competition and entrepreneurs.

7

Entrepreneurs

Utility executives tend to be cautious engineers who, protected from competition and guaranteed a profit, never had to hustle for customers or stretch the technological envelope. Most have little in common with Tom Casten, an entrepreneur who rages against the barriers that block energy-saving and pollution-cutting technologies. The Chicago-based businessman recently cut a deal to produce 900 megawatts of electric and thermal energy, enough to power a medium-sized town, from the waste heat and flared gas released by several steel smelters.

Entrepreneurs like Casten are demonstrating the tremendous explosion in power system innovation. Spurred by competition, such modernization can reduce pollution, stimulate economic progress, and enable a wealth of new electrotechnical applications.

Casten crusades against inefficiency. He waves his stocky arms when lamenting how the twelve nuclear reactors surrounding Chicago throw away their heat, enough to warm all of the city's major buildings. He points his finger aggressively when explaining how a coal-fired plant in Lemont, Illinois, discards enormous amounts of steam from its giant cooling towers, while across the street CITGO burns its own oil to obtain heat for powering its refinery. Describing today's electricity industry, Casten declares, "No other industry wastes two-thirds of its raw material; no other industry has stagnant efficiency; no other industry gets less productivity per unit output in 2004 than they did in 1904."[1]

Thomas Casten. Courtesy of Private Power, LLC.

Casten's alternative is to recycle energy, or to capture the heat and pressure that is normally wasted or flared from industrial processes. He has been waging this battle since 1977, when he formed the Cummins Co-generation Company, a division of Cummins Engine. He subsequently founded Trigen Energy Corporation, which provided heat and cooling via fourteen urban district-heating-and-cooling systems to more than 1,500 commercial buildings, hospitals, universities, and industrial facilities, as well as cogeneration units at Coors Brewery in Golden, Colorado; Kodak's headquarters in Rochester, New York; and four General Motors facilities and three chemical plants. Not unlike Thomas Edison, Casten eventually faced the machinations of financiers when a foreign investor took over Trigen and moved it away from energy projects.

The entrepreneur took his buyout money, launched Private Power, and began recycling heat from several steel mills along Lake Michigan. At U.S. Steel's Gary Works, Casten's venture developed, owns, and operates a 161-

megawatt cogenerator powered by the gas once flared from the giant blast furnaces. A separate unit provides ninety-five megawatts of electricity as well as process steam to Ispat Inland's steel-making operation in East Chicago, Illinois. Sixteen heat recovery boilers capture and utilize the waste heat from that steel company's metallurgical coke-making facility, and a desulfurization process and fabric-filter system make Ispat the steel industry's environmental standard. Recycled heat, according to Casten, could generate a substantial 45,000 megawatts of electricity and reduce carbon dioxide pollution by 320 million tons, and he declares, "It is every bit as environmentally friendly as heat and power from renewable energy sources, including solar energy, wind, and biomass."[2]

Casten's Indiana projects were done in cooperation with NiSource, a rather unique local utility that came to the realization it benefits from cooperating with, rather than opposing, energy entrepreneurs. From NiSource's perspective, Casten's smelter-based generators free up power that the utility can sell at higher rates (and profits) to its commercial or residential customers.

Casten works hard to find similarly far-sighted utilities, yet he complains that most monopolists maintain their inefficient ways because they want protection from competitors and change. After almost thirty years of trying to tweak the power system, he no longer believes a clever rate structure can encourage utilities to adopt efficiency or allow on-site generation. "At the very core of the onion," Casten declares, "the interests of energy producers are misaligned with the interests of energy consumers. . . . [Utilities] are not paid for being efficient and that kills demand-side management. . . . They work very, very hard to prevent their wires monopoly from ever being challenged."[3]

The entrepreneur glows with anger when railing against the monopolistic privileges bestowed on utilities, particularly their right to control electricity distribution lines. "Microsoft was threatened with breakup by the U.S. Justice Department," he declares. "Heinz was denied approval to acquire Beech Nut because it would concentrate market power over baby food. Europeans denied GE approval to acquire Honeywell. United Air Lines was denied approval to merge with U.S. Air. But the same governments keep laws giving local utilities the sole right to run a private wire." That right is unique to electricity monopolies since federal laws allow private firms to construct natural-gas pipelines, and developers can build telephone lines, steam tunnels, and Internet extensions to their neighboring buildings. Casten maintains that few businesses would construct their own electric lines, just as there are few independent gas pipelines, but the availability of competitive wires would transform the power industry and end the monopolies' ability to block local power with predatory line charges. When reviewing suggestions for improving the U.S. electricity system, Casten recommends, "Instead of new federal eminent domain for transmission wires, overturn the 50 state bans on private wires."[4]

Casten knows the cost-cutting benefits of competition firsthand. Only when he threatened to build a competitive natural-gas pipeline in order to supply Trigen's Philadelphia cogeneration unit did the monopolistic gas distribution company announce an 88-percent price cut.

Casten also complains that more than a dozen southern states still prevent their local industries from buying the electricity produced by third parties on their own sites. As a result, entrepreneurs are forced to sell their power only to utility monopolies, which set the transaction's terms to their favor.

On-site generators, according to Casten, offer enormous advantages. First, they reduce the need for unpopular transmission lines. "Remove the ban on private wires that bypass distribution monopolies and the result will be fewer wires," he says. "If industry met all future load growth with on-site power, the U.S. would not need any new transmission lines." Distributed generators, boasts the entrepreneur, also increase efficiency, reduce pollution, and provide more reliable power.

Casten's favorite on-site generator captures both heat and power. About 8 percent of U.S. electricity comes from such cogeneration plants, but the potential is much greater, particularly noting that Denmark generates 59 percent of its electricity from combined heat and power units, and the Netherlands and Finland each garner more than 40 percent of their current generation from such decentralized plants. U.S. use of distributed generation has doubled since the Public Utility Regulatory Policies Act of 1978, yet the progress varies across the country, largely as a result of differing state policies. Kentucky, South Carolina, and South Dakota, for instance, are dominated by politically powerful utility monopolies and allow virtually no distributed generation. Maine and Hawaii, in contrast, obtain more than 30 percent of their power from on-site units. Other active states include New Jersey (29 percent), Louisiana (24 percent), and California (22 percent).

The 200,000-mile network of high-voltage transmission lines, Casten argues, is the industry's current linchpin. While constructing a centralized power plant costs about $5,000 per megawatt, someone must pay an additional $1,260 per megawatt to string the associated transmission and distribution wires. Casten proposes distributed or on-site generators that do not require such additional costs as a solution. Installing units close to consumers also means less losses from those lines. The current centralized system leaks 9.5 to 10 percent of its power, and as mentioned earlier, line losses climb even higher when the wires are congested, rising to 20 percent or more during peak hours. Such losses mean that to deliver 1,000 megawatts, someone must build 1,200 megawatts of capacity.

This combination of generation and distribution expenses reflects Casten's frequent plea for the "right metrics." Rather than focus on a generator's capital costs, the entrepreneur argues that intelligent policies will result only if analysts acknowledge the costs associated with transmission and distribution construction, line losses, and the extra generation needed to meet peak loads. Wanting to advance a commonly accepted definition of electricity's delivered cost, Casten declares, "Recognize the locational value of power."[5]

Casten understands that not every consumer can generate his own electricity, and he appreciates why Samuel Insull in the early twentieth century built large power plants and integrated the different loads of streetcar companies, street-lighting firms, office buildings, and farms. Casten, however, argues that today's utility executives learned the wrong lesson from Insull's success. It is not that central generation of electricity is cheaper than distributed generation, he states. Insull's real lesson is that "grid-connected generation is superior to isolated generation, regardless of the size of generation plant."[6]

Yet an independent power producer trying to link to the grid is often blocked by utility monopolies. To give some perspective on the importance of interconnection, Casten notes that the United States has 80,000 megawatts of isolated standby generation, representing 12 percent of the system's peak load, but those resources cannot be used to decrease the grid's vulnerability because monopolists have not allowed the standby systems to operate in parallel with the transmission and distribution system.

Utilities impose another barrier to competition and on-site power when they calculate what to charge self-generating companies for backup power. Protecting their monopolies, they typically assume that only one distributed power plant will ever operate in a region and that it will fail during the time of peak electricity demand. Put another way, utilities assume that 100 percent of the on-site load will be out of service at the very same time, thereby having independents demand backup power when it is most rare and expensive. In reality, says Casten, the likely-outage figure is closer to 2 percent, meaning the monopoly's overcharge is 50 to 1. He compares utilities' high backup rates to a home insurance company trying to set its annual premium at a house's full replacement price.

"Today's power system was built to serve yesterday's needs," argues Casten.[7] In the past, a short power disruption—resulting perhaps by a tree falling on distribution wires—caused only flickering lights and slowed motors. Several seconds without power was tolerable, and most consumers could handle even several minutes of outage without large costs. Yet today's computer chips can suffer only eight-billionths of a second without power before they lose memory. Genetech's research center in Boston, for instance, would suffer damages of more than $100 million if its power supply were cut or became unstable for less than a second.

Most utilities respond to this reliability problem by trying to construct more centralized power plants, more transmission and distribution lines, and perhaps banks of batteries. Casten instead argues for integrating on-site generators into the grid.

Although he advances relatively small power units, Casten thinks big. He argues that today's energy-efficient and distributed technologies could reduce U.S. fuel use by a third, slash air pollution, and save a trillion dollars per decade. Such gains are not unrealistic if you compare the United States to its industrial competitors. According to Casten, "France, Germany, Japan, the United Kingdom, Spain, and Italy all use less energy per dollar of product than the U.S.—21 percent to 45 percent less. This gives manufacturers in these countries a competitive edge over U.S.-based production."[8] The challenge in the United States, he says, is to remove the policies that block the achievement of similar efficiencies.

Casten is both entrepreneur and lobbyist. He enjoys traveling to Washington, DC, to regale politicians about the opportunities associated with competition and cogeneration. An example of his effectiveness occurred during testimony before the House Resources Committee, which is populated with politicians that support the coal and oil industries. In the course of tough questioning from a particularly conservative lawmaker, the barrel-chested Casten noted that he was completing a successful cogeneration project at a Boy Scout camp. The politician, announcing that he, too, was an Eagle Scout, changed his attitude dramatically and began to plot with the competition advocate about how to remove the barriers to similar projects.

Casten argues that the partial competition advanced by the Public Utility Regulatory Policies Act led to seventeen straight years of electricity price reductions—a total savings of 32 percent. "Imagine," he declares, "what real competition can bring!"[9]

8

Modern Technologies

Technological advances are driving the power industry's restructuring. Compared with the decades-old, efficiency-stagnant generators protected by tradition-bound utility monopolies, an array of modern equipment offers opportunities for new and innovative players to enter the electricity market. Such technologies, if not blocked by outmoded policy, could vastly expand consumer options, increase productivity, and reduce pollution.

One of the hottest items is the cogenerator. This ingenious machine, a primitive model of which Edison employed at his Pearl Street Station power plant, produces both heat and electricity and can mean huge savings for consumers that might otherwise vent most of their energy to the great outdoors. A cogenerator captures the usually wasted heat to warm buildings, power chillers, dry paints and materials, and run an array of industrial processes. The benefit of cogeneration—sometimes called "combined heat and power"—is efficiency. The hybrid machines more than double the deployment of useful energy. A typical power plant producing only electricity is approximately 33-percent efficient, while a cogenerator using the same amount of fuel—but utilizing both electricity and heat—can be 80-percent efficient. Despite the economic downturn between 1998 and 2002, some 31,000 megawatts of cogeneration capacity were added in the United States, and the identified potential exceeds 200,000 megawatts.

Less noticed but also productive are back-pressure steam turbines that capture the energy when industries or institutions reduce pressures in their steam pipes. Many universities, hospitals, and industrial buildings, particularly in colder climates, employ district heating systems that distribute hot water or steam through pipes to buildings throughout their complexes. Few of these institutions capture the pressure reduction when valves cut the high-pressure steam coming from the generator to the low-pressure steam that can be handled by individual buildings. Lumber, pulp-and-paper, food, refining, and chemical firms also could employ similar back-pressure steam turbines to extract the energy released when they reduce steam pressure in order to run different industrial processes or when they release pressurized flue gas. Similarly designed expansion turbines take advantage of the pressure drop when natural gas in high-pressure pipelines is decompressed for local networks. These small expansion turbines are relatively inexpensive, the "fuel" is recycled and free, and their U.S. potential exceeds 6,500 megawatts or the output of thirteen large coal-fired power plants.

Huge energy savings can result from the widespread adoption of other seemingly simple technologies that increase energy efficiency. Compared to the basic incandescent bulb, for instance, compact fluorescent lamps consume one-quarter the energy and last seven times longer. Modern compressors and heat exchanges can reduce dramatically the operating costs of refrigerators, buildings can make better use of natural lighting and ventilation, and electronic devices can cut the standby consumption of computers and other equipment. Numerous energy management firms install sophisticated monitors and controls that trim costs and pollution, and scores of companies are devising more efficient and cleaner ways to produce paper, aluminum, steel, and chemicals.

Such efficient technologies already have reduced substantially the nation's energy intensity. This measure of energy used per unit of economic activity fell 42 percent from 1973 to 2000. In essence, the United States produced more with less power. The government's national laboratories calculate an even-larger energy-savings potential—almost 50 percent for lighting and space heating and cooling, and about 33 percent for refrigeration, water heating, and iron and steel production.[1] Further advancing the efficiency resource would mean less need for electricity generation and transmission and their accompanying economic and environmental costs.

Another modern technology is the combined-cycle gas turbine, made possible by advances in jet airplane engines that result from cash-strapped airlines demanding lower fuel costs and the military requiring better efficiency. These innovative turbines capture waste heat from the combustion turbine and use it to power a steam turbine. Put another way, the heat from burning natural gas or some other fuel is cycled twice through turbines in order to generate more electricity. (Unlike cogenerators, however, the remaining heat is vented and not captured.) Combined-cycle units, although they now generate only 3 percent of U.S. electricity, account for 88 percent of planned power plants. Because their relatively low emissions do not spark lengthy environmental reviews, a power-only, natural-gas-fired unit can be sited and licensed in less than eighteen months. Combined-cycle turbines, while still substantial in size, can be mass produced to meet near-term demands for power.

Improvements in truck turbochargers and hybrid electric vehicles have spurred a slew of microturbines, which feature a shaft that spins at up to 100,000 rpm and drives a high-speed generator. Because microturbines use recuperators to transfer heat energy from the exhaust steam back into the incoming air stream, they are far more efficient than other small combustion turbines. The recuperators also lower the exhaust temperature to the point where little nitrogen-oxide pollution is formed. Mass production should soon lower costs to only $250 per kilowatt, making them attractive to the residential market. Capstone Turbine, headquartered in Chatsworth, California, is selling gas-powered microturbines—ranging in size from 24 kilowatts (enough to power a home) to 500 kilowatts (enough to power a McDonald's)—whose operating costs are about a third of a comparable diesel generator's. Maintenance costs are relatively low because microturbines have only one moving part, the high-speed shaft spinning on air bearings. ABB, a large European engineering firm and generating-equipment manufacturer, has abandoned the construction of nuclear reactors in favor of producing and integrating efficient microturbines.

Such small units also can be good for the environment. Kawasaki's one-megawatt generator, which uses a catalytic combustor, is the world's cleanest gas turbine, emitting only two parts per million of nitrogen oxides compared to the roughly nine parts per million for the best 250-megawatt gas turbine. Small-scale fluid-bed boilers also allow for decentralized and relatively clean coal burning; these generators also emit little sulfur dioxide, and their excess steam can be captured for additional fuel efficiency.

Wind turbines are another increasingly sophisticated technology, and, although starting from a relatively small base, they represent the world's fastest-growing energy source, expanding some 30 percent annually. Progress in the United States, while substantial, has depended upon a federal tax credit equaling 1.8 cents per kilowatt-hour. Wind turbine performance has improved dramatically as a result of better rotor blades and controls. Larger turbines also are lowering costs, which average, depending upon wind speed, about \$0.04 to \$0.06 per kilowatt-hour.[2] Wind technologies can be deployed in centralized wind farms or on a smaller scale, as evidenced by the retail chain Target marketing a one-kilowatt Bergey wind machine for home use.

Among the more promising, but not yet widely commercialized, developments are fuel cells that produce an electric current and heat from chemical reactions rather than from combustion. They work by combining hydrogen with oxygen from the air, and their waste products are simply water and carbon dioxide. Although similar to a battery, fuel cells are recharged by the addition of hydrogen. Despite relatively high costs (more than \$3,000 per kilowatt-hour), fuel cells are attractive in niche applications because they emit negligible pollution, have very high electric efficiency, employ few moving parts, require low maintenance, and are quiet. Of the several types of fuel cells, perhaps the most attractive is the proton-exchange membrane (PEM), which uses a special polymer "filter" that looks like an ordinary sheet of plastic wrap. DaimlerChrysler and Toyota are already using PEM units in cars, while General Motors and Dow Chemical are installing a large-scale PEM fuel cell (up to 35 megawatts) at Dow's giant chlorine-production plant in Freeport, Texas.

Fuel cell advances over the past decade have been impressive. The value of platinum required for a PEM catalyst to power a small car has fallen from \$30,000 to a few hundred. The fuel-cell stack needed for an automobile has shrunk from the size of a giant refrigerator to a microwave. Washing-machine-sized units now can power an individual home. The head of DaimlerChrysler's fuel-cell program envisions a future in which cars parked in garages or at shopping malls can plug into the grid and sell power at a profit, thereby allowing virtually everyone to be an electricity producer. Noting the number of autos, such an approach would revolutionize the energy web, blur the lines between the electricity and automobile industries, and increase the opportunities for further innovation.[3]

In addition to powering fuel cells, hydrogen can store and carry energy directly. One advocate says, "Hydrogen as a widely used energy carrier is essential and inevitable,"[4] yet other researchers argue that using electricity directly remains more efficient than making hydrogen to transport power.[5] A transition to a hydrogen economy, although promising, would take time and demand substantial costs. According to the National Academy of Sciences, it would require "a comprehensive, long-range program of innovative, high-risk/high-payoff basic research in catalysis, nanomaterials, membranes, and separation."[6] That report makes a specific plea for expanded research into distributed hydrogen production and storage systems.

Another power innovation is the photovoltaic (PV) cell, a solid-state device that converts sunlight into electricity. PV costs have fallen fourfold in the last fifteen years and further reductions seem likely because of advances in the manufacture of silicon wafers. Firms are developing more efficient solar cells as well as modules that can be integrated into a building's structure. At current prices, approximately $0.25 per kilowatt-hour, photovoltaics can compete in niche markets, often in rural areas where it is more costly to extend transmission and distribution lines, yet they remain about three times the cost of conventional electricity.[7]

New technologies also are improving the production and processing of biomass, which includes wood, forestry and farm wastes, municipal garbage, and crops grown for energy use. These sources can be burned as well as converted into gaseous and liquid fuels. Biomass-powered electricity generation doubled in the United States from 1987 to 1999.[8] Sweden has planted willow tree plantations for power production, and it intends to obtain 40 percent of its energy from biomass by 2020.

External heat generators produce power not by explosive internal combustion but by an external heat source, such as a continuous-combustion burner. When burning fossil or biomass fuels, such systems avoid temperature spikes, making emissions very low and easy to control. The Stirling engine, one form of external heat generator, closely couples a burner to a heat exchanger that induces harmonic oscillations in a piston; the result is a highly efficient system that can deliver ten units of electricity and ninety units of useful heat from 105 units of natural gas. Thermo-photovoltaics generate electricity from infrared radiation, typically radiant heat obtained from a burner or concentrated solar energy. More esoteric are the space program's alkali metal thermal-to-electric converters that use a burner to vaporize potassium or sodium; in the last three years, efficiencies of these low-noise cells have risen from 2 percent to 20 percent.

Advocates of centralized power point to new nuclear designs, such as the pebble-bed modular reactor (PBMR) that would employ tennis-ball-sized "pebbles" filled with uranium oxide granules. Compared to reactors from the 1970s, the smaller PBMRs are promoted as safer, quicker to construct, and less expensive. Although PBMRs would emit no air pollution, they still would produce long-term radioactive wastes, and most investors (as well as the general public) remain skeptical of nuclear technologies after past accidents and cost overruns.

To continue burning the nation's substantial supply of coal, other engineers advance modern processes that convert coal into a gas. When subjected to heat and pressure, coal breaks down into a relatively clean-burning "syngas" of hydrogen and carbon monoxide, which can then be piped to turbines and burned. Without using the scrubbers that usually clean pollutants, four coal-gasification pilots—including a 250-megawatt station in West Terre Haute, Indiana—are releasing significantly less sulfur, nitrogen oxides, and mercury than conventional coal-powered generators. The gasification technology, however, remains a bit expensive, and risk-sensitive power companies have been reluctant to invest, although the climate may change if stricter air pollution regulations are enforced.

All of these innovations, of course, need to be compared to mature technologies that now dominate the electricity industry. Today's centralized coal plants that account for 56 percent of U.S. power have not improved their delivered efficiency in more than forty-three years, and their last significant enhancement—the supercritical boiler—was perfected in the mid-1950s.

Most modern innovations allow for on-site electricity production. In addition to avoiding transmission and distribution losses, such decentralized generation offers consumers the opportunity to optimize their power systems, increase efficiency, lower costs, enhance productivity, and reduce emissions. Today's dominant utility approach—centralized power plants for electricity and separate units for thermal energy to heat or cool buildings—might have made sense with state-of-the-art generation and distribution technologies of the 1950s and 1960s, but smaller and dispersed electricity systems now provide economic and environmental advantages.

Consider the benefits obtained by Aaron Feuerstein, who makes Polartec at his Malden Mills textile plant that employs 2,300 workers in Lawrence, Massachusetts. Increased demand for his product, used as an insulator in sleeping bags and coats, forced Feuerstein in 1992 to look for an efficient, low-cost, and reliable source of electricity, heat, and steam. He settled on two 4.3-megawatt gas-fired units that are saving Feuerstein more than $1 million annually in energy costs, and cutting Polartec's emissions of nitrogen oxides and carbon monoxide to less than fifteen parts per million.

Dow Chemical's operations are much larger than Feuerstein's, but they demonstrate the business community's growing adoption of innovative, on-site energy technologies. Dow is the world's largest consumer of fuel, and that expense has focused the company's attention on modern alternatives. The firm's recent efficiency improvements, for instance, are saving $40 million annually, and its cogenerators are supplying 95 percent of Dow's U.S. power needs.

Entrepreneurs are advancing innovative business plans as well as technologies. Noting that most consumers know little about energy and have no interest in managing their electricity usage, Real Energy presents an attractive offer—the independent generator will finance, install, and operate a cogenerator while the consumer simply enjoys guaranteed electricity savings of 10–15 percent. A moderately sized office building would obtain an annual, no-effort, no-risk benefit of $20,000 to $30,000. Other energy service companies, known as ESCOs, install and maintain efficient lighting, motors, and appliances; monitor an industrialist's or large commercial building's power usage; and, where possible, shop for the best electricity deals.

The economics of distributed generation, of course, vary from region to region, depending upon the local utility's rates and the consumer's electric and thermal needs. An analyst found that a gas-fired cogenerator in a 200-bed nursing home within one utility's service territory paid for itself in only 2.6 years, while a similar unit within another region faced a payback of 7.6 years.[9]

Support from the financial community is growing. A 2004 survey found that 94 percent of venture capital firms expressed an interest in distributed generation, particularly fuel cells, energy intelligence systems, and electronic components and communication technologies.[10]

Although the U.S. market for distributed generation is substantial, particularly in this era when industrial customers demand steady and high-quality power, perhaps the greatest on-site potential is with the world's 3 billion poor people who have no reliable access to electricity. Micropower saves the $1,500 per kilowatt that developing countries would be required to spend on transmission lines.

The traditional power industry's knee-jerk reaction to the 2003 blackout was: "Expand the grid." Specific problem areas certainly need to be upgraded, yet a growing number of engineers argue that the power cascade should provoke a dramatically new approach to delivering electricity.

They draw a comparison to computers and their evolution from centralized mainframes of the 1960s to today's decentralized web of networked laptops. These engineers foresee a radical new power network—one that's adaptive, self-healing, and compatible with distributed, on-site energy sources. It would have sophisticated sensors to anticipate crises, electronic circuits to redirect wayward currents, and a computerized "brain" to power down dishwashers and other noncritical electricity loads when the system is nearing its capacity. Such automatic adjustments would hardly be noticeable—slightly dimming overhead lights or raising the summer temperature by a degree or two—but throughout a skyscraper or at a factory they would result in substantial energy savings.

One innovation, the microgrid, already links small generators within industrial parks and housing complexes, and sophisticated software based on neural networks (a type of self-organizing system in which a computer teaches itself to optimize performance) can increase power quality and reduce the risk of overloads. The biggest barriers to such advancements are regulatory rather than technical. State laws, for instance, allow only utility monopolies to string wires across streets or among customers, yet microgrid advocates suggest that revised interconnection requirements would spark enormous benefits, as they did in the telephone industry in 1968 when the Carterphone legal decision enabled customers to connect to non–AT&T equipment and enjoy a world beyond the monopoly's black rotary telephones.

The University of California at Irvine, working with Southern California Edison and Southern California Gas Company, has created a "premium-power park" that deploys distributed generators and microgrids to supply the super-reliable power needed by many of today's innovative industries. In the jargon of utility engineers, today's grid provides "three-nines" reliability, or power delivered 99.9 percent of the time. That number sounds impressive, but disruptions of even 0.1 percent mean hours of blackouts, surges, and sags throughout a year, and those hours translate into millions in lost revenue for many businesses. The goal of electrical engineers, such as those in Irvine, is to achieve "nine-nines" reliability, or uninterrupted power 99.9999999 percent of the time. Noting the modern economy's need for such steady electricity, premium-power parks may be launched in urban centers throughout the country.

Superconductivity, another possible disruptive technology, could vastly increase the transmission grid's load and reliability. The Electric Power Research Institute predicts this advancement would at least triple the carrying capacity of power lines. Testing that notion, the U.S. Department of Energy and the Long Island Power Authority are sharing the $30-million cost for laying underground cable that will power 300,000 homes. Yet superconducting transmission lines remain expensive, largely because many of the prototypes contain a lot of silver. Engineers are experimenting with alternatives, including coated conductors that avoid the costly metal. Sumitomo Electric Industries, Japan's largest producer of cable, announced in late 2004 a process to make 3,000-foot-long sections of ceramic wire that transmits 130 times more electricity than normal copper lines. Optimists suggest such improved models will be ready for the marketplace by 2006 and that mass production will cut costs. Skeptics highlight the many needed engineering advances as well as question the willingness of utilities and regulators to invest in superconductive technologies.

Another transmission innovation is a new class of conductors that expand and sag far less than current wires. Those attributes are important because as electricity pulses, wires heat up, and if they sag too far, high-voltage electricity can arc to nearby trees or structures, possibly causing fires and shorting circuits. Since new low-thermal conductors produce less heat, they can carry more electricity. If engineering and price goals can be met, such an advancement would help to relieve transmission congestion and enable centralized power plants to send more power over longer distances.

Integrated transmission and distribution planning, however, may offer better returns. By focusing on customer needs rather than simply delivering electrons, several electric companies began in the 1990s to reevaluate their power-delivery options, particularly the use of efficiency measures or dispersed generators in order to reduce peak loads. Rather than spend $65 million to upgrade its grid, for example, New York State Electric & Gas Corporation invested only $45,000 on meters and radios that dispatch two small, backup generators when demand is high; such alternative planning provided a 99-percent capital savings.[11]

Improved consumer information can provide enormous benefits. When customers better understand their power usage and the varying cost of electricity over time, they make more efficient and cost-saving decisions. The largest customers of New York's Niagara Mohawk enjoy the sophisticated meters that provide real-time power prices, enabling them to purchase less-expensive electricity when the utility's generators are not stressed and have extra capacity. Rather than consumers paying the same rate whenever they use electricity throughout a month—the common practice that insulates buyers and sellers from the frequent and often substantial changes in power prices—a study by McKinsey Co. calculates that the availability of real-time pricing across the country would save some $15 billion each year.

Improved price signals, such as transmission tolls, also can encourage efficiency by reflecting the higher costs for moving power when lines are congested. Such charges would spur a shift to distributed generators that do not rely on the grid to deliver electricity.

The ability to trim consumption during peak hours can reduce a utility's costs significantly, largely because the extra, infrequently used generators are the most expensive to operate. The Electric Power Research Institute estimated that a 2-percent demand reduction in California during the summer of 2001 would have slashed power expenditures by $700 million; another study found a 10-percent reduction would have cut wholesale prices in half. Seeing a business opportunity, several companies are marketing electronic monitors that allow homes and industries to tweak their energy consumption, while others are selling software so utilities can shed load by instantaneously reducing by a couple of degrees the thermostats of thousands of businesses and residences.

Even the less visible segments of the electricity industry are enjoying technological updates. Consider the basic switch that controls the U.S. transmission system. Most are still mechanical, in that they must be opened to break electricity's circuit, and they are excruciatingly slow and unable to manage the flow of electricity. "Compared with the speed of light," complains Kurt Yeager of the Electric Power Research Institute, "those mechanical switches have an equivalent delay factor of about ten days. If I were running a railroad, for example, and I said it took me ten days to open or close a switch, I wouldn't move many trains."[12] In contrast, modern semiconductor-based switches act far more quickly, perform like a valve that can allow a manageable amount of current to pass, enable wires to carry far more electricity, and improve power reliability.

Consider also the meter. Until recently, utilities hired readers to walk through neighborhoods once a month and record each home's use of kilowatt-hours. Such meter readers have been one of the more glaring signs of utility backwardness in an era of sophisticated electronics. Modern meters now can be read remotely, and they can record an array of useful data, including energy usage by time period and various measures of power quality. In the next few years, according to one study, "the electric meter may evolve into a services gateway that will allow two-way communication between energy providers and consumers, opening up new ways for energy companies to maximize the efficiency of supply and customers to participate in energy markets."[13]

Storage is another key component. Today's electricity systems must delicately balance the demand and supply of power, activating generators when more consumers want more energy. Scores of power plants are turned on—and emit pollution—simply to meet consumer demands during the few busy hours, and they remain idle for the rest of the day and night. If new technologies could more effectively store electricity, the need for additional generators and wires would decrease and the use of intermittent power sources, such as solar and wind, would rise. Hydroelectric plants long have been used as large-scale storage systems, sometimes with water pumped uphill into reservoirs at night and released through turbines when power is needed. Yet because few good sites are available—and few communities want to flood valleys in order to create reservoirs—the United States has not added a pumped-hydro station for almost twenty years.

Another storage option is the electrochemical battery, which has been around for decades and today powers cellular telephones and an array of handheld devices. Its output, however, is small and its cost is impractical for storing substantial amounts of power. More recent storage developments are flywheels and ultra-capacitors that protect against brief voltage fluctuations by offering short bursts of power. A constantly spinning flywheel can convert its circular movement when needed into an electrical current. Flywheel batteries, for example, protect the semiconductor factory in Rousset, France, against voltage fluctuations that could destroy expensive and delicate manufacturing processes. New-generation batteries and compressed air storage also are gaining attention.

Today's technological revolution certainly challenges traditional power companies, but it could open new business opportunities. A dozen distribution utilities, for instance, are testing equipment that allows electric wires to carry telephone and Internet service. The concept of sending data across power lines is not new—numerous power companies long have used electric wires to monitor their substations—yet recent developments enable the transmission of much larger streams of data and voice. The speed equals DSL service, which is slower than most cable modem setups and therefore inadequate for high-quality video streaming, but power lines, unlike either of the current Internet options, offer symmetrical service that provides the same speed for both sending and downloading files. Several technical obstacles must be overcome, such as the annoying tendency for truck traffic to temporarily block signals and knock consumers offline. For electricity-distribution companies, however, broadband over power lines (known as BPL) could provide a new profit center without the need for substantial new investments. For consumers, BPL could mean lower prices and the set-up ease of simply plugging a modem into an electrical outlet. If engineers can develop the right compression technology, consumers also could obtain video over electric wires, and power companies would join the lucrative competition to provide digital communication and entertainment to millions of homes.

The appearance of so many innovative technologies is ironic since utilities spend so little on research. Compared to the pharmaceutical industry's 12 percent of revenue, power companies devote less than three-tenths of 1 percent on R&D, less, according to one researcher, than the research commitments of the dog food industry. The federal government has also cut its energy research and development by more than a third over the past decade, despite the rise of oil imports and the increasing costs of blackouts. In fact, new electric technologies result largely from developments within several separate industries. Airplane manufacturers, for instance, introduced the advanced turbines that power companies now utilize, while computer makers enabled the electricity industry to adopt more sophisticated switches and meters.

Some analysts argue that today's cornucopia of electric technologies reflect, at least in part, the entrepreneurial climate sparked by the Public Utility Regulatory Policies Act of 1978 and the Energy Policy Act of 1992. Others suggest that the development of modern equipment, particularly the cogenerator, forced policymakers to reform the regulated and centralized utility paradigm. No doubt today's opportunities result from some combination of policy and technology, and future benefits will depend upon innovations in both fields.

The fact that more efficient technologies are available or just on the horizon does not mean they all will be adopted, or that continued technology development will be a priority of a restructured electricity industry. Whether power innovations are boosted depends a great deal on how policy barriers are removed and open markets are advanced.

9

Barriers to Innovation

Overcoming the reluctance of monopolists and their regulators to accept innovative technologies and entrepreneurs is a challenge, even for an engineering super-sophisticate like the Massachusetts Institute of Technology. In 1985, MIT began to consider generating its own electricity. With its students using computers—to say nothing of stereos, hair dryers, and toaster ovens—the university faced soaring electricity costs from the local utility, Cambridge Electric Company (CelCo). Many of MIT's world-class research projects also could not afford the utility's disruptions or low-quality power. At the same time, MIT's heating and cooling system, which included 1950s-vintage boilers that burned fuel oil, was a major source of sulfur dioxide, nitrogen oxides, carbon monoxide, and volatile organic compounds.

The university reviewed numerous options and finally settled on installing its own 20-megawatt, natural gas-fired, combined-heat-and-power (CHP) system. The cogenerator was expected to meet 94 percent of MIT's power, heating, and cooling needs, and it was to cut the school's annual energy bills by $5.4 million. Even though MIT agreed to pay CelCo $1 million annually for its supplemental-power needs, the university expected to recoup its investment in a little less than seven years.

CelCo, not happy about losing business, demanded an additional "customer transition charge" of $3,500 a day ($1.3 million a year) as compensation for power it would no longer supply to MIT. The Massachusetts

Department of Public Utilities agreed with the utility monopoly, but the university appealed in federal court, arguing that it already was paying $1 million per year for backup power, that CelCo had known about MIT's plans for ten years and could have taken actions to compensate for the lost load, and that the utility's projected revenue loss was inflated. The judges eventually ruled that their court did not have jurisdiction. MIT then appealed to the Massachusetts Supreme Judicial Court, which in September 1997 reversed the state regulator's approval of the customer transition charge, remanded the case for further proceedings, and stated that no other CelCo ratepayers contemplating self-generation should have to pay similar costs.

The utility also lobbied environmental regulators to challenge MIT's cogenerator, even though the system promised to reduce annual pollutant emissions by 45 percent, an amount equal to reducing auto traffic in Cambridge by 13,000 round trips per day. Unfortunately for the university, the state's nitrogen oxide standard favored an expensive technology—designed for power stations more than ten times larger than MIT's generator—that posed a health risk because of the need to store large amounts of ammonia in the middle of campus. MIT engineers responded with a sophisticated life-cycle assessment that showed its innovative system enjoyed lower net emissions than the state-approved technology, yet they made no progress with state authorities until university lawyers appealed to the regional emissions-regulating agency.

MIT finally installed its own generator, which is saving money and reducing pollution, but the university's experience demonstrates the substantial effort and expense required to surmount barriers posed by utility monopolies and tradition-bound regulators. Because few companies interested in generating their own power possess MIT's resources or expertise, the university's lesson is that if state and federal lawmakers want to reduce costs and emissions, they must restructure the electricity industry in ways that remove the barriers to innovation and entrepreneurs.

Not all utilities oppose distributed generation. NiSource, the multibillion-dollar electric and natural gas company headquartered in Merrillville, Indiana, launched its own on-site power efforts with a microturbine at a Walgreen's drugstore and has since signed numerous contracts with independent power generators. "This [effort] can really benefit local distribution companies and pipelines," said CEO Gary Neale. "We no longer have winter and summer peaks because distributed generation means heat, electricity, and air conditioning year round. We don't see swings in load." From the utility's viewpoint, every distributed generation unit saves about $1,400 to $1,500.[1]

KeySpan Corporation, which also owns power plants and sells natural gas, installed in summer 2001 a natural-gas-fired cogenerator for Montefiore Medical Center in the Bronx. The hospital enjoys the energy savings, and KeySpan benefits from the sale of equipment and the delivery of natural gas.

Consumers, of course, can obtain the most direct savings and options from distributed generation. James O'Donahue, for instance, had grown tired of his local utility's high fees and unreliable service. The energy manager for Toray Plastics, a large manufacturer of tape, knew that blackouts caused by Rhode Island's electricity grid resulted in serious losses on his production line. Several years ago, Toray Plastics installed a generator that supplies 7.5 megawatts of electricity and recaptures the waste heat to run the plant's boilers. After the local utility tried to impose extra charges associated with backup power, O'Donahue installed more generators to meet Toray's entire 20-megawatt load. By cutting loose from the grid, says the executive, Toray Plastics remains economically competitive while meeting its environmental objectives.

Equity Office Properties Trust entered the power business by testing distributed generators at twelve of its 700 office buildings in Boston, New York, Chicago, Los Angeles, San Diego, and San Francisco. The power units provide some 30 percent of each building's needs and cost between $1 million and $5 million, an expense Equity is recovering over time by avoiding expensive electricity from the grid during times of peak demand. The property manager also sees the generators as lures to financial-service firms and other tenants seeking reliable power for their sensitive equipment.

Another on-site innovation sits in the basement of an otherwise ordinary-looking Manhattan high-rise on Avenue of the Americas at 45th Street. There, large tanks make and store about 380 tons of ice, which the building uses during summer months for cooling. Rather than run a power-hogging air conditioning system during expensive peak daylight hours, the Durst Organization produces ice at night, when electricity prices are lowest.

Energy service entrepreneurs also are helping consumers adopt distributed-generation solutions. Tom Aubee of Alternative Energy Corporation, for instance, understood that the South County Medical Center in Wakefield, Rhode Island, wanted cheaper power but did not want to run its own electric system. He proposed a fuel cell that would supply the hospital with 200 kilowatts of electricity, as well as heat and hot water. Aubee installed and maintains the system, and hospital administrators annually save $90,000 in fuel costs and 40,000 pounds of carbon dioxide emissions.

OPPOSING COMPETITION

To obtain additional savings across the country, what is needed is a policy revolution to accompany the emerging technological revolution. Energy laws and regulations must overcome regulatory inertia and become innovation-friendly. Current rules designed to support the status quo—centralized, steam-powered generators controlled by regulated monopolies—include restrictive interconnection standards, counterproductive environmental permits, and outmoded equipment depreciation schedules.

The chief barrier-busting proponents have been independent generators (who want to enter the electricity business), industrial and commercial customers (who want to shop for lower-priced power), and economists (who favor the marketplace over regulation). Relative to the telecommunications, airline, and trucking industries, they have made only limited progress, and the California and Enron debacles presented setbacks. Some of the manufacturers of on-site generators (such as Caterpillar) and industrial customers (such as Dow Chemical) are huge and enjoy substantial political clout, yet these innovation advocates have not been able to match the muscle of well-funded and well-positioned monopolists and their supporters.

Competition advocates enjoyed their first success in 1978 with passage of the Public Utility Regulatory Policies Act (PURPA), which enabled cogenerators and renewable energy suppliers to sell electricity to regulated utilities. In the mid-1980s, deregulating the natural gas market lowered the price and increased the availability of that relatively clean fuel. Finally, the Energy Policy Act of 1992 (EPACT) and subsequent rulings by the Federal Energy Regulatory Commission allowed unregulated independent generators to sell wholesale power over the grid to distant customers.

Numerous states, despite the policy disaster in California, have implemented utility restructuring plans that are increasing consumer options, saving money, and cutting pollution. The emerging competition, while still limited, has prompted the adoption of creative business deals as well as innovative technologies. In New Jersey, for instance, more than sixty manufacturers—including Bristol-Myers Squibb, Mobil, and Hoffman-LaRouche—banded together to purchase an initial 200 megawatts of independent power. This aggregation effort saved the industrialists $20 million during its first six months. New Jersey has also encouraged the market participation of entrepreneurial suppliers, which now provide about 78 percent of the power demand from the state's largest consumers.

Yet the forces aligned against further change are substantial, suggesting a colossal struggle for the future of electricity. The political alignments have become increasingly complex, particularly in response to evolving technologies and market mechanisms, but here are descriptions of some of the key defenders of the status quo.

Private Monopolies

Investor-owned utilities for some ninety years thrived by accepting government regulation in exchange for monopoly control over their service areas. Since their profits were calculated according to the size of their investments, private power companies had an incentive to build expensive generators and to encourage consumers to buy more appliances that devoured ever more electricity. With assured profits and steady growth, utilities often acted in concert as a powerful lobby. Yet with no competition, monopolists avoided technological advances, and the average efficiency of electricity generators stagnated. Their stable world has been shattered in recent years as independent generators, using innovative turbines, produce cheaper electricity.

The Edison Electric Institute trade association now faces internal squabbles and the loss of paying members as traditional utilities see different opportunities in a competitive market. Although most struggle to maintain their monopolies, a few utilities have created subsidiaries that compete in the service territories of other power companies, and they are demanding open access to the grid. Other utilities that want to concentrate on delivering power are reluctant to allow competitors on the transmission and distribution lines. This mixture of perspectives has launched several coalitions of utilities, often created by hustling lobbyists looking for deep-pocketed clients that needed representation in Washington.

Despite the internal squabbles, the utility industry remains the nation's largest in terms of capital investment, and it can afford to hire well-connected lobbyists in order to advance its interests on Capitol Hill and before the Federal Energy Regulatory Commission. The Edison Electric Institute's director, for instance, was George W. Bush's Yale classmate as well as a Republican "pioneer" who raised more than $100,000 in political donations for the presidential race. Most utilities maintain even more substantial political clout within their state legislatures and regulatory commissions, which is why they tend to favor state over federal initiatives.

A clear example of the utility industry's persistent political clout is the Bush administration's dramatic shift on clean-air policy. Coal-dominated utilities—particularly Atlanta-based Southern Company, North Carolina-based Duke Energy Corporation, and Ohio-based FirstEnergy Corporation—wanted to save money by rolling back pollution controls and eliminating the multimillion-dollar government lawsuits against them. They were particularly angry that the Clinton administration's Environmental Protection Agency sued nine coal-fired utilities that expanded older power plants without adding the required pollution controls. Feeling that the Edison Electric Institute was not sufficiently forceful on environmental issues, these coal-based utilities formed a splinter group, the Electric Reliability Coordinating Council, and hired lobbyist Haley Barbour, who had been chairman of the Republican National Committee and helped the GOP gain control of Congress.

A few weeks after Bush entered the White House, Barbour wrote to Vice President Dick Cheney, who was a former energy industry executive and now chaired an administration energy panel: "The question is whether environmental policy still prevails over energy policy with Bush-Cheney as it did with Clinton-Gore." Barbour encouraged the new administration to demonstrate that environmental concerns would not "trump good energy policy."[2] Along with Marc Raciot—another well-connected lobbyist who had been a governor and would become chairman of the Republican National Committee—Barbour quickly lobbied the president to reverse his campaign pledge to regulate the emissions of carbon dioxide, the key culprit of global climate change.

Two weeks before the vice president's energy task force was to release its final recommendations, the two lobbyists met privately with Cheney—

the Environmental Protection Agency administrator, who supported the lawsuits, was deliberately not invited. Just days before the report's unveiling, the Southern Company and other utilities contributed an additional $100,000 to the Republican Party. Reversing decades-old rules, the administration responded by declaring that utilities need not install pollution controls when they expand or upgrade their plants. Despite clear scientific evidence on the toxicity of mercury, the White House also advanced weak emission standards.

Many power companies are using similar political muscle to block competition. While distributed generators argue that small-scale units could improve the grid's reliability, most utility executives view independents as threats to their profits. As explained in more detail later, monopolists often refuse to interconnect with independent generators and impose on them high charges for backup electricity.

Government-Owned Monopolies

Among the strongest opponents of electricity reform, ironically, are the giant utilities owned by the federal government and created in the 1930s as social and business experiments. The Tennessee Valley Authority (TVA) and Bonneville Power Administration (BPA) successfully built dams, strung lines, and brought power to impoverished regions. Yet seventy years later, these taxpayer-supported utilities have become little more than bloated bureaucracies trying to protect their benefits by blocking reformers and competitors.

Part of public power's opposition to change results from the great deal provided to TVA and BPA beneficiaries. Agency officials vehemently scoff at the suggestion that federal utilities are subsidized, yet Oregon's former governor admitted BPA is a "publicly subsidized entity selling below-market power."[3] Bonneville executives privately estimate the utility's benefit to Pacific-Northwest consumers totals $16–34 billion. Noting that TVA pays no taxes, enjoys access to low-cost capital, and avoids scores of federal laws and state regulations, one observer concluded: "The Tennessee River flows through seven states and drains the nation."[4]

TVA long has opposed competition and dominated its own customers, which have been burdened with long-term, all-requirements contracts that they can terminate only by providing a ten-year notice. These are not ten-year contracts that expire; they are rolling provisions that after each new day cannot be terminated for another ten years. The contracts also prohibit consumer shopping and require that all power be purchased from TVA. The municipal utilities and rural coops that buy electricity from TVA, as a result, have been restricted from the benefits of competition; they cannot even obtain realistic price quotations for power to be supplied in ten years. The Federal Energy Regulatory Commission, of course, would not allow private utilities to use similar anti-competitive provisions, demonstrating again TVA's special treatment.

The Bristol Utility Board in southwest Virginia met strong resistance when it notified TVA that it wanted to consider competitive bids. Angry about high industrial electricity rates, the municipal utility gave TVA "years of forewarning" that it wanted to end its fifty-two-year relationship and to seek offers from multiple suppliers. TVA's price proposal turned out to be the very highest of twenty bids. Therefore, Bristol in 1997 signed a contract to purchase electricity for its 15,000 residents from Cinergy of Cincinnati, Ohio, saving the local government $70 million over seven years, double the city's annual budget. TVA responded by secretly trying to sell power directly to Bristol's industrial customers for 2 percent less than the best bid (and well below what it had previously charged or proposed). TVA also promptly imposed a $54-million "stranded-cost" charge for investments the federal agency claimed it made with the expectation that it would continue to supply power to Bristol. Representative Rick Boucher (D-VA), the local congressman, complained that TVA was using illicit tactics "to punish a former customer for exercising its legal right to obtain power from a less expensive supplier. TVA is seeking to make an example of the city of Bristol so as to discourage any other community presently served by TVA from considering the purchase of power from a TVA competitor." At a Boucher-instigated hearing before the House Judiciary Committee, die-hard liberals such as Representatives Barney Frank (D-MA) and John Conyers (D-MI) asserted that TVA's arrogant ways would make "FDR turn over in his grave."[5]

Despite such monopolistic practices, lawmakers from the Southeast perform TVA's bidding, as northwesterners do for Bonneville. Those politicians include the majority leader of the U.S. Senate and most members of the Senate Energy and Natural Resources Committee, providing federal utilities with significant influence over national energy policy. Northwest lawmakers, for instance, snuck a $700-million Bonneville benefit into the fiscal 2003 omnibus appropriation bill. The measure—to provide Bonneville with extra borrowing authority from the U.S. Treasury for transmission line improvements—had been rejected several times by congressional committees. Yet the well-placed Northwest delegation, without the benefit of public hearings or open debate, classified the borrowing measure as "emergency relief" for national defense and homeland security. According to Senator John McCain (R-AZ), that last-minute tactic demonstrated the need for "a top-to-bottom financial and management audit (of Bonneville Power Administration) . . . rather than opening up the federal Treasury and exacerbating another fiscal boondoggle."[6]

Smaller government-owned power companies—municipal utilities and rural co-ops—also fear emerging competition, aware that it makes little sense for public institutions to be in the power business when thousands of private businesses can generate and distribute electricity. Yet munis and co-ops maintain substantial political influence, as evidenced by California and other states exempting government-owned utilities from restructuring laws, as well as by Congress approving billion-dollar bailouts for rural co-operatives stuck with over-budget power plants.

Perhaps public power's greatest obfuscation comes from the co-ops and munis that argue they protect America's rural poor. These government entities fail to mention that they provide taxpayer-financed power to Aspen, Hilton Head, Palo Alto, and numerous other well-to-do enclaves. They do not acknowledge that private utility monopolies serve more farms and small towns than they do. Moreover, they ignore the ways competition and innovative technologies can increase efficiency and improve services in rural areas.

Rather than worry about how to compete in the new marketplace, public power's message—to maintain tax benefits and access to federal electricity—is direct, simple, and, to date, effective. From the perspective of public power managers, any federal restructuring raises the obvious and disturbing question—Shouldn't Congress restructure the government's own utilities as it orders changes for the rest of the electricity industry? To avoid such queries, public power opposes any expansion of federal controls that might disturb its status quo of subsidies without oversight.

Regulators

Public utility commissioners used to have an easy, if complex, job. Before the 1973 energy crisis, they watched electricity demand rise predictably, approved needed power plants to meet that demand, examined intricate financial statements, and periodically nicked electricity rates in order to demonstrate their commitment to consumers. Noting the ability of virtually every American to flick a switch and enjoy light, they performed their jobs well.

Yet regulators are having an identity crisis—what to do when there are no traditional monopolies to regulate. If restructuring accelerates, they may no longer control electricity prices, which would be determined instead by the market. Like the utility monopolies they have overseen, the reactions of regulators vary; some commissioners see competition as the best consumer protection and believe innovative and distributed generators will save money, improve reliability, reduce pollution, and enhance customer service and choice. Yet many state regulators, without admitting fear for their own jobs, advocate caution. They tend to distrust the intrusion of the marketplace's invisible and unpredictable hand, and they abhor virtually any federal oversight. Regulators from the Southeast and Pacific Northwest—which, as noted above, enjoy relatively-low electricity rates, in part because of federally-subsidized utilities—are the most aggressive critics of interconnection standards, transmission coordination rules, or other competition-promoting reforms.

The struggle between state and federal regulators has become increasingly pronounced. Although the days of a utility doing business only within a single state's borders have long passed, most local officials refuse to cede their authority or acknowledge that most electricity is part of interstate commerce and, therefore, primarily in the province of federal regulators.

Environmentalists

Conservation advocates long have criticized utilities for their pollution. Power plants, in fact, account for two-thirds of the nation's sulfur dioxide emissions, one-third of the nitrogen oxides that cause smog, one-third of the carbon dioxide (a greenhouse gas), and one-third of mercury emissions. Environmentalists also have waged an uphill, decades-long fight to have utility monopolies advance efficiency and renewable energy.

Identifying a pollution-reducing electricity policy for the twenty-first century, however, divides conservationists and causes intense (if arcane) rivalries. Most environmentalists, perhaps epitomized by the Natural Resources Defense Council (NRDC), favor regulations over markets since they worry that competition would curtail their ability to promote energy alternatives before government forums. Many conservationists also do not believe competition can spur conservation, rejecting a basic tenet of economics, and, having grown used to regulating centralized power plants, they fear reliance on distributed generation.

A few other conservation groups, notably Environmental Defense, promote market forces to achieve environmental benefits. They argue that accurate price signals, rather than government programs, are the best means to encourage efficiency. Although concerned about dirty diesel generators, these environmentalists support innovative distributed generation, as well as markets for pollution credits.

These debates within the conservation community will continue, but the pendulum is swinging away from government controls and toward market signals. Even one of NRDC's founders, Gus Speth, recently admitted that his group's faith in command-and-control measures was misdirected: "I'd have to say this was the single biggest failure in environmental management—not getting the prices right."[7]

NRDC also has served as an apologist for federal utilities. Below-market rates clearly discourage conservation and stimulate pollution, yet the environmental group staunchly defends the Bonneville Power Administration's subsidies as it encourages BPA to support a very limited number of renewable-energy projects. Despite clear federal restrictions, NRDC staff even use Bonneville's Washington office as a base from which to lobby Congress for additional taxpayer benefits. A few other conservation groups, such as Friends of the Earth and Taxpayers for Common Sense, see a need to reform federal utilities and have them charge market rather than subsidized rates.

Most environmentalists want the government to tilt the energy market toward their preferred technologies of solar, wind, and biomass. They support state and federal Renewable Portfolio Standards (RPS) that would require utilities to obtain a significant percentage of their power from such renewable resources. Seventeen states have adopted mandatory percentages, and nine western governors in June 2004 agreed their region by 2015 would develop 30,000 megawatts of electricity—approximately 15 percent of current demand—from renewable sources. Yet solar energy advocates have encountered strong opposition from Republicans in the House of Representatives who describe an RPS as unfair tinkering with the marketplace (these conservatives, ironically, do not view federal insurance for nuclear reactors as similarly unfair).

The environmental community's myopic focus on Renewable Portfolio Standards reveals its preference for government dictates rather than the removal of market barriers to alternative energy. With a singular attention on solar, wind, and biomass, many conservationists also oppose the recycling of energy that is now vented or wasted. That perspective is shortsighted since solar collectors installed in 2003 produced less than 100 megawatt-years of renewable energy while recycled energy generated nearly 10,000 megawatt-years of clean power and enjoys the potential for an-order-of-magnitude increase.

Consumer Organizations

Consumer groups, like some environmental organizations, exist to battle corporations, and that attitude has led to a preference for government regulations over competitive markets. The Consumer Federation of America for many years even opposed the deregulation of natural gas prices, although that step clearly encouraged producers to find more supplies and consumers to enjoy lower prices.

Ironically, consumer advocates support the go-slow approach of utility monopolies they historically have criticized. Rather than recognize that electricity flows in multistate (rather than localized) markets, they also oppose the Federal Energy Regulatory Commission's efforts to coordinate electricity transmission. And rather than acknowledge that the number of electricity-generating companies long will exceed the number of highly competitive auto manufacturers, they complain that competition may allow power companies to consolidate and obtain market-manipulating power.

Major consumer organizations also are in league with, and depend upon contributions from, public power interests. Instead of seeing reform of federal utilities as a means to save money for all taxpayers, they complain that the fortunate few consumers of subsidized federal power may have to pay slightly more for electricity in a competitive market.

Few consumer organizations, moreover, are trying to help residential consumers aggregate their demand through buying clubs or coops. That role is being taken up slowly by small and mid-sized businesses—such as hotels, restaurants, retailers, gas station dealers—that want to collectively purchase power in order to save money.

Modelers

For the electricity industry to change, it needs clear perspectives on its future. Unfortunately, today's predictions by economists and modelers tend to reflect the status quo and assume that the future will be much like the past. Such projections could be worse than inaccurate because they discourage policymakers from considering laws and regulations that promote innovation and efficiency.

Energy modelers have not been particularly precise. During the 1960s, their projections tended to underestimate future energy growth, by 12 percent according to one examination.[8] Predictions made in the 1970s, in contrast, overestimated energy consumption, by 43 percent according to another study.[9] While more-recent energy-demand projections proved to be fairly accurate, boastful economists largely ignore the fact that they overestimated electricity and petroleum prices by about 25 percent. One would have expected cheaper-than-anticipated energy to cause more consumption. The fact that energy use remained low with relatively low prices suggests, first, that modelers did not account for technological and market changes that kept energy demand in check, and, second, that modelers underestimated the potential within the U.S. market for energy efficiency.

Modelers focus mostly on prices, in part because costs have a clear impact on consumer demand, but also because prices are measurable (and modelers, essentially, are measurers). As a result, the modeling community often ignores the numerous nonprice factors—such as environmental quality, national security, and technological change—that influence energy production and consumption.

Modelers also largely avoid "externalities," such as the medical costs that result from fossil-fuel-fired power plants emitting pollution. Such expenses are more than zero but less than infinite, but most modelers, wanting to avoid uncertainty, stick with zero, an approach that is both unrealistic and distorting.

Models, moreover, sometimes conflict with common sense. One key program used in the United States, for instance, estimates that the use of renewable energy technologies will not grow rapidly even if their price is zero. Although it is hard to understand how free energy would not be popular in the market, such projections limit the review of policy reforms and reinforce the status quo.

Politicians

Republicans and Democrats tend to favor different energy technologies. Most conservatives support "hard" applications such as nuclear reactors and coal-fired power plants, while liberals prefer "soft" measures such as energy conservation and solar, wind, and other renewable resources. Republicans often criticize Renewable Portfolio Standards, but see no contradiction in advancing federal insurance and taxpayer-subsidized research for nuclear power. Democrats, meanwhile, support clean air but most oppose reactors that emit no air pollution.

The political alignments, however, are not always so neat. Those Republicans who emphasize market-based competition express interest in distributed generators and oppose the utility monopolies that retard entrepreneurs. Yet some staunch conservatives, such as Stephen Moore of the Club for Growth, despite blackouts and bankruptcies, suggest the nation's electricity system "seems to be working" and he argues against competition.[10] Meanwhile, some Democrats side with government-owned utility monopolies even though they retard efficiency.

Regionalism, in fact, plays a larger role than party-affiliation in the politics of electricity. The flow of power may not recognize state borders, but politicians do, and Republicans as well as Democrats from the Southeast and Pacific Northwest try desperately to preserve their benefits and block the development of multistate electricity markets. They enjoy the relatively low-cost electricity that results from federally subsidized hydroelectric dams and, in the case of the Tennessee Valley Authority and numerous investor-owned utilities, from dirty coal-fired power plants that have been exempted from strict and expensive pollution controls.

Southerners and northwesterners are winning several policy battles, largely because they fervently fear competition and are organized. Other regions have seen benefits from freer markets, but those gains are dispersed throughout the economy and tend not to garner substantial political support for the effective policies. Consider the restrictions southern and northwestern lawmakers have placed on the Federal Energy Regulatory Commission

(FERC). With its budget threatened, FERC in May 2003 backed away from its so-called Standard Market Design proposal to create regional electricity markets. Offering major concessions to the South and Northwest, federal regulators unveiled a plan that would allow regions to develop their own regulatory designs. Even these concessions, however, were not enough to stall the politicians' march to preserve the status quo, as the northwesterner-dominated Senate Energy Committee approved legislation that would restrict FERC from even considering standardized electricity coordination. The results are fragmented markets and a regulatory hodgepodge that limits power trading.

POLICY BARRIERS

Bringing innovation to the power industry requires a paradigm shift in thinking. More than four generations of Americans have come to accept the notion that electricity is best produced by monopolies at centralized generators. Most take for granted the traditional system in which distant power plants throw away much of their heat, while more fuel is burned elsewhere to produce that same thermal energy. Few appreciate that improved small-engine and turbine technologies have made it more efficient and economical to build dispersed power plants that provide both heat and power to consumers. Although utilities have been protected from market discipline for almost 100 years, few challenge the wildly inaccurate assumption that the United States already has achieved maximum efficiency.

Crafting the rules for an innovation-based electricity market is an uncertain and complex process. The California experience certainly demonstrates that costly consequences can result from good intentions, yet other states have introduced rules that are increasing consumer options and limiting any producer's market power. In essence, they represent experiments at integrating competition and regulation. These ground rules will be tested and revised, causing difficulty for some participants in the electricity industry, but the reforms demonstrate an ongoing effort to restructure an inefficient system based on centralized power plants and regulated monopolies.

The 2003 blackout highlighted the grid's importance, the fact that electricity does not stop at state lines, and the need for better coordination among power transmitters. On that warm August day, PJM Interconnection was one of the rare power coordinators able to isolate most of its grid from the cascading power failure. It may offer a model for a competition-enhancing institution.

Created in 1927 to help mid-Atlantic utilities finance and integrate a fairly large hydroelectric plant, PJM now features an independent board that creates rules and markets for electricity exchanges. PJM, referred to as a "regional transmission organization" (RTO), operates a vast wholesale energy market stretching from New Jersey to West Virginia and northern Illinois. It is the world's largest centralized electricity dispatcher, coordinating the output of 800 power plants and 25,000 miles of transmission lines that serve about 35 million people. Some 300 sellers and buyers of electricity participate in PJM's markets, which have led to increased efficiency, reliability, consumer savings, and investments in the transmission grid.

PJM serves as an independent middle man, enabling generators and consumers to participate in a real-time electricity market. That market—made possible by tools with awkward-sounding names, such as locational marginal pricing, day-ahead and real-time bidding, and security-constrained dispatch—is competitive and nondiscriminatory, and it balances demand and generation to maintain the 60-Hertz frequency required by sensitive motors and computers. According to Phillip Harris, PJM's president, "We don't care if the needed balance is achieved by reducing demand or by increasing supply. Our job is to ensure that generators and consumers have accurate and timely pricing information so they can make informed decisions for themselves."[11]

No doubt independent system operators like PJM can be better platforms for wholesale competition, in part by having the authority to require the construction of new transmission lines in order to mitigate congestion, yet they are necessary for fair and transparent trading. Although centralized, such transmission systems enable distributed generators to link to a grid and buy and sell power. Without such unbiased institutions, a dominant utility would control the transmission lines in order to benefit its own generators and block competitors. As mentioned earlier, the Federal Energy Regulatory Commission is trying to duplicate the PJM model across the country, yet it faces strong opposition from southern and northwest monopolies that want to maintain their exclusive control over power transmission.

Competitive markets also will require the elimination of numerous regulatory, financial, and environmental obstacles to innovation. Consider the following barriers:

- Dominant power companies limit competition by blocking competitors from connecting to the grid, or by imposing obsolete and prohibitively expensive interconnection standards and metering requirements that have no relation to safety.
- States ban the stringing of independent wires across any public street, forcing distributed generators to negotiate with their competitors in order to send power to their customers. Developers can build telephone lines, steam tunnels, and Internet extensions to their neighboring buildings, but stringing their own electric wires across a street, rather than relying on the utility monopoly, would send them directly to jail.
- The balkanization of state electricity regulation fails to appreciate the interstate nature of electricity sales and discourages efficiency and reliability.
- Utility lobbyists have won state regulatory approval to recover most of their investments in power plants and transmission lines that would not survive in a competitive market. These so-called stranded costs are being recovered through either a fee on future electricity sales or a charge to those individuals or businesses exiting the utility's system. High exit fees, as demonstrated by the MIT example, discourage independent generation.
- Fifteen, mostly southern, states prohibit independent sales of electricity to third parties. An entrepreneur, as a result, can install a cogenerator at a chemical plant but cannot sell the resulting electricity to that facility; instead, he must market his power to the local utility.
- Most states allow only the local utility monopoly to supply backup electricity to an independent generator down for maintenance, and regulators have endorsed high backup rates that assume all distributed generators will fail at the same time during periods of peak demand. Since the need for backup power at any given moment is only about 2 percent of total contracted power, these arrangements impose exorbitant rates on competitors. Unlike insurance premiums of only $2 for $1,000 of coverage, utility monopolies essentially get to charge $1,000 per year for a $1,000 life-insurance policy.
- Many consumers can cost-effectively generate some of their own electricity, but monopolists penalize customers who purchase less than all of their power from them.

- Regulated electricity rates average monthly costs and do not send accurate pricing signals to consumers. Regulators, by allowing utilities to pass through all fuel costs to the customers, also provide no incentive for power companies to improve efficiency or install distributed generators.

- Market power abuses can occur when one or two companies own most of the transmission as well as generation facilities in a particular region.

- Depreciation schedules for electricity-generating equipment are, on average, three times longer than those for similar-sized manufacturing equipment. They made sense when a utility monopoly wanted to operate its facilities, whatever the efficiency, for thirty or more years. However, they discourage the introduction of innovative technologies that spur efficiency and productivity.

- Because regulated monopolies obtain a profit on any investment, they have an incentive to build large, expensive, and site-constructed power plants. Such regulation also offers little incentive for utilities to retire those rate-based generators, even when new technologies are more economical, efficient, and environmentally sound.

- The Clean Air Act of 1970 exempted existing electric generating plants from stringent air-pollution rules. More than thirty years later, these "grandfathered" coal-fired facilities keep polluting while emission reductions must be borne by the small subset of new generators. Federal regulations, moreover, fail to recognize that efficient power plants, which emit 20 times less pollution, will curtail the need to generate electricity at dirtier facilities.

- State rules fail to recognize the locational value of generators, even when distributed placements reduce transmission and distribution costs dramatically.

- The U.S. currently measures air emissions based on fuel inputs, usually stated as pounds of pollutants per unit of fuel. Unfortunately, this input-based approach rewards power plants that burn a lot of fuel, regardless of their efficiency. In contrast, output-based regulations would calculate emissions based on the amount of electricity generated, thereby rewarding those innovative generators that supply more electricity but less pollutants.

- Giant utilities continue to reserve most transmission capacity for themselves. Although federal regulations clearly require that all generators enjoy ready access to the electricity grid, most transmission/generation owners give priority to their own customers, which they refer to as their "native load."

Several other countries have systematically eliminated such policy barriers. Portugal, for instance, embraces distributed generation as a means to increase reliability and to avoid the high costs of transmission wires, line losses, and pollution. Denmark, the Netherlands, and Finland advance co-generation and, as a consequence, use half the U.S. average of fuel per kilowatt-hour while they maintain robust industrial economies. Similar policy innovations are needed for the United States to obtain the benefits of technological advances.

10

Innovation-Based Restructuring

The U.S. electricity industry faces numerous uncertainties. The recession during the twenty-first century's early years curtailed power demand and put enormous financial pressure on entrepreneurs and others thinking of entering the power business. Even traditional utilities suffered falling credit quality,[1] and GE Power Systems saw its power-plant-construction orders fall from $24.5 billion in 2001 to $14.2 billion in 2002. Some power executives question if they will make new investments when electricity demand calls for more generators. Yet, as stated by the Federal Energy Regulatory Commission's chairman, "There's a good deal of money to be made, as long as the hometown guys [monopolists] aren't creating a disadvantage. [Electricity] is too important a commodity for people to just sit on the sidelines."[2]

Stressed utilities confront conflicting advice from Wall Street. When power companies in the early twenty-first century abandoned many of their disparate business ventures and declared their intention to "return to basics," an analyst for Fitch Ratings applauded: "Back to basics is a valid strategy that can help utilities maintain a stable rating and cut costs."[3] Yet the managing director of Standard & Poor's declared, "The difficulty in the back-to-basics strategy is how can a company grow and compete for capital against other industries."[4] An analyst for Bernstein & Co. agreed: "[Back-to-basics] is a smokescreen for continued complacency."[5]

The future of power trading is uncertain, although deep-pocketed players began to return to the markets a few years after Enron's failure. Basic trading—when generators sell their excess power on the "spot" market—never lagged. What collapsed after the Enron scandals—some estimates suggest a 70-percent decline—were the speculative bets on long-term electricity prices. Yet several commercial banks (such as Bank of America and Deutsche Bank) and investment banks (such as Goldman Sachs and Morgan Stanley) began in 2003 and 2004 to enter the power trading market, as the locus of activity shifts from Houston to Wall Street. These financial institutions, with stronger balance sheets and higher credit ratings than merchant marketers, are diversifying their commodities-trading operations and selling electricity products, such as wholesale contracts, to buy or sell power at certain prices at specific times. Merrill Lynch, for instance, spent approximately $1 billion to purchase Entergy-Koch Trading, and other financial giants are buying generators that sell power under long-term contracts.

Another unknown is public policy. The nation's power industry teeters between regulation and competition, not yet abandoning the era of monopolies and not yet embracing innovation and entrepreneurs. The result, as evidenced by the 2003 blackout, is instability. "We sit here today on this fault line, not clear how we move off of it or when we move off of it," observed James Rogers, chairman of Cinergy Corporation, a large Ohio-based utility.[6] No one suggests that electricity competition will eliminate regulation since government overseers still will need to enforce market rules and protect against abuses, yet rebalancing the mix of competition and regulation requires numerous experiments.

Utility oversight is split between the federal government and states, creating a regulatory fragmentation that makes it difficult to create a uniform market across the United States, thereby impeding development of the electric infrastructure. According to one study, "Unlike the European marketplace, which is moving rapidly towards a common vision of customer choice and competitive markets, the U.S. is caught in a position of indecision between the desire to revert to vertically-integrated markets and the reality that in many regions the market has already evolved too far to go back."[7]

Even state-based markets are not created equal. As evidenced by California's experience, single-price, bid-based schemes offer lucrative opportunities for large electricity suppliers to "game" the system. Texas, in contrast, curtails the ability of a few generators to abuse their power, and it allows customers equal opportunity to participate in the market as generators.

Since utilities long have been regulated locally, opportunities to deploy innovative technologies vary from state to state. Maine for about twenty-five years has adopted policies friendly to distributed generation, resulting in a recycled energy use of almost thirteen times the national average. Other progressive states include Delaware, Alabama, and Vermont. However, six states—including Alaska, Kansas, Missouri, Nevada, Utah, and Wyoming—have favored utility monopolies and centralized power plants, and they feature no recycled power.

Oversight of the electricity industry also may be shifting from regulators to judges as market transactions replace direct regulation. Although rules for the emerging market are being made by contracts and interpreted by courts, the law and its precedents are fuzzy even on the basic issue of whether electricity is a "good" governed by the Uniform Commercial Code or a "service" ruled by common law precedent. According to Steven Ferrey, professor of law at Suffolk University, "With a fundamental shift across the country from government-regulated, electric power monopolies to restructured, competitive markets, whether electricity is a good or service will determine both the legal rules by which the markets must operate and the outcome of the plethora of pending disputes. The multibillion-dollar stakes of this choice of law are high."[8]

The electricity industry also faces several environmental uncertainties, the greatest of which relates to carbon dioxide. Any attempt to minimize emissions in order to reduce the threat of global warming must focus particular attention on utilities, the largest emitters of the gas. According to Granger Morgan of Carnegie Mellon University, carbon dioxide is the "900-pound gorilla" that threatens the electricity industry's status quo.[9] Climate change could impose severe strains on the power market. One heat-belt utility concluded that each increased Fahrenheit degree in average temperature requires it to add 300 megawatts of generating capacity.

Strict limits on carbon dioxide emissions, meanwhile, could require a shift away from the burning of coal to generate electricity, yet they also could advance an emerging industry that captures and sequesters carbon from coal in order to produce hydrogen. A coal gasification plant in the Dakotas already sends hydrogen gas to Canada, and pipelines from New Mexico deliver hydrogen to oil-drilling operations in Oklahoma and Texas, where the gas is pumped into the ground to accelerate petroleum recovery. ExxonMobil is funding a hydrogen research effort at Stanford University, and BP is doing something similar at Princeton. If these large chemical companies become major producers of valuable hydrogen, they could sell the clean-burning gas to conventional utilities or they could use their hydrogen to enter the electricity business, becoming strong competitors among today's players.

The not-in-my-backyard (NIMBY) factor also confronts companies wanting to build transmission lines or liquefied-natural-gas ports. Proposals for high-voltage wires often provoke heated reactions from homeowners worried about falling property values and illnesses caused by electromagnetism. Transmission-line developers, moreover, can no longer rely on favorable state regulation since the federal government now oversees transmission wires used for wholesale trading.

Another uncertainty is the capability of electricity industry managers. For most of the twentieth century, utility executives dealt with predictable power demands and subsequently built bigger power plants and lines. The nation's most talented engineers went into other fields, believing electricity offered few challenges or rewards. Most U.S. engineering colleges shifted their curriculum to computers, and few now even teach the fundamentals of power generation and transmission. Engineers who remained within utility monopolies were unprepared for the shattered momentum that began in the 1960s, and they now face fresh competition from a new generation of entrepreneurs building small-scale and efficient generators.

Yet perhaps the industry's greatest unknown is the future state of technology. For the first time in almost a century, an array of innovations are changing the industry's basic and fundamental arrangements. New devices include solid-state electronics that control the flow of power to end-use devices; highly efficient generators and motors; advanced sensor, communication, and computation technologies that allow greater flexibility in control and metering; high-temperature superconductivity that enables virtually "lossless" transmission; efficient long-term storage technologies; short-term capacity to avoid surges; fuel cells that convert hydrogen into electricity; low-cost renewable electricity; and gasification. Several of these technologies are on the market, while others remain under development. Some allow for more effective use of the grid, some reduce the emissions of air pollutants and greenhouse gases, and some promise greater systemwide efficiency.

The interplay of advanced technologies and innovation-based policies could take the power industry down divergent paths. Clarity on the dominant trends may be a few decades away, and the intervening years may witness numerous regional experiments. The Dutch, for instance, are advancing distributed generation. Iceland is moving toward a hydrogen-based economy. Northeastern U.S. states are considering a trading program for carbon-dioxide emissions, while Texas is becoming the nation's wind-energy capital.

Differing paths notwithstanding, one of the most likely trends favors dispersed over centralized generation. Most of today's technological innovations suggest a continuing shift away from an electricity system based on giant generators linked to customers by a vast transmission and distribution network. More promising is a system that moves toward a grid that links decentralized turbines, cogenerators, energy recyclers, fuel cells, or renewable technologies. In fact, the scale of electricity generation has been changing dramatically. Over the past two decades, after large power plants lost their economies of scale, the trend has been toward smaller units that can be sized more readily and economically to meet a particular need.

Localized power avoids or reduces distribution bottlenecks and curtails the need for massive investments in high-voltage (and unpopular) transmission lines. Some 10 percent of electricity is sacrificed during the typical long-distance transmission process as a result of heat and resistance. During peak hours, the number rises to 20 percent, meaning that congestion-related losses require the construction of extra generators and lines. Such costs would shrink if electricity producers were close to power consumers.

Terrorist attacks, harsh weather, and simple accidents have highlighted the vulnerability of the centralized power system with its large power plants and far-flung transmission wires. Smaller, dispersed units, in contrast, provide more security and resiliency. To state the obvious, a destroyed micro-generator has smaller impacts than damage to a nuclear reactor or high-voltage line. Centralization's vulnerability was revealed clearly in January 2002 when a failed wire from Brazil's giant Itaipu hydroelectric dam cut the nation's electricity supply by 18 percent and darkened six major cities in five states.

Distributed generators can provide the highly reliable and high-quality power demanded increasingly by the array of businesses that cannot afford energy disruptions. On-site units also can avoid most power outages and surges that result from problems with the grid, as evidenced by Kodak's factory continuing to operate during the massive 2003 blackout.

Small-scale diesel generators long have been used to provide backup power at hospitals, schools, and other institutions, and the Federal Aviation Administration relies on almost 3,000 units for emergency power at its air traffic control centers. Diesel proponents note that the 40,000 megawatts now available increase the electricity system's reliability. When mounted on tractor trailers, these power-plants-on-wheels also can respond effectively to hurricanes and other emergencies. Diesel generators, however, are far less efficient and spew far more pollutants than modern gas-fired turbines. According to the Regulatory Assistance Project, "It is important for state and federal environmental regulators to address the need for efficiency and emission standards for small-scale power plants before the rapid proliferation of the less efficient, more polluting technologies creates a serious and unexpected new source of air pollution."[10]

Perhaps decentralization's key benefits are financial. Smaller modules, put simply, are less risky economically because they take less time to devise and construct, obtain greater efficiencies, enjoy portability, and face reduced vulnerability to fuel shortages and price volatility. Small generators, which can be built in increments that match a changing electricity demand, allow for more reliable planning. Large units, in contrast, take a dozen years to complete, during which time forecasts can alter dramatically, perhaps eliminating or reducing the need for the investment. Big plants also invariably "overshoot" because they add huge supplies that remain idle until the expected demand "catches up."

Even fervent distributed-generation advocates do not envision the total abandonment of today's centralized generators or long-distance transmission lines. Their goal is a more equal hybrid of central power and distributed energy. Compared to the present system's virtually total reliance on large plants and long lines, a mixed approach would provide substantial economic, environmental, and security benefits. The American Gas Association forecasts that small distributed generators by 2020 will account for 20 percent of the nation's new electric capacity.

Although the U.S. market for distributed generation is substantial, perhaps the greatest potential is with the world's 3 billion poor people who have no reliable access to electricity. On-site generators, as noted before, can save the $1,500 per kilowatt that developing countries would be required to spend on transmission lines. They could allow those nations to leapfrog the power grid, eliminating the need to build an expensive system based on giant generators and high-voltage wires, much the way that some countries are using cell phone technology to leapfrog the need to string expensive telephone landlines. If electricity consumption in developing countries continues to rise rapidly, dispersed technologies—such as efficient turbines, recycled energy, wind turbines, and fuel cells—also may be the best means to minimize carbon dioxide emissions and limit demand for oil and natural gas from the world's volatile regions.

INNOVATION

Sustaining innovation is critical if nations are to achieve economic growth and raise their standards of living. Most people would say they can recognize innovation when they see it, yet such advances are difficult to measure. By using proxies, economists estimate that technological modernization provides strong rates of return—on the order of 20 to 30 percent for firms, and more than 50 percent for the country as a whole.[11] While rewards can be generous, innovation demands both technical and financial risks, as evidenced by the fact that most developments never reach the market. According to one analysis, "Competition is a harsh taskmaster for inventions, but it has been proven repeatedly to be superior to command-and-control economic regimes at rewarding innovation and encouraging entrepreneurship."[12]

Competition alone, of course, does not generate innovation. Modernization requires an interplay of several factors, including entrepreneurial traditions; first-class schools, universities, and research centers; well-developed angel and venture capital sectors; and market systems.

Some industries—including electricity and natural gas—long were assumed to be natural monopolies because competitive firms could not afford the enormous capital investments associated with wires and pipelines. Of course, parts of those energy systems—such as electricity generators—never needed to be controlled by a single provider. Other industries—such as airlines and freight—never fit the natural-monopoly model, but they were deemed too important to be left to the machinations of competition and the threat that some customers could complain about inadequate service.

Monopolies provided neither innovation nor efficiency, and even limited competition has tended to reduce costs and improve services in formerly regulated industries, including air travel, trucking, rail, long-distance telecommunications, and British electricity. For example, the curtailment of regulation quickly prompted airline fares to drop 15–22 percent and telecommunication rates to fall 30 percent (tellingly, local phone rates, which remained under monopoly regulation, rose by the same amount). Other impacts have varied by industry, but competition clearly leads to improved productivity and the introduction of multifunctional technologies, with the explosion of telecommunication choices beyond the ubiquitous black rotary phone being the classic example.[13]

Congress restructured the airline industry in 1978, and the initial impacts were dramatic—within a little more than a decade, ticket prices fell 15–22 percent, the number of airline competitors increased from forty-three to seventy-six, and the industry share controlled by the top five carriers dropped from 69 percent to 57 percent. Restructuring prompted several innovations, included the refinement of a hub-and-spoke system that allowed airlines to increase their loads and expand their flight frequencies, as well as computerized reservation-and-ticketing systems that boosted consumer benefits. Price-conscious airlines also demanded more efficient turbines, which inadvertently sparked dramatic changes in the electricity industry.

Government had overseen freight railroads since 1887, when Congress tried to rein in the power of shippers over American farms and businesses. By the 1950s, however, regulation was stifling the railroad industry, and several lines declared bankruptcy. Lawmakers in 1980 finally endorsed deregulation with the Staggers Rail Act. A similar progression occurred within the trucking industry, which was deregulated with the Motor Carrier Act of 1980. According to the Brookings Institution, these restructurings provided some $20 billion of annual benefits to both shippers and customers.[14] Innovation also abounded as the entire freight transport system became more intermodal, with airlines and railroads increasingly carrying containers that were offloaded onto trucks near their final destinations. This trend increased transportation efficiency and revolutionized the business of mail and package delivery.

Although much of the telecommunications industry remains regulated, competition has advanced over the past three decades. The federal court's 1968 "Carterfone" antitrust decision offered the first major blow to AT&T's monopoly, allowing the connection of non-AT&T equipment to the public network. The 1982 "Consent Decree" divested AT&T of its regional Bell operating companies and helped to open the long-distance telecommunications market to competitors. The subsequent deployment of new hardware and services—including digital switches and wireless telephones—has been striking. Consider that messages now can travel by airwaves, cable, fiber optics, microwave, as well as traditional copper wires. The cost of sending a unit of data has plummeted to less than 10 percent of its price when a monopoly controlled the market.

Competition also altered Britain's government-owned utility monopolies. Part of the privatization effort, admittedly, resulted from the Thatcher administration's desire to break the power of the National Union of Mineworkers, which had clashed for years against conservative politicians. Still, competitive power companies in the early 1990s quickly shed costs, cutting employment from more than 130,000 to less than 90,000[15]; slashed wholesale power rates by a third; and introduced new service innovations, such as hedged contracts. In the decade after reforms began, Britain's electricity industry displaced coal-fired generators with scores of combined-cycle, natural-gas-powered turbines, reducing pollution substantially. Similar restructuring efforts in other developed countries, according to the International Energy Agency, "have generally delivered their expected benefits," and they promise more significant gains over the long-term.[16]

What do these case studies suggest for competition within the U.S. electricity industry? Many monopolists and other opponents of utility restructuring argue that electricity is different, that it is a necessity of life and not just another commodity, and that it is one of the few products that cannot be easily stored. They argue that this vital resource should not be subjected to market forces. Yet numerous other items and services—including food, banking, interstate trucking, and telecommunications—can be considered vital to modern life and they are provided effectively by competitive businesses rather than government-regulated monopolies.

Chapter 3 traced the U.S. electricity industry's early evolution from chaotic competitors to regulated monopolies. Although initial competition sparked technological and business revolutions, the unregulated power market in the late nineteenth century began to show strains. A customer moving across the street, for instance, often found that his appliances no longer worked. Electricity entrepreneurs eventually began to merge and consolidate, as well as develop questionable relationships with local officials. Georgia, New York, and Wisconsin responded to these concerns in 1907 by establishing public service commissions that began to regulate electric utilities. Twenty more states quickly followed, and power companies became integrated monopolies—generating, transmitting, and distributing electricity to consumers in their exclusive service territories. For much of the twentieth century, these utilities provided reliable power in exchange for guaranteed profits on their investments.

Sam Insull argued that monopolies made sense in a maturing electricity industry since only a single company could afford to pay for a community's expensive generators and wires. State officials decided to regulate utilities in order, at least in theory, to capture the low costs available only to the monopolist as well as to control unfair pricing behavior.

Yet utility monopolies proved to be sluggish. According to one analyst, the lack of competition "causes an industry to accumulate substantial managerial slack—that is, firms do not minimize the cost of producing a given level of output."[17] Cushioned from external change, regulated utilities reacted more slowly and less effectively than companies facing competition. When OPEC raised oil prices in the 1970s, for instance, power monopolies simply passed on the higher energy prices to consumers rather than advance efficiency measures or alternative technologies that would reduce their costs.

Regulated utilities, moreover, displayed little innovation. The power industry's R&D intensity—its research-and-development expenditures as a percentage of net sales—is meager, only 0.2 percent and declining, compared to an all-industry average of 3.4 percent.[18] Most recent electricity-related advances, including combined-cycle generators and microturbines, occurred within the machinery industry, which has an R&D intensity of over 5 percent.

Regulated utilities also suffered stagnant efficiency. The industry's percentage of electricity obtained from each unit of fuel rose from below 10 percent as the twentieth century began to only 33 percent in the mid-1950s. Yet there's been no further improvement. A five-decade lull in efficiency is remarkable compared to the substantial advances associated with the computer, telecommunications, and other innovative industries.

A research study of Ohio's electric utilities concluded that regulation retards technological modernization. The analysts found that monopolies fail to implement their capital and production systems effectively.[19] Investment analyst Hugh Holman was even more blunt. "After decades of regulatory protection, the utility industry operates from a moribund technology base," he declared. "Competition will create incentives for innovation, leading potentially to a total reshaping of the industry's technology base."[20]

Competition, of course, cannot guarantee wonders. While it often attracts a wave of new entrants into an industry, that free-for-all period can be followed by an era of consolidation. Another sobering consequence is that cost-conscious competitive firms often reduce, at least initially, their research and development expenditures. Restructuring also may lead to the rapid introduction of new technologies, usually the result of a pent-up demand, but it may not portend ongoing innovation.

Markets tend to particularly benefit large consumers who have the resources to look and bargain for good prices. At its worst, competition is blind to the plight of poor families who spend up to one-quarter of their income on energy. An estimated 30 million American households during the winter months must choose between food and fuel, and every year dozens of older people die from hypothermia, largely because they cannot afford power. The federal government's Low Income Home Energy Assistance Program (LIHEAP) provides almost $2 billion annually to supplement the fuel bills of poor families, but even at that level the initiative can help only 12 percent of those eligible for assistance.

The market, moreover, does not address "externalities" and noneconomic factors. To obtain foreign oil, for instance, the government invests billions of dollars in armaments that protect fragile oil-supply lines, yet energy prices do not reflect these costs; instead, they are hidden in the form of higher taxes. A rational national defense strategy would view investments in efficiency and power innovations as alternatives to money spent on fighter jets, submarines, and troops. Electricity's market price, moreover, does not include the health expenses associated with pollution from power plants.

A skewed market, as demonstrated in California, also can enable a single firm, or even a small set of firms, to manipulate prices. Other abuses in the 1930s prompted lawmakers to approve the Public Utility Holding Company Act (PUHCA) and limit a power company's size and scope. A growing number of industry executives and experts argue that PUHCA is outmoded and, worse, stifles needed investment in generators and wires. Famed financier Warren Buffet, for instance, claims he would commit billions of dollars to the electricity industry—above the $5.1 billion he spent in May 2005 to purchase Oregon-based PacifiCorp—were it not for PUHCA's restrictions. Yet a report by Standard & Poor's argues that the law is needed to stop market abuses at least until real electricity competition is assured throughout the country. "PUHCA has prohibited investors such as Berkshire Hathaway from investing in more than one utility," concluded that study, but the law "also prevented Enron Corp. and AES Corp. from owning more than one U.S. electric utility."[21]

Competition certainly increases risk. While regulated monopolies are virtually guaranteed a set profit, market-dependent firms face highly volatile costs. During the 2003 summer, peak power prices in one region swung from a low of $14.26 per megawatt-hour to a high of $64.58. To manage that risk, electricity generators and traders are devising several financial instruments, which have such strange names as exchange-based futures and options, ISO-based financial transmission rights, and over-the-counter derivatives. Although electricity markets are less robust than the risk-management opportunities within the deregulated natural-gas industry, NYMEX recently offered a futures market for power sold within the PJM interchange and other exchanges are matching buyers and sellers of electricity swaps, options, and other futures-like instruments.

Despite competition's shortcomings, the market enjoys substantial advantages over regulated monopolies. According to researchers at the Brookings Institution and George Mason University, industry restructurings have generated cost savings and technological innovations in the natural gas, trucking, railroad, airline, and long-distance telecommunications businesses. "In virtually every case," they concluded, "the economic benefits from deregulation or regulatory reform have exceeded economists' predictions."[22]

Consider again the competition-sparked innovations in the telecommunications market. Within a relatively short period, consumer options increased from a black rotary phone to cellular, call waiting, voice mail, paging, long-distance commerce, and video conferencing. Similar consumer gains could occur in the electricity industry.

While the Enron and California debacles obtained notoriety, Pennsylvania officials calculate that their state's partially competitive market has spurred the development of district-heating systems and windmills, and saved residential and industrial customers approximately $8 billion. One study found that states with restructured utilities benefited from increased power supplies and lower rates. "Deregulating jurisdictions have attracted more new generation supply than non-reformers," concluded the 2004 report, "with 80 percent faster per-capita growth in the U.S. over the latest five years." Addressing electricity prices, the survey stated that "retail residential prices for

U.S. state reformers dropped 80 percent faster than non-reformers over the latest five years, and non-residential prices dropped 65 percent faster."[23]

Other countries are proceeding to competition rapidly. Noting that electricity restructuring will continue to be a force worldwide, another survey concluded: "The European Union plans to bring retail choice to all customers over the next few years, and full retail customer choice with the equivalent of [Independent System Operators] has been in effect in Australia, New Zealand, and Britain for a number of years. Other countries, such as Chile and the Nordic countries of Norway and Sweden, have operated competitive generation markets for over a decade. And the Canadian provinces of Alberta and Ontario have implemented competitive markets."[24]

CONCLUSION

Electricity—which provides flexibility, convenience, and controllability—holds enormous promise. This precious energy source altered our landscape and lives, and electrotechnologies have revolutionized the flow of information, the processing of steel, and the construction of automobiles. Modern electricity-powered applications offer even greater precision and reliability; higher quality, portability, and modularity; enhanced speed and control; expanded productivity and consumer options; and "smarter" and miniaturized designs. Yet innovations in electricity generation and delivery hold enormous promise only if they are not blocked from the marketplace.

Available and affordable technologies—if combined with barrier-busting policies—could double the U.S. electric system's efficiency; cut the generation of pollutants and greenhouse gases; increase reliability and economic development; stimulate new conveniences; spawn a multibillion-dollar export industry; bring power to millions of the world's poor; and reduce consumer costs.

Just the environmental benefits alone are enormous since power plants spew almost half of all North American industrial air pollutants, and forty-six of the top fifty emitters are electricity generators. In contrast, new gas turbines emit 500 times less nitrogen oxide per kilowatt-hour than today's older power plants, and modern refrigerators use only 10 percent of the electricity consumed by a unit built in 1975.

Businesses increasingly realize they need more reliable power than the status quo can provide. Hewlett-Packard estimates that a fifteen-minute outage at one of its chip manufacturing facilities would cost $30 million, or half the plant's annual power budget. According to a microchip executive, "My local utility tells me they only had 20 minutes of outages all year. I remind them that these four five-minute episodes interrupted my process, shut down and burnt out some of my controls, idled my workforce. I had to call in my control service firm, call in my computer repair firm, direct my employees to 'test' the system. They cost me eight days and millions of dollars."[25] No wonder more and more corporations are installing their own on-site generators in order to control costs and increase security. The First National Bank of Omaha, for instance, purchased stacks of fuel cells after the local utility's one-hour power outage shut down its data processing network at a cost of $6 million.

Many developed countries have promoted competitors over monopolists, and they are enjoying numerous benefits. In the four years since Australia began its utility deregulation, wholesale power prices fell 32 percent in real terms, and air quality improved. Six years after the United Kingdom began to deregulate electricity sales and to shift from coal to natural gas, carbon dioxide emissions from power generation fell 39 percent and nitrogen oxides 51 percent. Even limited competition in the United States since the Public Utility Regulatory Policies Act of 1968 helped prompt a 32-percent drop in wholesale electricity prices.

Unless we alter today's centralized and monopolized paradigm, when the rest of the world electrifies and begins to enjoy the drudgery-reducing benefits of modern appliances, the resulting environmental damage will be staggering. We have a moral obligation, therefore, both to provide power to the world's poor and to radically alter the ways electricity is generated and delivered.

Timing is critical if the United States is to capture additional economic and environmental benefits. In the next several years, much of the nation's aging electrical, mechanical, and thermal infrastructure will need to be replaced, offering a unique opportunity to substitute efficient generators for outmoded power plants and old industrial boilers.

Yet electricity remains the most politicized energy source, as evidenced by the numerous subsidies and regulations that temper its supply and demand. Utility managers argue that state regulators approve dangerously low returns on utility investments, but consumer advocates maintain rates are too high. Power executives criticize regulators for delaying the construction of new power plants and lines, while environmentalists think too many facilities are being licensed. Entrepreneurs complain monopolists block innovative technologies. Tax experts say federal subsidies encourage outmoded systems and waste precious resources. In short, political confrontation surrounds most aspects of electricity production and delivery. That fact alone highlights the need for a more market-based, efficient, and innovative system.

The industry that supplies electricity is changing. Once dominated by integrated monopolies, the generation of power has become increasingly competitive as entrepreneurs deploying innovative technologies offer lower-cost and more-reliable electricity. Independent power companies now provide almost one-third of the nation's electricity, up from only 1.7 percent in 1993.[26] From another perspective, the wholesale exchanges by non-utilities soared from 40 million kilowatt-hours in 1986 to 259 million kilowatt-hours in 1998, for an average annual growth rate of 16.8 percent.[27]

The major struggle within the electricity market over most of the past century pitted public against private monopolies. The battles once waged by George Norris and Sam Insull continue today, yet a more significant struggle has emerged between competitors and monopolists, where entrepreneurs promoting an open market face stiff opposition from both public and private utilities. The issue is no longer whether the nation's interest is better served by profit-seeking monopolies or by government-owned monopolies. Today's debate is about what balance of competition and regulation will deliver more consumer choices, cost savings, environmental sustainability, and reliable electrical service.

Maintaining the status quo is no longer an option, in part because the current monopoly-based structure has forced Americans to spend far more than needed on outmoded and polluting energy services. Achieving the benefits of innovation requires the elimination of numerous regulatory, financial, and legal barriers. If federal and state lawmakers can restructure the electricity industry based on the principles of technology modernization, market efficiency, and consumer choice, they will bring about immense benefits for both the economy and the environment.

Notes

CHAPTER 1: AN INDUSTRY IN TRANSITION

1. Walt Patterson, *Transforming Electricity* (London: Earthscan Publications, Ltd., 1999).

2. International Energy Agency, *2002 World Energy Outlook Reference Case* (Paris: IEA, 2002).

3. Thomas R. Casten, "Presidential Campaign Energy Policy Thoughts," July 11, 2004 (unpublished paper).

4. Electric Power Research Institute Consortium for Electric Infrastructure to Support a Digital Society, *The Cost of Power Disturbances to Industrial & Digital Economy Companies* (Palo Alto, CA: EPRI, June 2001).

CHAPTER 2: EARLY COMPETITION

1. Carl Van Doren, *Benjamin Franklin* (New York: Viking Press, 1938).

2. Matthew Josephson, *Edison: A Biography* (New York: McGraw-Hill, 1959).

3. Paul Israel, *Edison: A Life of Invention* (New York: Wiley, 2000).

4. Blaine McCormick, *At Work with Thomas Edison* (Irvine, CA: Entrepreneur Press, 2001).

5. Israel, *Edison*.

6. Robert Friedel and Paul Israel with Bernard S. Finn, *Edison's Electric Light: Biography of an Invention* (New Brunswick, NJ: Rutgers University Press, 1986).

7. Jill Jonnes, *Empires of Light* (New York: Random House, 2003).

8. Robert Conot, *A Streak of Luck* (New York: Seaview Books, 1979).

9. Israel, *Edison.*

10. Ibid.

11. Ibid.

12. Francis Jehl, *Menlo Park Remembrances* (Dearborn, MI: Edison Institute, 1937).

13. Memo from Samuel Insull in response to questions from Mr. Martin. Insull Collection at Loyola University, Chicago.

14. Friedel and Israel with Finn, *Edison's Electric Light.*

15. Charles Batchelor's technical notes, October 27, 1889, Thomas Edison Papers at www.edison.rutgers.edu

16. Harold Evans, *They Made America: Two Centuries of Innovators from the Steam Engine to the Search Engine* (Boston: Little, Brown, 2004).

17. *New York Herald*, December 21, 1879.

18. Conot, *A Streak of Luck.*

19. *New York Herald*, January 1, 1880.

20. Edison diary entry, July 12, 1885. Thomas A. Edison Papers at www.edison.rutgers.edu

21. Friedel and Israel with Finn, *Edison's Electric Light.*

22. Robert Silverberg, *Light for the World* (Princeton: D. Van Nostrand, 1967).

23. Conot, *A Streak of Luck.*

24. "Moonlight on Broadway," *New York Evening Post*, December 21, 1880.

25. Josephson, *Edison: A Biography.*

26. Steve Silberman, "The Energy Web," *Wired*, July 2001, quoting Elbert Hubbard.

27. Thomas R. Casten, *Power Failure* (August 1, 2001 draft).

28. Silverberg, *Light for the World.*

29. Ibid.

30. Ibid.

31. Ibid.

32. Conot, *A Streak of Luck.*

33. Silverberg, *Light for the World.*

34. Conot, *A Streak of Luck.*

35. Israel, *Edison: A Life of Invention.*

36. Silverberg, *Light for the World.*

37. Josephson, *Edison: A Biography.*

38. Silverberg, *Light for the World.*

39. Letter from George Westinghouse to Thomas Edison dated June 7, 1888. Thomas A. Edison Papers at www.edison.rutgers.edu

40. Letter from Thomas Edison to George Westinghouse dated June 12, 1888. Thomas A. Edison Papers at www.edison.rutgers.edu

41. Terry S. Reynolds and Theodore Bernstein, "Edison and 'the Chair,' " *IEEE Technology & Society*, March 1989.

42. Jonnes, *Empires of Light*.

43. "Mr. Brown's Rejoiner, Electrical Dog Killing," *Electrical Engineer*, August 1888.

44. "Surer Than the Rope," *New York Times*, December 6, 1888.

45. "Far Worse Than Hanging," *New York Times*, August 7, 1890.

46. George Westinghouse, Jr., "A Reply to Mr. Edison," *North American Review*, November 1889.

47. Josephson, *Edison: A Biography*.

48. Forrest McDonald, *Insull* (Chicago: University of Chicago Press, 1962).

49. Conot, *A Streak of Luck*.

50. McDonald, *Insull*.

51. Francis E. Leupp, *George Westinghouse: His Life and Achievements* (Boston: Little, Brown, 1918).

52. Henry G. Prout, *A Life of George Westinghouse* (New York: Scribner's, 1926).

53. Ibid.

54. "World's Fair Doings," *Daily Interocean*, May 24, 1892.

55. Harold C. Passer, *The Electrical Manufacturers, 1875–1900: A Study in Competition, Entrepreneurship, Technical Change, and Economic Growth* (Cambridge: Harvard University Press, 1953).

56. "World's Fair Doings," *Daily Interocean*, May 17, 1892.

57. J. P. Barrett, "Electricity," in G. R. Davis, *World's Columbian Exposition* (Chicago: Elliott Beezley, 1893).

58. Jonnes, *Empires of Light*.

59. John J. O'Neill, *Prodigal Genius: The Life of Nikola Tesla* (New York: David McKay, 1944).

60. Ibid.

61. *New York Times*, July 16, 1895.

62. *New York Times*, October 19, 1931.

63. John J. O'Neill, *Prodigal Genius: The Life of Nikola Tesla* (New York: McKay, 1944).

64. Nikola Tesla, *My Inventions: The Autobiography of Nikola Tesla* (Williston, VT: Hart Bros., 1982).

65. O'Neill, *Prodigal Genius*.

66. Inez Hunt and Wanetta Draper, *Lightning in His Hand: The Story of Nikola Tesla* (Denver: Sage Books, 1974).

67. Nikola Tesla, "My Inventions," *Electrical Experimenter*, February 1919.

68. *New York Herald*, 1897.

69. Margaret Cheney and Robert Uth, *Tesla: Master of Lighting* (New York: Metro Books, 1999).

70. O'Neill, *Prodigal Genius*.

71. Nikola Tesla, "The Problem of Increasing Human Energy," *Century Magazine*, July 1900.

72. Cheney and Uth, *Tesla: Master of Lighting*.

73. Prout, *A Life of George Westinghouse*.

74. *New York Times*, July 16, 1895.

75. H. G. Wells, "The End of Niagara," *Harper's Weekly*, July 21, 1906.

76. Merrill Denison, *Niagara's Pioneers* (Buffalo: Niagara Mohawk Power Corp., 1953).

CHAPTER 3: MONOPOLISTS

1. Forrest McDonald, *Insull* (Chicago: University of Chicago Press, 1962).

2. Ibid.

3. Burton Berry, "Mr. Samuel Insull," Insull Collection at Loyola University Chicago (unpublished, but copyrighted in 1962 by Samuel Insull, Jr.).

4. McDonald, *Insull*.

5. Harold Platt, *The Electric City: Energy and the Growth of the Chicago Area* (Chicago: University of Chicago Press, 1991).

6. Samuel Insull's undated memo in response to questions from Mr. Martin. Insull Collection at Loyola University Chicago.

7. McDonald, *Insull*.

8. Robert Silverberg, *Light for the World* (Princeton: D. Van Nostrand, 1967).

9. Samuel Insull's undated memo in response to questions from Mr. Martin. Insull Collection at Loyola University Chicago.

10. McDonald, *Insull*.

11. Ibid.

12. "Proceedings," National Electric Light Association, 1898.

13. Address given by Samuel Insull to the NELA convention in Chicago on June 4, 1913. Printed as "Broad Questions of Public Policy," in William E. Keily, ed., *Central-Station Electric Service, Its Commercial Development and Economic Significance as Set Forth in the Public Addresses (1897–1914) of Samuel Insull* (Chicago: privately printed, 1915).

14. Richard F. Hirsh, *Power Loss* (Cambridge: Massachusetts Institute of Technology, 1999).

15. McDonald, *Insull*.

16. M. L. Ramsay, *Pyramids of Power: The Story of Roosevelt, Insull, and the Utility Wars* (New York: Bobbs-Merrill, 1937).

17. George W. Norris, *Fighting Liberal: The Autobiography of George W. Norris* (New York: Macmillan, 1945).

18. Ibid.

19. *Chicago American*, November 3, 1934.

20. Burton V. Berry, "Mr. Samuel Insull," 62-page manuscript written after the author and Insull sailed together in April–May 1934 from Europe to Chicago. Available at Insull Collection, Loyola University Chicago.

21. Ibid.

22. Federal Trade Commission, *Utility Corporations* (Senate Document 92, 70th Congress, 1st Session, 1928).

23. Ramsay, *Pyramids of Power*.

24. T. J. Brennan et al., *A Shock to the System: Restructuring America's Electricity Industry* (Washington, DC: Resources for the Future, July 1996).

25. Berry, "Mr. Samuel Insull."

26. McDonald, *Insull*.

27. "Insull Owns Full Story: Puts Courtroom in Tears!," *Chicago Herald Examiner*, November 2, 1934. "Insull Takes Entire Blame," *Chicago American*, November 1, 1934.

28. Norris, *Fighting Liberal*.

29. Ibid.

30. Ramsay, *Pyramids of Power*.

31. Ibid.

32. Norris, *Fighting Liberal*.

33. Ramsay, *Pyramids of Power*.

34. Norris, *Fighting Liberal*.

35. Alfred Lief, *Democracy's Norris* (New York: Stockpole Sons, 1939).

36. Ramsay, *Pyramids of Power*.

37. Ibid.

38. Federal Trade Commission, *Utility Corporations*.

39. Ramsay, *Pyramids of Power*.

40. Norris, *Fighting Liberal*.

41. Ibid.

42. Ibid.

43. Ibid.

44. Ibid.

45. Ramsay, *Pyramids of Power*.

46. Ibid.

47. Stephen E. Ambrose, *Eisenhower* (New York: Simon and Schuster, 1991).

48. Edwin Vennard, *Government in the Power Business* (New York: McGraw-Hill, 1968).

49. "Freedom Is Not Lost by Guns Alone," advertisement in photographic collection of the National Rural Electric Cooperative Association.

50. David E. Nye, *Electrifying America: Social Meanings of a New Technology, 1880–1940* (Cambridge: MIT Press, 1990).

CHAPTER 4: THE GOLDEN ERA AND SHATTERED MOMENTUM

1. John Anderson Miller, *At the Touch of a Button* (Schenectady, NY: Mohawk Development Service, 1962).

2. Charles Freeman, *The Miracle of Electric Light and Power* (Exton, PA: The Newcomen Society, 1952).

3. Miller, *At the Touch of a Button.*

4. Walter C. Patterson, *Nuclear Power*, 2d edition (New York: Penguin Books, 1983).

5. Ibid.

6. Dwight D. Eisenhower, *Mandate for Change* (New York: Doubleday, 1963).

7. H. Peter Metzger, *The Atomic Establishment* (New York: Simon and Schuster, 1972).

8. Patterson, *Nuclear Power.*

9. Brookhaven National Laboratory, *Theoretical Possibilities and Consequences of Major Accidents in Large Nuclear Power Plants* (Washington, DC: Atomic Energy Commission, 1957).

10. H. Peter Metzger, *The Atomic Establishment* (New York: Simon and Schuster, 1972).

11. Peter Pringle and James Spigelman, *The Nuclear Barons* (New York: Holt, Rinehart and Winston, 1981).

12. "Demand for Engineers Is 'Easing,' " *Electrical World*, October 12, 1964.

13. H. A. Cavanaugh, "The Management Report," *Electrical World*, September 1984.

14. "The Disaster That Wasn't," *Time*, November 19, 1965.

15. Ibid.

16. J. T. Peters, "That Vital Commodity, Quality," *Public Utilities Fortnightly*, May 10, 1973.

17. Equipment Availability Task Force Prime Movers Committee, "Report on Equipment Availability for the Ten-Year Period 1966–1975" (Washington, DC: Edison Electric Institute, 1976).

18. Amory Lovins, *Small Is Profitable* (Snowmass, CO: Rocky Mountain Institute, 2002).

19. Richard Morgan and Sandra Jerabek, *How to Challenge Your Local Electric Utility* (Washington, DC: Environmental Action Foundation, 1974).

20. Harvey Wasserman, *Energy War: Reports from the Front* (Westport, CT: Lawrence Hill & Co., 1979).

21. Office of Science and Technology, *Electric Power and the Environment* (Washington, DC: Executive Office of the President, October 1970).

22. *Otter Tail Company v. United States*, 93 S. Ct. 1022 (at 1035), 1973.

23. Anthony Sampson, *Seven Sisters* (New York: Viking Press, 1975).

24. John M. Blair, *The Control of Oil* (New York: Pantheon Books, 1977).

25. Robert Stobaugh and Daniel Yergin, eds. *Energy Future* (New York: Random House, 1979).

26. "Con Edison: Archetype of the Ailing Utility," *Business Week*, May 25, 1974.

27. Leonard Hyman, *America's Electric Utilities: Past, Present, and Future* (Arlington, VA: Public Utilities Reports, 1983).

28. "Will the Light at the End of the Tunnel Go Dim?" *Business Week*, March 1976.

29. "A Financial Crisis for the Utilities," *Business Week*, April 27, 1974.

30. Peter Sandman and Mary Paden, "At Three Mile Island," *Columbia Journalism Review*, July/August 1979.

31. *Report by President's Commission on the Accident at Three Mile Island* (Washington, DC: Government Printing Office, 1979).

32. Sandman and Paden, "At Three Mile Island."

33. Ibid.

34. *Report by President's Commission on the Accident at Three Mile Island.*

35. David Comey, "The Incident at Browns Ferry," from *Countdown to a Nuclear Moratorium* (Washington, DC: Environmental Action Foundation, 1976).

36. Mark Hertsgaard, *Nuclear* (New York: Pantheon Books, 1983).

37. Chip Brown, "Whoops," *Washington Post*, December 3–7, 1984.

38. Daniel Jack Chasan, "The Fall of the House of WPPSS," *The Weekly* (Seattle, WA) October 1984.

39. Peter W. Bernstein, "A Nuclear Fiasco Shakes the Bond Market," *Fortune*, February 22, 1982.

40. I. C. Bupp and Charles Komanoff, *Nuclear Power at the Turning Point* (Cambridge, MA: Cambridge Energy Research Associates, November 1983).

41. John R. Emshwiller, "Electricity Costs Rise Sharply as Utilities Add New Nuclear Facilities," *Wall Street Journal*, August 11, 1982.

42. John Noble Wilford, "Laxity and Safety Rules Raise Expense of Nuclear Reactors," *New York Times*, February 27, 1984.

43. Matthew Wald, "Despite High Costs, Some Utilities Feel Compelled to Finish Reactors," *New York Times*, February 28, 1984.

44. Ibid.

45. James Cook, "Nuclear Follies," *Forbes*, February 11, 1985.

46. "Utility Stockholders: Little Guys Have the Most to Lose," *Business Week*, May 21, 1984.

CHAPTER 5: PARTIAL COMPETITION

1. Richard Hirsh, *Power Loss* (Cambridge: MIT Press, 1999).

2. "Utilities View Carter Energy Message as Mix of Good Intentions and 'Trauma' For the Industry," *Electrical Week*, April 25, 1977.

3. "Utilities Muster for Big Rate-Reform Fight," *Electrical Week*, August 1, 1977.

4. "Senate Energy Committee May Sharply Pare Carter's Rate-Reform Plan," *Electrical Week*, September 12, 1977.

5. Hirsh, *Power Loss.*

6. Ibid.

7. William C. Hayes, "The National Energy Act Isn't," *Electrical World*, December 15, 1978.

8. *FERC v. Mississippi*, 102 S. Ct. 2126 (1982) in *Supreme Court Reporter* 102 (St. Paul, MN: West Publishing Co., 1986), 2133.

9. Interview with James Bruce, then chairman of Idaho Power Company.

10. *American Paper Institute, Inc., Petitioner, v. American Electric Power Service Corporation, et al.; Federal Energy Regulatory Commission, Petitioner, v. American Electric Power Service Corporation, et al., Nos. 82–34, 82–226,* 103 S. Ct. 1921 (1983).

11. Quote by Erroll Davis, CEO of Wisconsin Power & Light, in Peter Nulty, "Utilities Go to War," *Fortune*, November 13, 1995.

12. Comment by Stephen Wiel, former commissioner of the Nevada Public Service Commission, as quoted in Hirsh, *Power Loss.*

13. "Least-cost Planning: Much Ado About Nothing?" *Electrical World*, June 1987.

14. Ibid.

15. Hirsh, *Power Loss.*

16. Paul Joskow, "Expanding Competitive Opportunities in Electricity Generation," *Cato Review of Business and Government*, Winter 1992.

17. "DOE's Moore Urges EEI to Embrace PUHCA Change, Move on Transmission," *Electric Utility Week*, June 17, 1991.

18. Robert Barton, "Coalition Joins to Support Electrical Industry Reform," *Oil Daily*, August 12, 1992.

19. Joseph Paquette, "PUHCA Proposal Could Harm Millions," *Energy Daily*, February 14, 1992.

20. Electric Reliability Coalition advertisement in *Hartford Courant*, September 12, 1991.

CHAPTER 6: STRESSES

1. David Owens, interview with author, May 15, 2003.

2. Ken Silverstein, "Light Ahead," *UtiliPoint Issue Alert*, July 27, 2004.

3. "Fitch Sees Signs of Utility, Merchant Sector Recovery in 05," *Intelligence Press*, December 16, 2004.

4. Ken Silverstein, "Strongest Utilities Flex Muscles," *UtiliPoint Issue Alert*, May 15, 2003.

5. "States Gear Up for Rate Battles as Price Caps End," *Wall Street Journal*, August 17, 2004.

6. "1988: The Big Issue is Deregulation," *Electrical World*, January 1988.

7. John Emshwiller and Rebecca Smith, "Behind Enron's Fall: A Culture of Operating Outside Public's View," *Wall Street Journal*, December 5, 2001.

8. Rebecca Smith, "Enron Files for Chapter 11 Bankruptcy, Sues Dynergy," *Wall Street Journal*, December 3, 2001.

9. "Documents Show Investment Officer Had Key Role in Enron Demise," *Chicago Tribune*, February 20, 2002.

10. Ken Silverstein, "Enron Tapes Inflame Californians," *UtiliPoint Issue Alert*, June 7, 2004.

11. Comment by Gerald Mestralett of Suez as quoted in Vijay Vaitheeswaran, *Power to the People* (New York: Farrar, Straus and Giroux, 2003).

12. M. L. Ramsay, *Pyramids of Power: The Story of Roosevelt, Insull, and the Utility Wars* (New York: Bobbs-Merrill, 1937).

13. Paul L. Joskow, "California's Electricity Crisis," Working Paper 8442, National Bureau of Economic Research, August 2001.

14. California Public Utility Commission News Release, "CPUC Proposes Competition for Electric Utilities and Open Electric Supply Market for Consumers," April 20, 1994.

15. Mark Maremont, "Shock Treatment for California Utilities?" *Business Week*, May 9, 1994.

16. Vijay Vaitheeswaran, *Power to the People* (New York: Farrar, Straus and Giroux, 2003).

17. Press release from the governor's office, "Wilson Signs Historic Legislation Restructuring Electric Industry: Ending California's Utility Monopoly Creating the Nation's First Plan to Deregulate Electricity," September 23, 1996.

18. Amory B. Lovins, *Small Is Profitable* (Snowmass, CO: Rocky Mountain Institute, 2002).

19. John Woolfolk and Steve Johnson, "California Tallies Cost of Power Deregulation Fiasco," *San Jose Mercury News*, July 10, 2001.

20. Steven Pearlstein, "On California Stage: A Cautionary Tale," *Washington Post*, August 21, 2001.

21. Congressional Budget Office, *Causes and Lessons of the California Electricity Crisis*, September 2001. http://www.cbo.gov/showdoc.cfm?index=3062& sequence=0#pt5

22. Electric Consumer Research Council, "The Economic Impacts of the August 2003 Blackout," February 2, 2004.

23. U.S./Canada Power Outage Task Force, "August 14, 2003 Outage Sequence of Events," September 12, 2003.

24. "Overseers Missed Big Picture As Failures Led to Blackout," *New York Times*, September 13, 2003.

25. Ibid.

26. Peter Behr, "System's Crash Was Predicted," *Washington Post*, August 15, 2003.

27. "Report: One Nuclear Weapon Could Take Out 70 Percent of Electric Supply," *Electricity Daily*, August 19, 2004.

28. Steve Silberman, "The Energy Web," *Wired*, July 2001.

29. Northeast American Electric Reliability Council, "Reliability Assessment 1998–2007," September 1998.

30. Peter Behr, "System's Crash Was Predicted," *Washington Post*, August 15, 2003.

31. William W. Hogan, "The California Meltdown," *Harvard Magazine*, September–October 2001.

CHAPTER 7: ENTREPRENEURS

1. Thomas R. Casten and Brennan Downes, "Economic Growth and the Central Generation Paradigm," November 2004 (unpublished paper).

2. Thomas R. Casten, interview with author, May 11, 2004.

3. "What Tom Casten Wants His New Firm to Do?" *Restructuring Today*, March 27, 2002.

4. Thomas R. Casten, "Power Failure," April 23, 2001 (unpublished paper).

5. Casten, interview with author.

6. Ibid.

7. Ibid.

8. Ibid.

9. Ibid.

CHAPTER 8: MODERN TECHNOLOGIES

1. Interlaboratory Working Group, 1997, *Scenarios of U.S. Carbon Reductions: Potential Impacts of Energy Technologies by 2010 and Beyond.* Oak Ridge, TN: Oak Ridge National Laboratory; and Berkeley, CA: Lawrence Berkeley National Laboratory.

2. J. G. McGowan and S. R. Connors, "Windpower: A Turn of the Century Review," *Annual Review of Energy and the Environment,* November 2000.

3. Steve Silberman, "The Energy Web," *Wired,* July 2001.

4. "Leapfrogging the Power Grid," *Nature,* February 19, 2004.

5. Institute for Lifecycle Environmental Assessment, *Carrying the Energy Future: Comparing Hydrogen and Electricity for Transmission, Storage, and Transportation* (2004) at www.ilea.org

6. National Academies of Science, *The Hydrogen Economy: Opportunities, Costs, Barriers, and R&D Needs* (Washington, DC: National Academics of Science, February 2004).

7. B. Rever, "Grid-Tied Markets for Photovoltaics: A New Source Emerges." *Renewable Energy World,* January 2001.

8. W. Short, "Renewable Energy Technologies: Progress, Markets, and Industries." Presentation at the 2nd Renewable Energy Analysis Forum, National Renewable Energy Laboratory, Golden, CO, May 29, 2002.

9. Jerry Jackson, "Turning Utility DG Threats into Business Opportunities," *EnergyPulse,* June 3, 2004. (www.energypulse.net)

10. Monica Perin, "Venture Capital Survey Tracks Energy Technology Investments," *Houston Business Journal,* December 3, 2004.

11. N. Lenssen, "Local Integrated Resource Planning: A New Tool for a Competitive Era" (Boulder, CO: E source, November 1995).

12. *Sierra Club Roundtable,* May/June 2002.

13. Bob Shively and John Ferrare, *Understanding Today's Electricity Business* (San Francisco: Enerdynamics, 2004).

CHAPTER 9: BARRIERS TO INNOVATION

1. "Neale Touts Distributed Generation to Meet Bottlenecks," *Pipeline & Gas Journal,* August 10, 2001.

2. Christopher Drew and Ricard A. Oppel, Jr., "How Power Lobby Won Battle of Pollution Control at E.P.A.," *New York Times,* March 6, 2004.

3. Comment by Oregon Governor John Kitzhaber, from *Rethinking Bonneville* (Washington, DC: Northeast-Midwest Institute, 2001).

4. Comment by Wendell Wilkie, former presidential candidate and private utility executive, from *Restructure TVA* (Washington, DC: Northeast-Midwest Institute, 1998).

5. Richard Munson, *Restructure TVA: Why the Tennessee Valley Authority Must Be Reformed* (Washington, DC: Northeast-Midwest Institute, 1998).

6. Richard Munson, *Bonneville in Crisis* (Washington, DC: Northeast-Midwest Institute, 2003).

7. Vijay Vaitheeswaran, *Power to the People* (New York: Farrar, Straus and Giroux, 2003).

8. Hans Landsberg, "Historical Perspective on Demand Forecasts" in M. F. Searl (ed.), *Energy Modeling—Art, Science, Practice: Working Papers for a Seminar on Energy Modeling* (Washington, DC: Resources for the Future, 1973).

9. P. Craig, A. Gadgil, and J. Koomey, "What Can History Teach Us?: A Retrospective Analysis of Long-term Energy Forecasts for the U.S.," in R. H. Socolow, D. Anderson, and J. Harte (eds.), *Annual Review of Energy and the Environment 2002* (Palo Alto, CA: Annual Reviews, Inc.).

10. Stephen Moore, "Lights Out on Regulators," *Washington Times*, September 29, 2004.

11. Phillip Harris, interview with author, May 24, 2004.

CHAPTER 10: INNOVATION-BASED RESTRUCTURING

1. Standard and Poor's, "U.S. Utilities Ratings Decline Continued in 2003, but Pace Slows," January 29, 2004.

2. Richard Stavros, "In His Own Words: A Face-to-Face Interview with FERC Chairman Pat Wood III," *Public Utilities Fortnightly*, April 2004.

3. Quote by Richard Hunter, managing director at Fitch Ratings, in "Analysts Suggest Back-to-Basics Strategy Is Just Common Sense," Reuters, June 3, 2004.

4. Quote by Ronald Barone in "Utility Downgrades by S&P Lessen; Financial Stress May Be Ending," *Electricity Daily*, June 4, 2004.

5. Quote by Hugh Wynne in "Analysts Suggest Back-to-Basics Strategy is Just Common Sense," Reuters News Service, June 3, 2004.

6. Sudeep Reddy, "Power Industry Working toward Recovery after Difficult Decade," *The Dallas Morning News*, February 12, 2004.

7. Bob Shively and John Ferrare, *Understanding Today's Electricity Business* (San Francisco: Enerdynamics, 2004).

8. Steven Ferrey, "Inverting Choice of Law in the Wired Universe: Thermodynamics, Mass, and Energy," *William and Mary Law Review*, 45(5), April 2004.

9. Granger Morgan, interview with the author, January 30, 2003.

10. The Regulatory Assistance Project, "Distributed Resources," *Issuesletter,* February 2000.

11. Council of Economic Advisers, *Economic Report of the President* (Washington, DC: U.S. Government Printing Office, February 1994).

12. Tina Kaarsberg, Julie Fox Gorte, and Richard Munson, *The Clean Air-Innovative Technology Link: Enhancing Efficiency in the Electricity Industry* (Washington, DC: Northeast-Midwest Institute, 1999).

13. Clifford Winston, "U.S. Industry Adjustment to Economic Deregulation," *Journal of Economic Perspectives* 12(3), Summer 1998.

14. Clifford Winston, Thomas M. Corsi, Curtis M. Grimm, and Carol A. Evans, *The Economic Effects of Surface Freight Deregulation* (Washington, DC: The Brookings Institution, 1990).

15. Michael C. Brower, Stephen D. Thomas, and Catherine Mitchell, *The British Electric Utility Restructuring Experience: History and Lessons for the United States* (National Council on Competition and the Electric Industry, October 1996).

16. International Energy Agency, *Competition in Electricity Markets* (Paris: IEA, 2001).

17. Winston, "U.S. Industry Adjustment to Economic Deregulation."

18. National Science Foundation, "Research and Development in Industry." (http://www.nsf.gov/sbe/srs/srs99411/start.htm)

19. Philip Israilevich and K. J. Kowalewski, "The Effect of Regulation of Ohio Electric Utilities," *Federal Research Bank of Cleveland Economic Review,* First Quarter, 1987.

20. Hugh F. Holman, "Rejoice Re: Juice: Finding Profit in the Restructuring of the Electric Utility Industry," 1999. Unpublished paper.

21. "S&P Analyst Says Congress Should Keep PUHCA," *Energy Daily,* February 23, 2004.

22. Winston et al., *The Economic Effects of Surface Freight Deregulation.*

23. Mark Mullins, "Power Jolt Required: Measuring the Impact of Electricity Deregulation," The Fraser Institute, October 25, 2004.

24. Bob Shively and John Ferrare, *Understanding Today's Electricity Business* (San Francisco: Enerdynamics, 2004).

25. Scott Sklar, "New Dawn for Distributed Energy," *Cogeneration and On-Site Power Production,* July–August 2004.

26. Margaret Kriz, "Power Struggle," *National Journal,* June 28, 2003.

27. Energy Information Administration, *The Changing Structure of the Electric Power Industry 2000: An Update.* (http://www.eia.doe.gov/cneaf/electricity/chg_stru_update)

Index

About the Author

RICHARD MUNSON is Director of the Northeast-Midwest Institute, a non-partisan policy research center in Washington, D.C. Having founded the National Solar Lobby and Center for Renewable Resources in the 1970s, he has spent the last twenty-five years spearheading innovative public policy approaches to help meet America's energy needs. He frequently testifies before Congress, collaborates with regional energy and power providers, briefs local and state governments on their energy options, and provides consumer information on energy choices. His articles on the business and politics of the electricity industry have appeared in publications ranging from *The Washington Post* and *Los Angeles Times* to the journals of the National Academy of Sciences, environmental organizations and utility associations. He is the author of *The Power Makers, Cousteau: The Captain and His World*, and *The Cardinals of Capitol Hill*.